PLANT BIOSYNTHESIS

For
B. Pharmacy and M. Pharmacy

DR. S. S. KHADABADI
M. Pharm., Ph.D., FIC, LLB
Principal,
Govt. College of Pharmacy,
Amravati – 444604.

DR. S. L. DEORE
M. Pharm., Ph.D.
Assistant Professor,
Govt. College of Pharmacy,
Amravati – 444604

B. A. BAVISKAR
M.Pharm.
Govt. College of Pharmacy,
Amravati – 444604.

N1632

Plant Biosynthesis

ISBN 978-93-80725-07-9

Third Edition : August 2015
© : Authors

The text of this publication, or any part thereof, should not be reproduced or transmitted in any form or stored in any computer storage system or device for distribution including photocopy, recording, taping or information retrieval system or reproduced on any disc, tape, perforated media or other information storage device etc., without the written permission of Authors with whom the rights are reserved. Breach of this condition is liable for legal action.

Every effort has been made to avoid errors or omissions in this publication. In spite of this, errors may have crept in. Any mistake, error or discrepancy so noted and shall be brought to our notice shall be taken care of in the next edition. It is notified that neither the publisher nor the authors or seller shall be responsible for any damage or loss of action to any one, of any kind, in any manner, therefrom.

Published By :
NIRALI PRAKASHAN
Abhyudaya Pragati, 1312, Shivaji Nagar,
Off J.M. Road, PUNE – 411005
Tel - (020) 25512336/37/39, Fax - (020) 25511379
Email : niralipune@pragationline.com

Printed By :
Repro Knowledgecast Limited,
Thane

☞ DISTRIBUTION CENTRES

PUNE
Nirali Prakashan : 119, Budhwar Peth, Jogeshwari Mandir Lane, Pune 411002, Maharashtra
Tel : (020) 2445 2044, 66022708, Fax : (020) 2445 1538
Email : bookorder@pragationline.com, nirallocal@pragationline.com

Nirali Prakashan : S. No. 28/27, Dhyari, Near Pari Company, Pune 411041
Tel : (020) 24690204 Fax : (020) 24690316
Email : dhyari@pragationline.com, bookorder@pragationline.com

MUMBAI
Nirali Prakashan : 385, S.V.P. Road, Rasdhara Co-op. Hsg. Society Ltd.,
Girgaum, Mumbai 400004, Maharashtra
Tel : (022) 2385 6339 / 2386 9976, Fax : (022) 2386 9976
Email : niralimumbai@pragationline.com

☞ DISTRIBUTION BRANCHES

JALGAON
Nirali Prakashan : 34, V. V. Golani Market, Navi Peth, Jalgaon 425001,
Maharashtra, Tel : (0257) 222 0395, Mob : 94234 91860

KOLHAPUR
Nirali Prakashan : New Mahadvar Road, Kedar Plaza, 1st Floor Opp. IDBI Bank
Kolhapur 416 012, Maharashtra. Mob : 9850046155

NAGPUR
Pratibha Book Distributors : Above Maratha Mandir, Shop No. 3, First Floor,
Rani Jhanshi Square, Sitabuldi, Nagpur 440012, Maharashtra
Tel : (0712) 254 7129

DELHI
Nirali Prakashan : 4593/21, Basement, Aggarwal Lane 15, Ansari Road, Daryaganj
Near Times of India Building, New Delhi 110002
Mob : 08505972553

BENGALURU
Pragati Book House : House No. 1, Sanjeevappa Lane, Avenue Road Cross,
Opp. Rice Church, Bengaluru – 560002.
Tel : (080) 64513344, 64513355,Mob : 9880582331, 9845021552
Email:bharatsavla@yahoo.com

CHENNAI
Pragati Books : 9/1, Montieth Road, Behind Taas Mahal, Egmore,
Chennai 600008 Tamil Nadu, Tel : (044) 6518 3535,
Mob : 94440 01782 / 98450 21552 / 98805 82331,
Email : bharatsavla@yahoo.com

niralipune@pragationline.com | www.pragationline.com
Also find us on www.facebook.com/niralibooks

Dedicated to …

OUR BELOVED PARENTS

PREFACE TO THE THIRD EDITION

The first edition of our book "Plant biosynthesis" has brought in a flood of approval from teachers and students alike. Our goal, from the beginning was to provide the basics of the subject in simple and lucid language.

The present edition has been completely revised and restructured. In revising the book we took the opportunity to correct, rewrite and rearrange material, improve the index, focus on the most fundamental and add only the most essential to improve readability and comprehension of the subject. Major effort has gone into adding and updating the bibliography, with the aim of referring to the most recent publications. Biosynthetic pathways of vitamin B12, folic acid, Reserpine, imidazole alkaloid-pilocarpine have been added in this second edition of this book.

We have tried our level best to neither lengthen nor complicate this book and have kept the content to the point and specific.

We are grateful to Miss Lalita Bhagure in aiding us in the preparation of this second edition and all our students for their helpful comments and for their many constructive suggestions. We express our gratitude to our publisher Dinesh Bhai and Jignesh Furia and their staff for their meticulous toil in producing the second edition of this book. We will also like to thank the chief editor Nirja Sharma who has always been a pleasure to talk to and work with. Many others have offered minor corrections and suggestions since the first edition was published, for which we are also grateful.

Last but not least, we are grateful to our family for their encouragement and loving support.

Authors

PREFACE TO THE FIRST EDITION

The sophisticated analytical techniques and modern information facilities are encouraging researchers to deal with different aspects of plant derived products. The common questions of how and where these interesting compounds are synthesized by plants can be explained with biosynthesis study.

Based on teaching and research experience in pharmacognosy and phytochemistry, we realized that very few books are available on plant biosynthesis. Hence, despite the wide scope of the subject the authors have provided the basics of biosynthesis along with a few representative secondary metabolite pathways in a simple, lucid and concise manner. The study of biosynthetic pathways is useful either to develop synthetic, semi-synthetic new moieties or bring out bio-transformations.

This sincere attempt is to cater the needs of graduate and post graduate students of Pharmacy. It is hoped that this book will be very useful to the students and professionals of Pharmacognosy, Natural Chemistry and Botany.

There are a number of individuals who have helped us with the book. Specifically, we acknowledge the help of Dr. N. S. Vyawahare and kind co-operation of our publisher Shri Dineshbhai Furia and Shri Jigneshbhai Furia.

Finally, we look forward to comments and kind suggestions from our readers to improve the book.

Amravati

15th May, 2010　　　　　　　　　　　　　　　　　　　　　　　　　　　**Authors**

CONTENTS

1. Plant Metabolism   1.1 – 1.38
- Plant Physiology and Biochemistry: Primary and Secondary Metabolism, Building Blocks, Common Reactions
- Role of Enzyme and Cofactor
- Role of Vitamins: Biosynthesis of vitamin B12 and Folic acid
- Elucidation of Biosynthetic Pathway
- Chemistry of Primary Metabolites : Amino Acids, Proteins, Enzymes, Vitamins, Nucleic Acids, Sugars, Lipids
- Chemistry of Secondary metabolites : Phenolic compounds, Tannins, Resins, Alkaloids, Glycosides, Terpenoids

2. Biogenesis   2.1 – 2.7
- Introduction
- Photosynthesis: C_3, C_4, CAM
- Glycolysis
- Citric acid cycle (Kreb's Cycle)
- Pentose Phosphate Pathway

3. Carbohydrates   3.1 – 3.5
- Introduction: Classification, Glycosidic Linkage, Anomerisation
- Biosynthesis of Sugars
- Oligosaccharides
- Polysaccharides: Starch
- Vitamin C Biosynthesis

4. Acetate Pathway   4.1 – 4.11
- Introduction: Fatty Acids, Saturated fatty acids, Unsaturated fatty acids
- Saturated Fatty Acids Biosynthesis
- Unsaturated Fatty Acids Biosynthesis
- Aromatic Polyketides Biosynthesis: Anthraquinones- Emodin, Aloe emodin, Rhein, Sennoside, Frangulin Cascaroside, Hypercin, Khelin, Visnagin

5. Shikimic Acid Pathway   5.1 – 5.14
- Shikimic Acid Biosynthesis
- Phenylpropanoides
- Coumarin Biosynthesis: Furanocaumarins, Vanillin, Psoralen, Angelicin, Bergapten, Umbeliferon, Scopoletin, Scopolin.
- Lignans and Lignin Biosynthesis: Podophylotoxin
- Volatile Oil Biosynthesis: Anethole, Eugenol, Myristicin,
- Flavonoid Biosynthesis: Naringin, Resveratrol, Daidzein, Hesperidin, Genistein, Kaemferol, Quercetin, Pelargonidin, Silybin
- Miscellaneous: Lawsone, Alizarin, Aloe emodin, Vitamin K, Vitamin E

6. Isoprenoid Pathway / Acetate Mevalonate Pathway   6.1 – 6.32

- Introduction: Isoprenoid pathway, D-L-deoxyxylulose-3-phosphate pathway
- Classification of Terpenoids
- Monoterpenoide Biosynthesis: Pinene, Limonene, Phellandrene, Linalool, Fenchone, Camphor, Cineol, Thujone, Geraniol, Carvone, Menthol
- Monoterpenoid irridoide Biosynthesis: Loganin, Secologanin, Valtrate, Gentiopicroside
- Sesquiterpenoide Biosynthesis: Gossypol, Artemisinin, Humulene, Cadinene
- Diterpenoide Biosynthesis: Forskolin, Ginkgolide, Abietic acid, Steviol, Taxol
- Triterpenoide Biosynthesis: α-Amyrin, β-Amyrin, Lupeol, Euphol, Cucurbitacin-E
- Modified Triterpenoid Biosynthesis:
- Steroids and Steroidal Saponin Biosynthesis: Diosgenin, Hecogenin, Tigogenin, Sarsapogenin, Ginsenoside,
- Cardioactive sterol Biosynthesis: Digitoxigenin, Digoxigenin, Gitoxigenin, Scillaren A, Hellebrigenin
- Phytosterol Biosynthesis: Stigmasterol, Sitosterol, Ergosterol, Fucosterol
- Pentacyclic triterpenoid Biosynthesis: Quillaic acid, Glycyrrhezetic acid, Limonoids, Quassinoids, Azadirachtin.
- Tertaterpenoide Biosynthesis: Lycopene, α-Carotene, β-Carotene, Capsanthin, Lutein, Vitamin A

7. Alkaloid Biosynthesis   7.1 – 7.18

- Introduction: Alkaloid Classification, Biosynthetic Origin of Alkaloids
- Tropane Alkaloids : Hygrine, Hyoscyamine, Hyoscine
- Quinoline Alkaloids: Quinine, Quinidine, Cinchonine, Cinchonidine, Cinchonamine
- Isoquinoline/Opium Alkaloids: Thebaine, Morphine, Codeine, Papaverine, Berberine
- Amine Alkaloids: Ephedrine, Pseudoephedrine
- Purine Alkaloids : Caffeine, Theophylline, Theobromine
- Indole Alkaloids: Lysergic acid, Ergotamine, Ajmalicine, Yohimbine, Catharanthine, Vincristine, Vinblastine, Strychnine, Brucine
- Imidazole Alkaloids: Pilocarpine, Pilosine

Abbreviations   A.1 – A.1

Further Readings   F.1 – F.4

***

CHAPTER 1

PLANT METABOLISM

- Plant Physiology and Biochemistry: Primary and Secondary Metabolism, Building Blocks, Common Reactions involved in biosynthesis
- Role of Enzyme and Cofactor
- Role of Vitamins: Biosynthesis of Vitamin B12 and Folic acid
- Elucidation of Biosynthetic Pathway
- Chemistry of Primary Metabolites : Amino Acids, Proteins, Enzymes, Vitamins, Nucleic Acids, Sugars, Lipids
- Chemistry of Secondary Metabolites : Phenolic compounds, Tannins, Resins, Alkaloids, Glycosides, Terpenoids

1.1 PLANT PHYSIOLOGY AND BIOCHEMISTRY

Plant Physiology is a sub discipline of Botany concerned with the morphological functioning, or physiology, of plants while Plant Biochemistry is the science explaining the molecular function of a plant. Thus, plant biochemistry and physiology studies biological and chemical processes of individual plant cells involved in photosynthesis, respiration, transpiration, nutrition, hormonal changes, tropisms, photoperiodism, photomorphogenesis, circadian rhythms, metabolism of primary and secondary compounds, seed germination, dormancy, stomata function and as well new concepts and methods involved. The first two chapters of this book, 1 and 2, elaborate the basic points of plant physiology and biochemistry.

It is a well known fact that a plant is a biosynthetic laboratory producing a number of metabolites which are used by humans for diet, health and recently biofuels. These plant metabolites are characterised by an enormous chemical diversity with excellent economic value and potential for new drug development. Plant metabolites include carbohydrates, proteins, lipids, tannins, resins, latex, volatile oils, alkaloids, glycosides, mineral crystals, pigments and enzymes.

Plants produce a vast amount of sugar molecules by photosynthesis which are necessary for the basic life processes of the plant cells. Excessive quantities of these sugar molecules are stored as a reserve food and further oxidized to provide energy and building blocks (Table 1.1) for all metabolic processes. This whole complex process, collectively called as *metabolic pathway*, is a combination of many biochemical reactions which are mediated and regulated by enzymes to give either primary or secondary metabolites. The prerequisites for biosynthesis are precursor compounds, chemical energy in the form ATP, reduction equivalents in the form of NADH, NADPH and catalytic enzymes, which may require cofactors to assist the modifications. The reactions which commonly occur during biosynthesis are as given in Table 1.2.

Table 1.1: Building Blocks for Biosynthesis

Building Blocks	Source
C_1	L-Methionine
C_2	Acetyl CoA
C_5 (isoprene)	Mevalonate/deoxyxylulose phosphate
C_6C_3 (phenylpropene)	L-phenylalanine, L-tyrosine
C_6C_2-N	L-phenylalanine, L-tyrosine
C_2N (indole)	L-Tryptophan
C_4N (pyrrolidine)	L-Ornithine
C_5N	L-Lysine

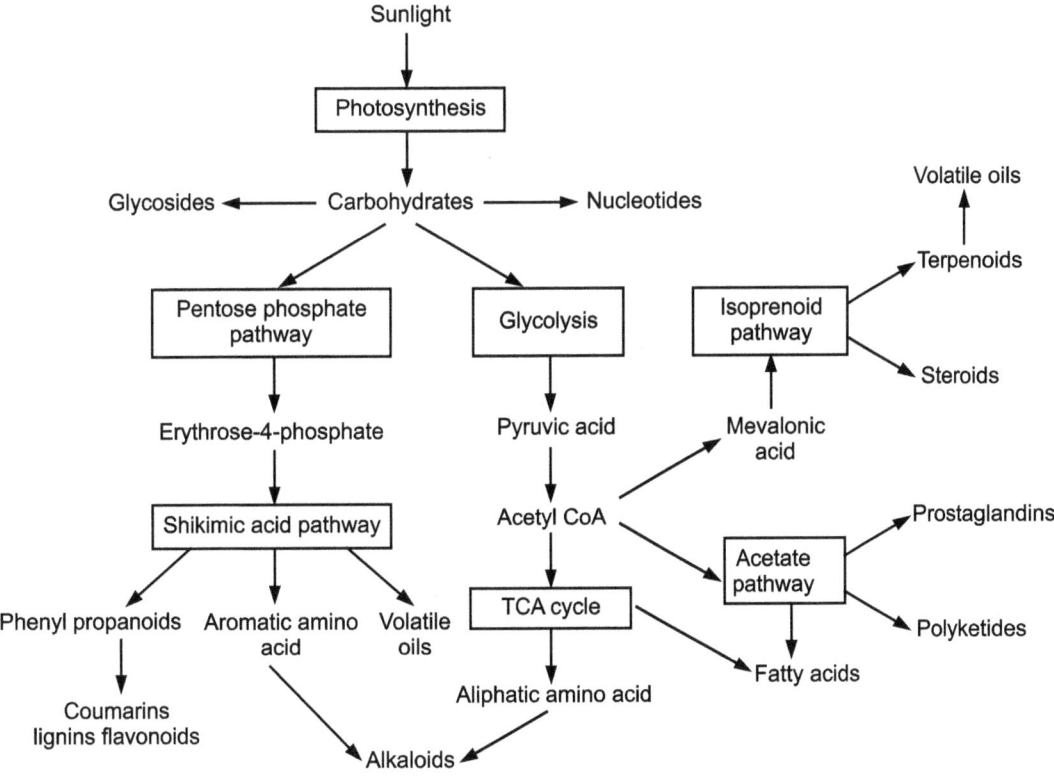

Fig. 1.1 Primary and secondary metabolite biosynthesis.

The group of pathways synthesizing simpler but still essential molecules for normal physiological growth and energy requirement together is called *primary metabolism* and products (e.g. sugars, amino acids, coenzyme A, mevalonic acid, and lipids) are called *primary metabolites*.

Secondary metabolites are supposed to be useless for plants and are stored in various parts of plants, restricted in their distribution and are derived biosynthetically from primary metabolites. These are organic compounds that are not directly involved in the normal growth, development, or not necessary for the cells themselves but may be useful for the plant as a whole. Since these don't have a primary function they are called *secondary metabolites*. Examples of secondary metabolites are alkaloids, glycosides, tannins, flavonoides, terpenoides and essential oils.

Figure 1.1 elaborates the general flow chart of primary and secondary metabolite biosynthesis. Most interestingly, secondary metabolites have a number of applications; as food, adjuvant and medicines; so it becomes necessary to study the biogenetic pathways of these important metabolites. The integration of new technologies in the molecular genetics and biochemistry of higher plants promises a continuation of the rapid progress that has made it possible to understand the fundamentals of biosynthesis like role of common reactions, vitamins, cofactors and enzymes.

Table 1.2 : Reactions Regulating Biosynthesis

Reactions	Mechanisms
Alkylation reactions (Nucleophilic substitution and Electrophillic addition).	Introduction of C_1 and C_5 units.
Alkylation reactions (Electrophillic addition).	Addition of C_5 units to form terpenoids and steroids.
Wagner Meerwein rearrangement.	1, 2 shifts of hydride, methyl and alkyl groups.
Aldol and Claisen reactions -(enolate anion from Carbonyl reaction).	Carbon-carbon bond formation and condensations to form acetoacetyl CoA.
Schiff base formation and Mannich reaction (imine / iminum ion formation).	Formation of C-N bond.
Transamination reactions.	Exchange of amino group from amino acid to keto acid with the help of co-enzyme pyridoxal phosphate (PLP).
Decarboxylation reactions	Removal of carbonyl group with the help of PLP to form C_6C_2N or C_2N.
Oxidation and reduction reactions	Dehydrogenases : Remove two hydrogen atom, Oxidases : remove one H to form water, di/monooxygenases : addition of one or two oxygen, Dioxygenases : Cleavage of bonds, Mono or Diamine oxidases : Transform amine to aldehyde.

Reactions	Mechanisms
Phenolic oxidative coupling	Coupling of one or two phenolic rings via enzyme oxidase or cytochrome P_{450} dependent proteins.
Glycosylation reactions	Sugar is attached to aglycone moiety. UDP : Sugar which is in alpha configuration causes SN_2 displacement reaction to yield Beta glycosides.

1.2 ROLE OF ENZYMES AND COFACTORS

The very first role in biosynthesis of natural products is of enzymes. An enzyme affects the chemical modifications very rapidly and efficiently. An enzyme is an organic catalyst produced by the living cells capable of catalyzing reactions even outside the cells. Chemically all enzymes are proteins in nature. However, sometimes non-protein moieties such as cofactors and coenzymes are also required by some enzymes which assist in the biochemical transformations. Coenzymes are organic molecules and cofactors are inorganic substances. Cofactors can be divided into two broad groups' organic cofactors and inorganic cofactors. (Table 1.3)

Table 1.3 : Organic and Inorganic Cofactors involved in Biosynthesis

Organic Cofactor	Group(s) Transferred
Lipoic acid	Electrons, acyl groups
Folic acid	Methyl, methylene and amino groups
Vitamin K	Carbonyl group and electrons
Vitamin C	Electrons
Nicotine adenine dinucleotide (NAD)	Electron (hydrogen atom)
Nicotine adenine dinucleotide phosphate (NADP)	Electron (hydrogen atom)
Flavine adenine dinucleotide (FAD)	Electron (hydrogen atom)
Coenzyme A (Co A)	Acyl groups
Coenzyme Q (Co Q)	Electrons (hydrogen atom)
Thiamine pyrophosphate (Vit. B_1)	Aldehydes
Pyridoxal phosphate (Vit B_6)	Amino groups carboxyl groups
Biotin	Carbon dioxide
Cyanocobalamine (Vit. B_{12})	Alkyl groups
Nucleotide sugars	Monosaccharide

INORGANIC COFACTOR	
Zinc (Zn)	Carbonic anhydrase, Alcohol dehydrogenase
Magnesium (Mg)	Pyruvate phosphokinase
Iron (Fe)	Cytochromes, Ferredoxin, hemoglobin
Copper (Cu)	Cytochrome oxidase
Potassium (K)	Pyruvate phosphokinase

1.3 ROLE OF VITAMINS

Vitamins are the very essential nutritional factors of human diet and are present in many plants. Besides nutritional value they play an important role in the biosynthesis of many primary and secondary metabolites. Vitamin B_1 is a coenzyme for pyruvate dehydrogenase which catalyses decarboxylation of pyruvate to acetyl CoA and transfers two carbons between carbohydrates in pentose phosphate pathway. Vitamin B_2, riboflavin, is the component of FMN, and FAD which have a role in oxidation and reduction reactions. Vitamin B_5, (Panthothetic acid) part of structure of Coenzyme-A is used in biosynthesis of fatty acids and carbohydrates. Vitamin B_6, (pyridoxol, and pyridoxiamine), is the part of PLP (pyridoxal 5' –phosphate) which causes, transamination and decarboxylation. Vitamin H transfers the carboxyl group e.g. carboxylation of acetyl CoA to malonyl CoA or propionyl CoA to methyl malonyl CoA.

1.4 ELUCIDATION OF BIOSYNTHETIC PATHWAY

The elucidation of pathways is the first step of biosynthesis study. New advances in chemistry and analytical techniques has made possible the exploration of various biosynthetic pathways with a very clear picture of precursors, intermediates, products, enzymes and reactions involved.

Use of radio labelled tracers is the most preferred technique of elucidation due to its specificity and selectivity. It involves the following steps :

1. Selection of suitable radioisotope e.g. ^3H, ^2H, ^{13}C, ^{14}C, ^{18}O, ^{32}P.
2. Labelling of precursor or intermediate.
3. Insertion of radiolabelled metabolite in plant part.
4. Time-to-time determination of radioactivity.
5. Establishment of precursor-intermediate-product relation.

The selection of a radioisotope depends on its half-life so that it should withstand the long and unpredictable time period of biosynthesis. ^{14}C (Half-life : 6000 years) and ^3H (Half-life : 12 years) are the most commonly used radio isotopes. Nowadays, stable isotopes like ^{13}C are also utilized to elucidate biosynthesis with the help of sophisticated NMR analysis.

The labelling of any metabolite by a radioisotope is a tedious and complex procedure involving many chemical steps. After labelling the desired metabolite, the next step is to introduce it into the suitable organ of a plant (e.g. root, stem, leaves) by proper method (e.g. immersion, injection and spraying). Tissue cultures of plant parts are also preferred for introduction of the labelled metabolite. The whole pathway elucidation as well as the exact site of biosynthesis can be studied by tissue culture. Intact roots can be grown in tracer solution. The plant can even be grown in an atmosphere containing $^{14}CO_2$ or $^{13}CO_2$ tracers.

After a sufficient period of time, the metabolite or intermediate or products are isolated to check the radioactivity by suitable detectors, e.g. Geiger-Muller Counter, Scintillation Counter.

If radioactivity is detected then the precursor-product relationship can be confirmed. Similarly, each step should be elucidated and enzymes catalyzing these steps should be identified.

Tracer technique is also useful to confirm the exact precursor or intermediate from the number of possible precursors or intermediates. The whole sequence can also be generated by use of tracer technique.

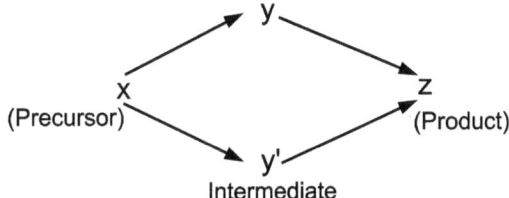

The grafts of two different plants are also helpful to compare which plant part is synthesizing the expected secondary metabolite in higher concentration.

Note : Previously, we discussed what is exactly the primary and secondary metabolism and metabolites. Now, we will study each of them in detail.

1.5 AMINO ACIDS

Amino acids are colourless solids containing an amine group, a carboxylic acid group and a side chain that varies between different amino acids. Amino acids have both basic (amine) and acidic (carboxylic acid) functionalities and therefore act as an acid and a base at the same time. Amino acids have a zwitterionic nature and specific pKa's unique to each amino acid. The ions produced at the isoelectric point (point at which molecule is electrically neutral) have both positive and negative charges and are known as a 'zwitterions'. Zwitterions have minimal solubility at their isoelectric point and hence by adjusting the pH to its particular isoelectric point, amino acids can be precipitated.

The amino acid biosynthesis starts with glutamate, which is obtained from alpha-ketoglutarate and ammonia in the mitochondria. Other amino acids are formed by transaminases which moves amino group to another alpha-keto carboxylic acid. For example, aspartate aminotransferase converts oxaloacetate to aspartate. The 20 principal amino acids normally considered to be involved in plant protein biosynthesis are shown in Fig. 1.2.

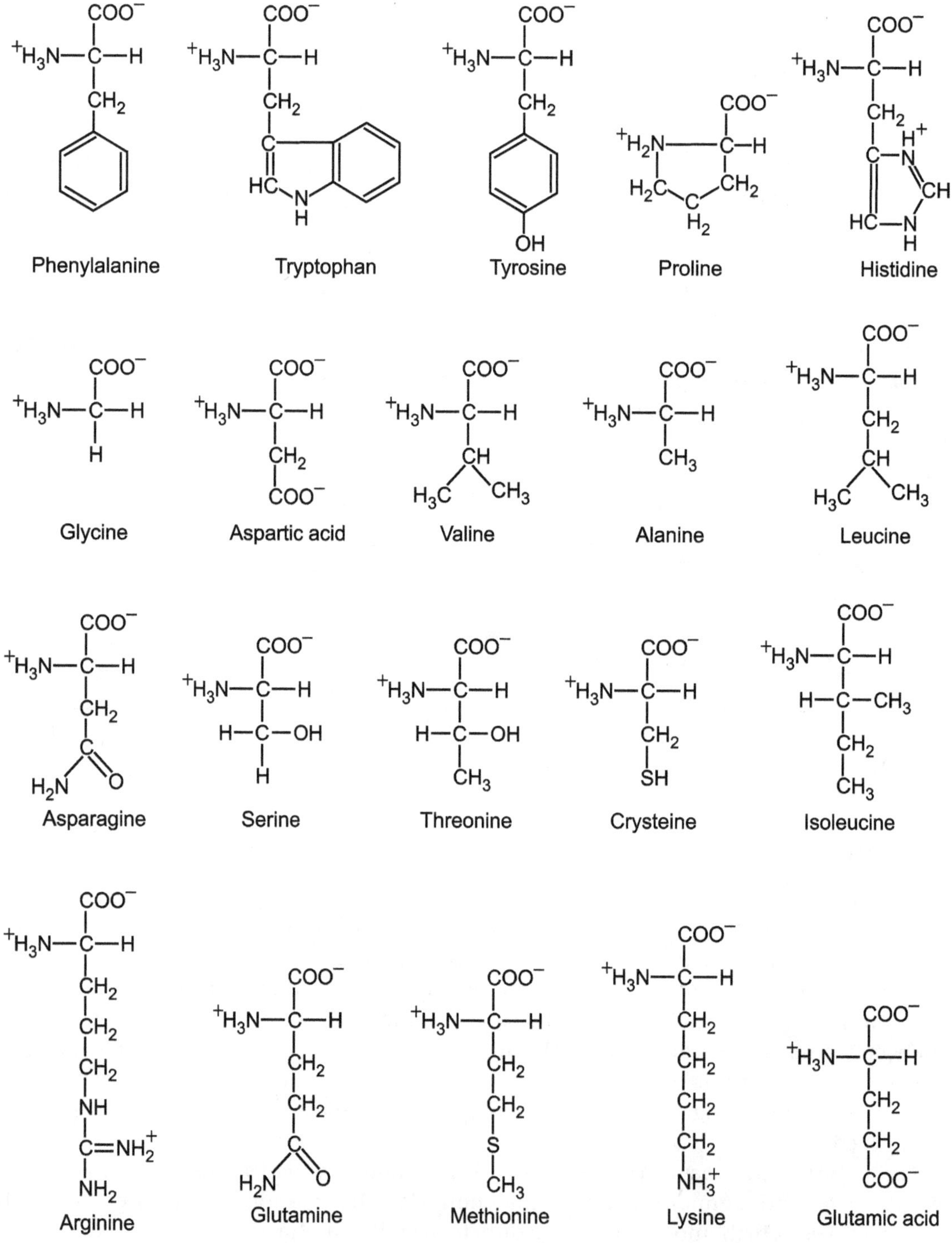

Fig. 1.2 : 20 Amino Acids involved in Protein Biosynthesis

1.6 PROTEINS

Proteins, also known as polypeptides, are the high-molecular-weight polymers of large chains of amino acids. The amino acids in a polymer are joined together by peptide bonds between the carboxyl and amino groups of adjacent amino acid residues. Generally, the proteins are three dimensional in nature due to the fact that each amino acid which forms proteins has its own enantiomeric structure. Proteins are actually the genetic information storing components of plants. These are involved in storage, transport, form structural components and carry out the reactions in the form of enzymes. The two steps (transcription and translation) in the biosynthesis of proteins depend on information encoded by genes.

In transcription, an mRNA chain is generated in the cell nucleus, with the help of DNA. The next process is known as translation which occurs in the cytoplasm, where the ribosomes attach to mRNA. The sequence of amino acids in a protein is defined by the sequence of a gene, which is encoded in the genetic code. Each protein has its own unique amino acid sequence that is specified by the nucleotide sequence of the gene encoding this protein. The genetic code is a combination of three-nucleotide sets i.e. codons and each three-nucleotide combination designates an amino acid, for example : AUG (adenine-uracil-guanine) is the code for methionine.

1.7 ENZYMES

One of the most important proteins in nature are enzymes which can be defined as organic catalysts produced by the living cells but capable of acting outside cells or even in-vitro. Enzymes are also called as biological catalysts. Chemically all enzymes are proteins. However, there are additional non-protein moieties usually present which may or may not participate in the catalytic activity of the enzyme. E.g. minerals : Cu, Fe, Zn. Other factors often found are metal ions (cofactors) and low molecular weight organic molecules like vitamins (coenzymes). These may be loosely or tightly bound by non-covalent or covalent forces.

Distinct advantages of enzymes over conventional chemical catalysts are specificity and selectivity not only for particular reactions but also in their discrimination between similar parts of molecules (regiospecificity) or optical isomers (stereo specificity). Reaction can be catalyzed to the exclusion of side-reactions, eliminating undesirable by-products. Thus, higher productivities plus reduced material costs can be obtained. Product is generated in an uncontaminated state thereby reducing purification costs. Often a smaller number of steps may be required to produce the desired end-product. They catalyze only the reactions of very narrow ranges of reactants (substrates). Biologically active enzymes may be extracted from any living organism, over 50% are from fungi and yeast and over 30% are from bacteria with the remainder divided between animal (8%) and plant (4%) sources. Enzymes are useful as biocatalysts in various industries (Table 1.4) like food, pharmacy and chemical or in analysis (enzyme electrode or probe) and medicine (treatment of cancer, hepatic and renal failure). Plant enzymes are useful in proper food digestion or predigestion where protease digests proteins, amylase digests carbohydrates, lipase digests lipids and cellulose digests fibers. Low levels of enzymes are toxic to the colon and leads to the chronic digestive disorders hence many over the counter nutritional supplements are now provided with these enzymes. The study and knowledge of enzymes is prerequisite of plant biosynthesis.

Table 1.4 : Natural Enzymes

Enzyme	Source	Action	Use
Papain	Latex of *Carica papaya*, Caricaceae	Proteolytic	Meat tenderization
Bromelain	Fruits and stems of *Ananas comosus*, Bromeliaceae	Proteolytic	Anti-inflammatory for soft tissues
L-asparginase	*Escherichia coli* and *Erwinia chrysanthemi*	L-asparginase	Acute leukaemia
Pepsin	Stomach of *Sus scrofa*(hog), Suidae	Proteolytic	Predigestion of food
Trypsin	Pancreas of *Bos taurus* (Bovine), Bovidae	Proteolytic	Wounds and ulcers as causes lysis of blood clots
Chymotrypsin	Pancreas of *Bos taurus* (Bovine), Bovidae.	Proteolytic	Opthalmolgy as a zonal lysis in cataract removal
Urokinase	Mammalian urine or kidney tissue cultures	Fibrinolytic (conversion of plasminogen to plasmin)	Thrombolytic (plasmin dissolves pulmonary thrombosis or clots in eye)
Streptokinase	*Streptococcus heamolyticus*	Fibrinolytic (conversion of plasminogen to plasmin)	Thrombolytic (plasmin dissolves pulmonary thrombosis or clots in eye)
Haluronidase	Mammalian testes and semen	Hydrolysis of mucopoly-sachharides	Increases permeability of tissue for IM or SC injections
Pancreatin	Pancreas of *Sus scrofa* (hog), Suidae ; pancreas of *Bos taurus* (Bovine), Bovidae.	Proteolytic, Amylolytic,	Predigestion of food
Amylase	Human saliva	Amylolytic	Predigestion of food

1.8 VITAMINS

Vitamins, amines of life, are the organic compounds derived from plants which are required as nutrients in tiny amounts by human beings for normal growth and development. Vitamins are either water-soluble (8 B vitamins and vitamin C) or fat soluble (A, D, E and K). Common names, chemical names, biosynthetic origin, and deficiency diseases are given in Table 1.5. Vitamin B_{12} is biosynthesized in microorganism from precursor 5-aminolaevulinic acid (ALA) which is obtained from glutamate to give further the porphyrin moiety. Representative structures of vitamins are given in Fig. 1.3.

Table 1.5 : Vitamins and their Biosynthetic Origins

Common Name	Chemical Name	Deficiency Disease	Biosynthetic Origins
Vitamin A	Retinol, retinal	Night-blindness	Mevalonate pathway
Vitamin B_1	Thiamine	Beriberi	DXP pathway
Vitamin B_2	Riboflavin	Ariboflavinosis	GTP and Ribulose-5-phosphate
Vitamin B_3	Niacin, niacinamide	Pellagra	Tryptophan
Vitamin B_5	Pantothenic acid	Paresthesia	Methylenne tetrahydrofolate and beta alanine
Vitamin B_6	Pyridoxine, pyridoxamine, pyridoxal	Anemia, peripheral neuropathy	DXP pathway
Vitamin B_7	Biotin	Dermatitis, enteritis	Pimelic acid
Vitamin B_9	Folic acid	Birth defects	Shikimate pathway
Vitamin B_{12}	Cyanocobalamine, methylcobalamine	Megaloblastic anemia	Glutamate
Vitamin C	Ascorbic acid	Scurvy	D-glucose
Vitamin D	Ergocalciferol, cholecalciferol	Rickets and Osteomalacia	Mevalonate pathway
Vitamin E	Tocopherols, tocotrienols	Deficiency is very rare	Shikimate pathway
Vitamin K	phylloquinone, menaquinones	Hemorrhage	Shikimate pathway

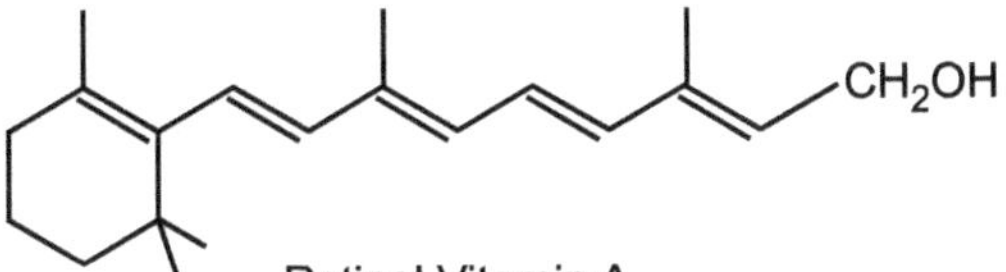

Retinol Vitamin A_1

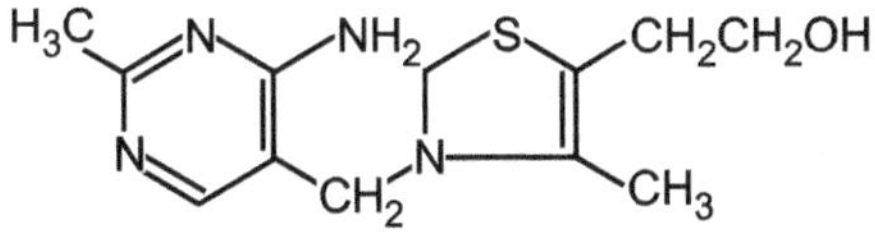

Vitamin B_1 Thamine

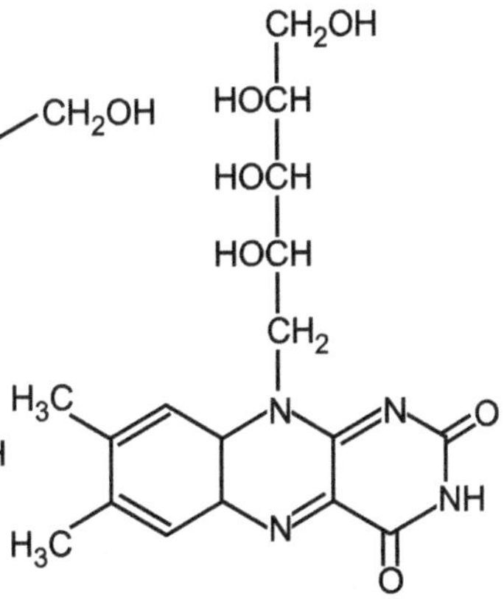

Vitamin B_2 Riboflavin

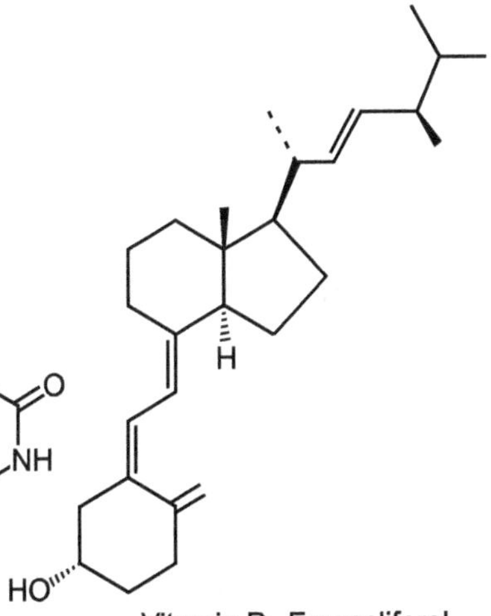

Vitamin D_2 Ergocaliferol

Contd. ...

Contd. ...

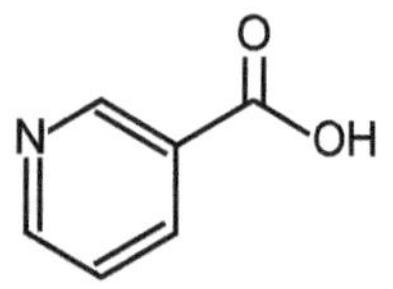

Vitamin B$_3$ Nicotinic acid

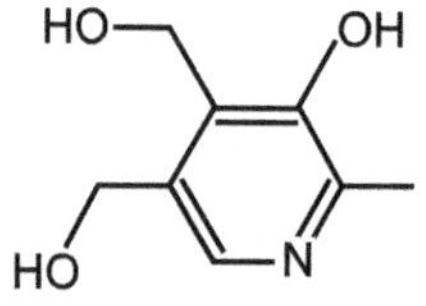

Vitamin B$_6$ Pyridoxine

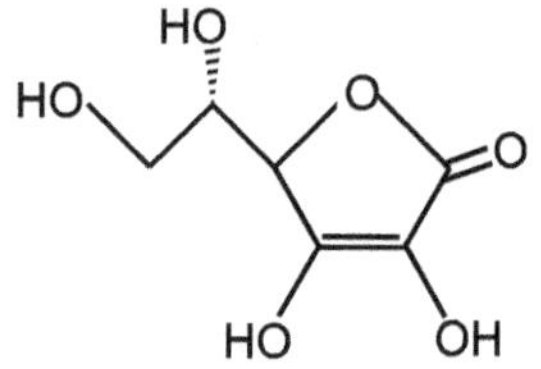

Vitamin C Ascorbic acid

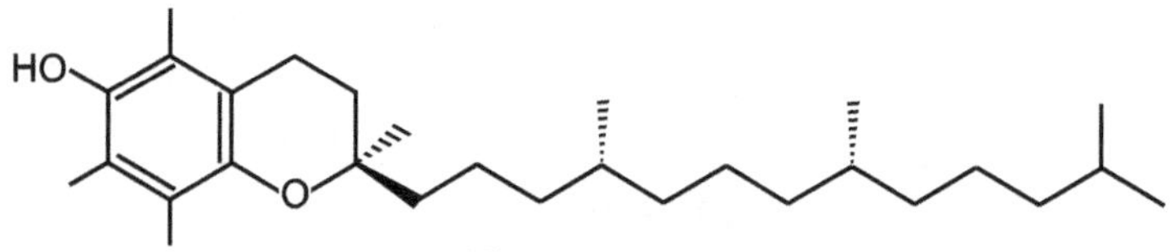

Vitamin E Tocopherol

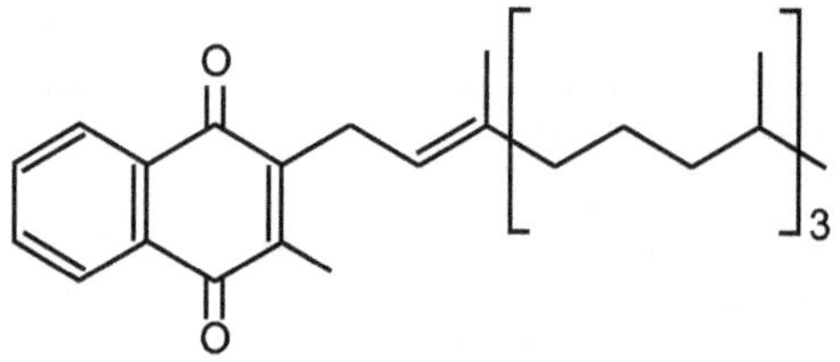

Vitamin K$_1$ Phylloquinone

Fig. 1.3 : Vitamins

Cyanocobalamin is a water soluble vitamin commonly known as Vitamin B12. Biosynthesis of the basic structure of the vitamin in nature is only accomplished by simple microbial organisms such as some bacteria and algae, but conversion between different forms of the vitamin can be accomplished in the human body.

Vitamin B12 is used in the body in two forms: Methylcobalamin and 5-deoxyadenosyl cobalamin. The enzyme methionine synthase needs methylcobalamin as a cofactor. This enzyme is involved in the conversion of the amino acid homocysteine into methionine. Methionine in turn is required for DNA methylation. 5-Deoxyadenosyl cobalamin is a cofactor needed by the enzyme that converts L-methylmalonyl-CoA to succinyl-CoA. This conversion is an important step in the extraction of energy from proteins and fats. Furthermore, succinyl CoA is necessary for the production of haemoglobin, the substance that carries oxygen in red blood cells.

It has complex structures containing corrin ring, which has two of the pyrrole rings directly bonded. Insufficient vitamin B12 consumption can lead to pernicious anaemia (lack of or inhibition of intrinsic factor i.e. gastric glycoprotein), a disease that results in nervous disturbances and low production of red blood cells.

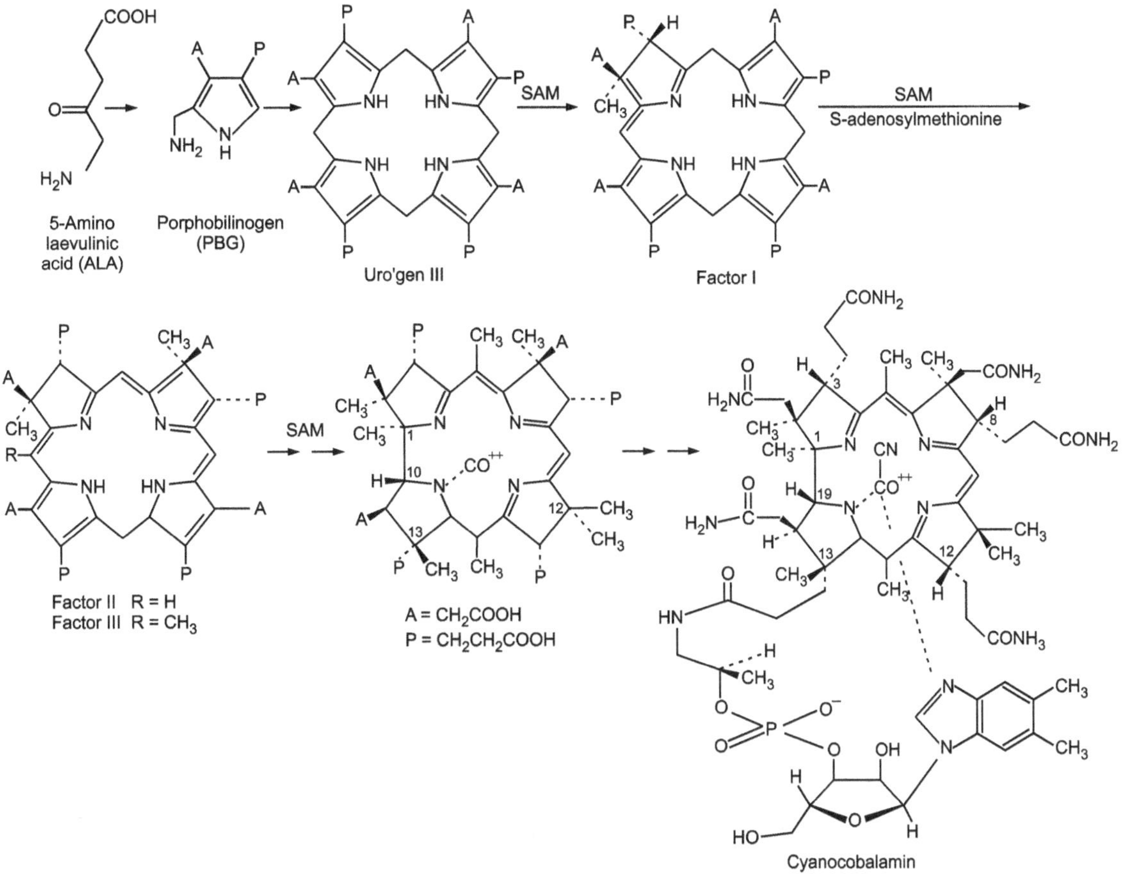

Fig. 1.4 : Cyanocobalamine biosynthesis

Folic acid is also known as Vitamin B9 and folate. Folic acid is itself not biologically active, but its biological importance is due to tetrahydrofolate and other derivatives after its conversion to dihydrofolic acid in the liver. Folate and folic acid derive their names from the Latin word folium (which means "leaf"). Leafy vegetables are a principal source.

Folate is necessary for the production and maintenance of new cells, for DNA synthesis and RNA synthesis, and for preventing changes to DNA, and, thus, for preventing cancer.

Similar to bacteria and yeasts, plants make folates de novo from pterin, p-aminobenzoate (PABA), and glutamate moieties. In contrast, humans and other mammals lack a complete folate-synthesis pathway and thus need dietary folate. The pterin hydroxymethyldihydropteroate is formed from GTP, and PABA from chorismate. The pterin and PABA units are condensed, glutamylated, and reduced to give tetrahydrofolate, and a polyglutamyl tail is added

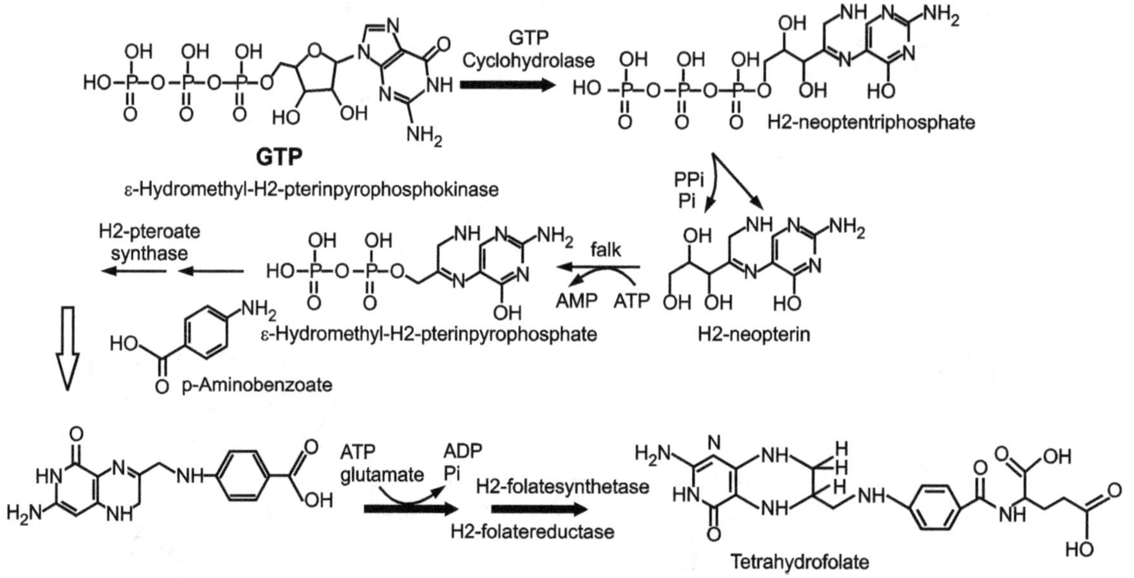

Fig. 1.5 : Folic acid biosynthesis

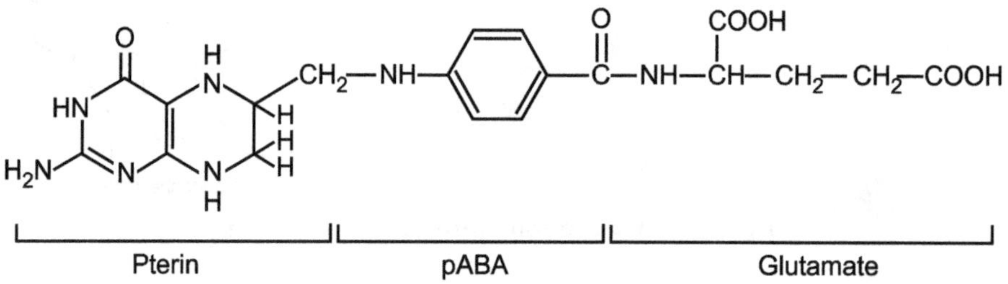

Fig. 1.6 : Tetrahydrofolate

1.9 NUCLEIC ACIDS

Nucleic acids store and transfer genetic information. A nucleic acid is a macromolecule made of chains of monomeric nucleotides. A nucleotide consists of a nucleoside and one phosphate group. Nucleosides are the nucleobases attached to a ribose or deoxyribose sugar ring. Nucleobases (Fig. 1.4) are the pyrimidine bases (Cytosine, thymine) and purines (guanine, adenine) which are found predominantly in deoxyribonucleic acid (DNA), while in ribonucleic acid (RNA) thymine is replaced by uracil.

Nucleotides are part of many important cofactors (Fig. 1.5) like Coenzyme A, flavin mononucleotide (FMN), flavin adenine dinucleotide (FAD), adenosine triphosphate (ATP) and nicotinamide adenine dinucleotide (NAD). The nuleotide derivatives are found to be involved in cytokinins (plant growth regulator), purine alkaloids (e.g.caffeine, theobromine) and pyrimidine glycosides (e.g. vicine and convicine).

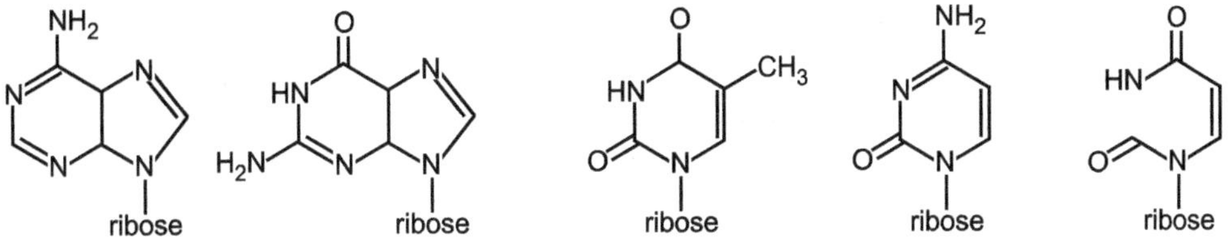

Fig. 1.7 : Nucleobases of Nucleic Acids

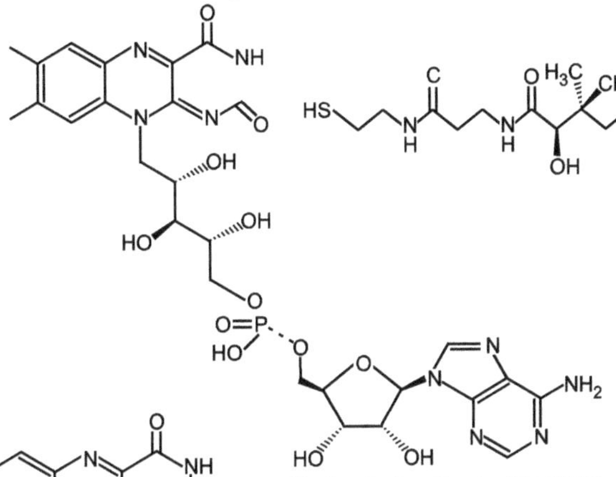

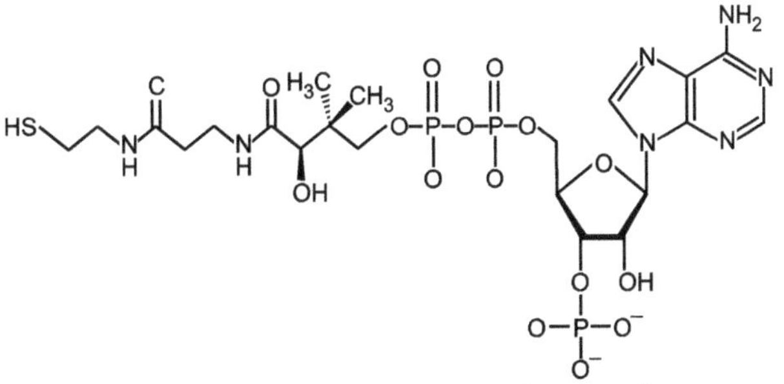

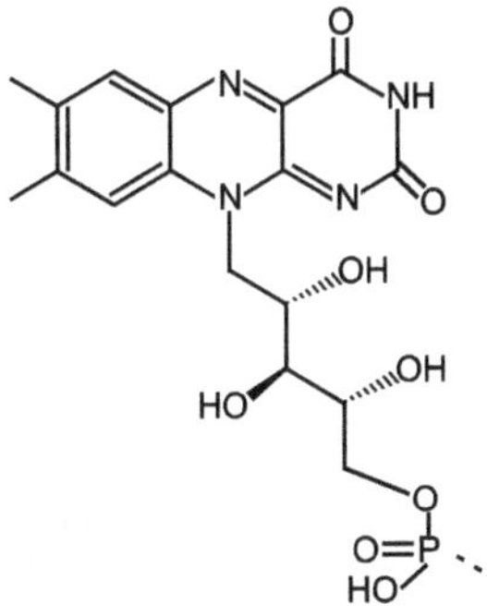

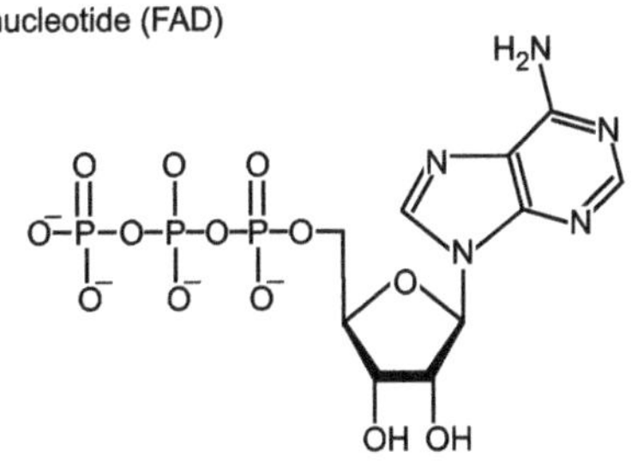

Fig. 1.8 : Nucleotide Derived Co-factors

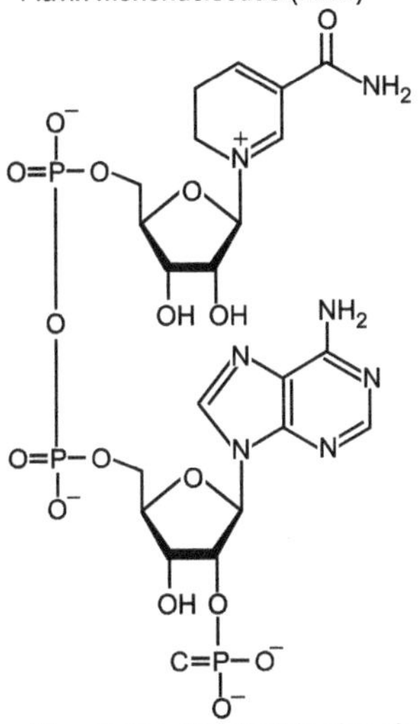

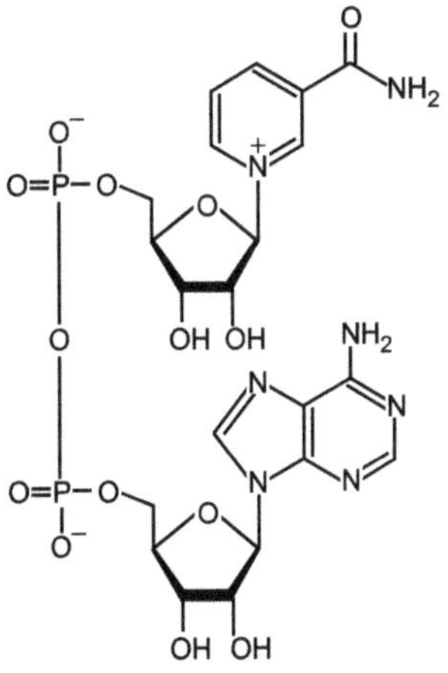

1.10 SUGARS

Sugars, primary products of photosynthesis, are the most abundant natural organic compounds defined as polyhydroxy aldehydes or ketones and the products derived from them. Sugars mainly function as sources of energy, structural components or as reserve food material. Besides these, sugars are the parts of very important secondary metabolites, glycosides, alkaloids and phenols. Ribose is a part of the backbone of genetic material i.e. RNA, DNA. They are also found linked to proteins and lipids to form glycoproteins and glycolipids. Carbohydrates can be monosaccharides, oligosaccharides and polysaccharides. Monosaccharides have two major groups : the aldoses and the ketoses. Fig. 1.6 shows all common as well as rare sugars (e.g. digitoxose, thevatose, cymarose etc.).

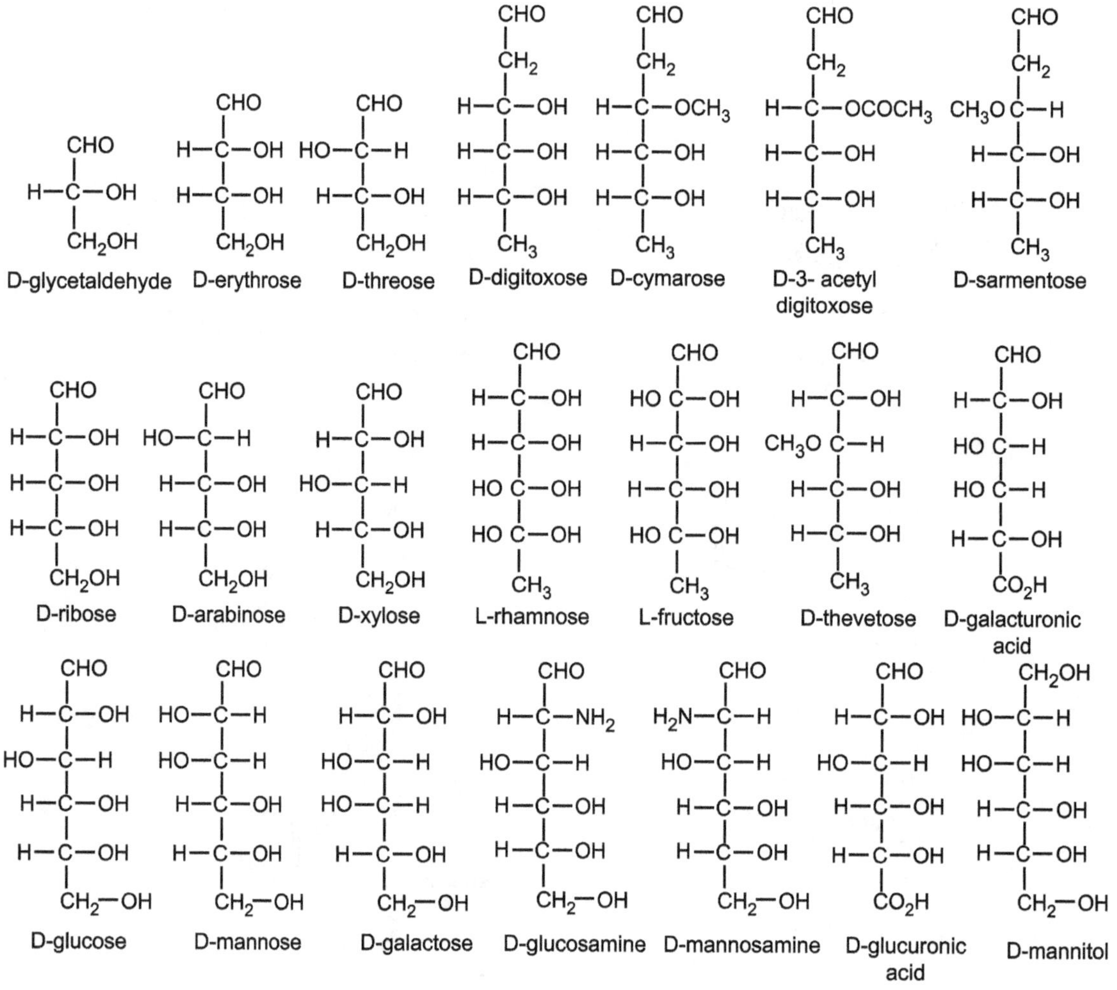

Fig. 1.9 : Sugars

1.11 LIPIDS

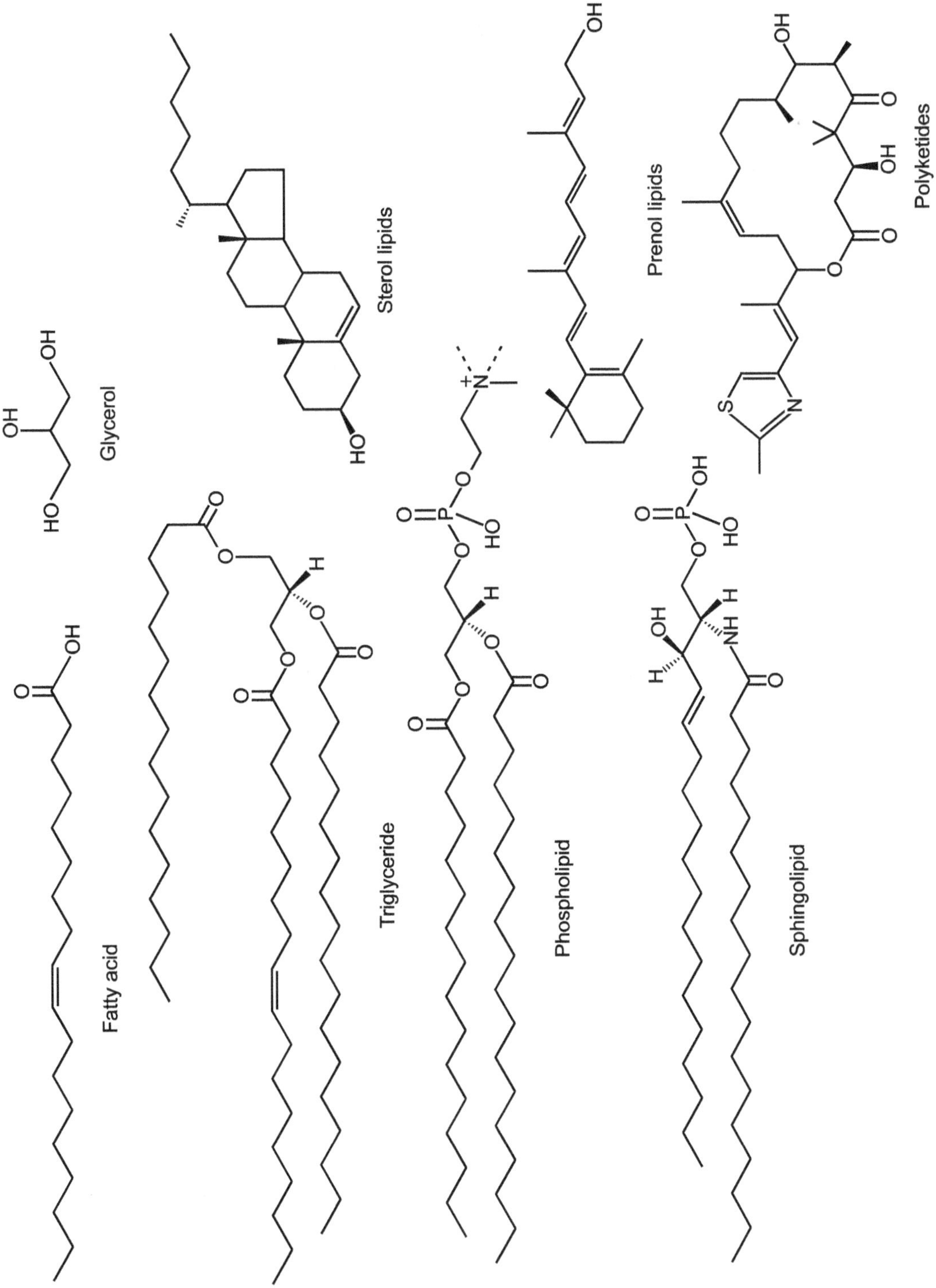

Fig. 1.10 : Types of Lipid

Lipids are hydrophobic compounds used to supply energy. They are incorporated as structural components of the brain and cell membranes. They carry fat-soluble vitamins (A, D, E, K) and are vital parts of the cell signaling. They are also found to have potential source of antioxidant compounds. Lipids can be called as oils, fats, fatty acids which include glycerols, waxes, monoglycerides, diglycerides, triglycerides, phospholipids, sphingolipids, sterols (chlolesterol), prenols (retinol) and polyketides. A few representative structures are shown in Fig. 1.7. Fats may be either solids or liquids at room temperature. Chemically, these are triesters of glycerol and fatty acids. Fatty acids consist of the carboxyl group (-COOH) at one end of the aliphatic side chain. Hydrolytic removal of glycerol from fats or oils produces fatty acids. Saturated fatty acids (SFAs) do not have double bonds between the carbons. Monounsaturated fatty acids (MUFAs) have only one double bond. Polyunsaturated fatty acids (PUFAs) have more than one double bond. Phospholipids (e.g. lecithin, cephalin, phosphatidate) are made of only two fatty acids, glycerol, phosphoric acid and simple organic molecules such as choline, serine or ethanolamine. Similarly sphingomyelin is derived from sphingosine instead of glycerol. Waxes (e.g. bees wax, carnauba wax, paraffin) are types of lipids that contain a long-chain of alkanes, alkyls, alkane esters, fatty acids, fatty alcohols or even terpenes. They are usually distinguished from fats by the lack of triglyceride esters of glycerin. Fatty acids biosynthesis starts with acetyl-CoA which polymerize and is reduced by enzyme fatty acid synthases to give fatty acids and its derivatives.

1.12 PHENOLIC COMPOUNDS

Phenolic compounds, aromatic ring bearing one or more hydroxyl substituents, from plants include a wide range of substances like simple phenols, phenolic acids, flavonoids, tannins, phenylpropanoids, anthocyanins and quinones (Fig. 1.8). Salicylic acid, p-hydroxybenzoic acid, protocatechuic acid, gallic acid, vanillic acid and gentisic acid are widely distributed plant phenolic acids. Quinones are coloured compounds containing the basic chromophore of benzoquinone which consists of 2 carbonyl groups in conjugation with 2 C-C double bonds. Quinones are divided into benzoquinones, naphthaquinones, anthraquinones and isoprenoid quinones. The phenylpropanoids contain a three-carbon side chain attached to a phenol with one or more C_6-C_3 residues. Most common among them include the hydroxycoumarins (umbelliferone and scopoletin), hydroxycinnamic acids (caffeic and coumaric acids), phenylpropenes (eugenol, anethole and myristicin), and lignans (pinoresinol, podophyllotoxins). Lignans are the polymers of cinnamic acid and derived products. Lignins, very long chain polymers, are the dimmers of lignans. Lignins, gums, mucilage, cellulose, pectin combine to form dietary fiber which acts as a bulk laxative, reduces blood cholesterol and even shows anticancer properties. Cellulose is biosynthesized from UDPG (Uridine Diphosphate Glucose obtained from disaccharides). Due to the structural support of cellulose and lignins, trees can grow tall. Flavonoids form the largest group of phenols in the form of glycosides and are hence discussed separately in glycosides.

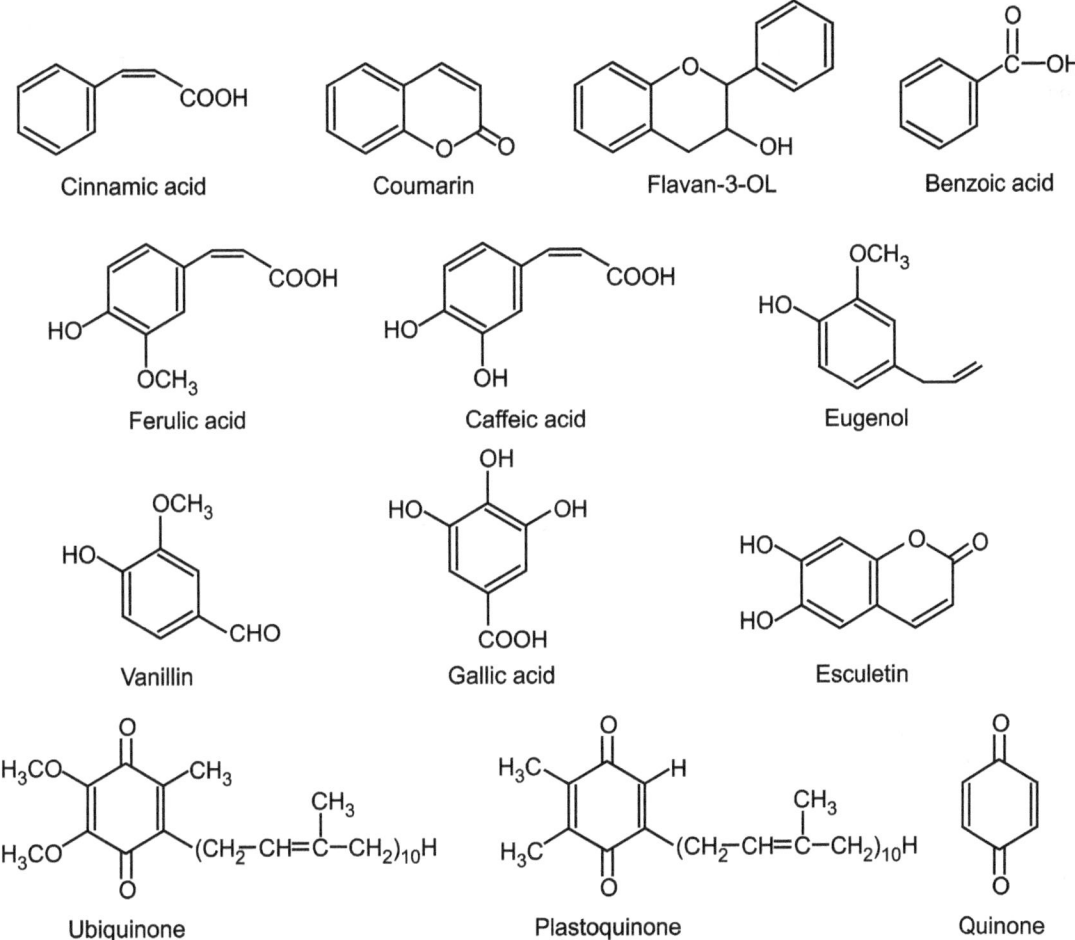

Fig. 1.11 : Common Plant Phenolic Compounds

1.13 TANNINS

Tannins are common polyphenols that either bind or precipitate the proteins to form water-insoluble polymers. This property is useful for the conversion of animal skins into leather. Tannins (Fig. 1.9) are of two types – hydrolysable and non-hydrolysable (condensed tannins). Citrus fruits, red wine and tea leaves are important sources of natural tannins.

Hydrolysable tannins, confined to dicots, consist of a polyhydric alcohol, such as glucose, to which is linked gallic acid or ellagic acid and ellagitannins in ester linkages. The hydrolysable tannins centrally involve a glucose moiety. As the name implies, these compounds are easily hydrolyzed in alkali, giving rise to a polyhydric alcohols.

The non-hydrolysable or condensed tannins are essentially derived from the polymerization of the flavan-3-ols like catechin, epicatechin and their derivatives. The name pro-anthocyanidin is used alternatively for condensed tannins because on treatment with hot-acid, some of the C-C linking bonds are broken and anthocyanidin monomers are released. Tannins are potent free radical scavengers and thus useful as anticancer substances. A variety of hydrolysable tannins have been shown to act as hormone receptor antagonists or inhibitors of particular enzymes like protein kinases.

1.14 RESINS

Resins are the complex mixtures of volatile or non-volatile terpenoids and or phenolic compounds which are secreted in specialized structures in plants. They consist of functional groups like acids, alcohols, phenols, esters and sometimes chemically inert compounds known as resenes. Resins are often associated with gums (gum-resins), volatile oils like alpha-pinene, beta-pinene, delta-3 carene and sabinene (oleo-resins) or both oil and gum (oleo-gum-resins). Balsams (e.g. Benzoin, Perubalsam, Tolubalsam and Styrax) are resinous mixtures that contain cinnamic acid, benzoic acid, or both, or esters of these acids.

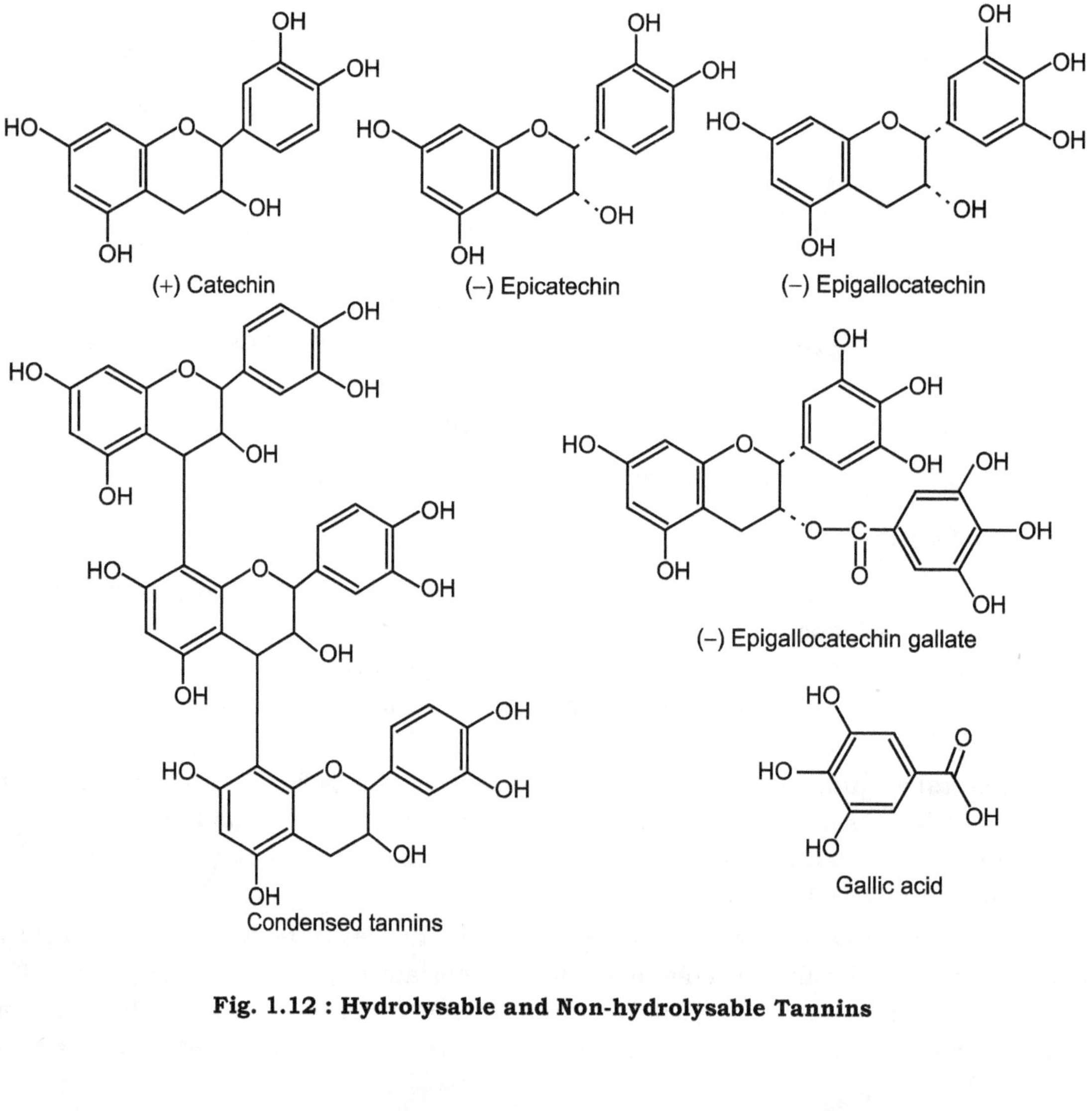

(+) Catechin

(−) Epicatechin

(−) Epigallocatechin

Condensed tannins

(−) Epigallocatechin gallate

Gallic acid

Fig. 1.12 : Hydrolysable and Non-hydrolysable Tannins

1.15 ALKALOIDS

The term "alkaloids" or "pflanzenlkalein" was coined by Meissner, a German pharmacist in 1819. The term alkaloids is derived from the word "alkali like". But now due to advancement in knowledge in Chemistry, alkaloids are defined as "physiologically active basic compounds of plant origin, in which at least one nitrogen atom forms part of a cyclic system". Table 1.6 discusses a few exceptions of alkaloids which do not confine to the above definition. The main criterion for the classification of alkaloids is the type of fundamental (normally heterocyclic) ring structure present in alkaloids. They are broadly categorized into two divisions. Heterocyclic (divided into 12 groups according to the nature of their heterocyclic ring) and non-heterocyclic (Proto alkaloids or biological amine). For details see Chapter 7.

Table 1.6 : Exceptions of Alkaloids which do not confine to the above definition

Cholines, Ephedrine	N-atom in side chain not in ring.	Ephedrine, Choline
Piperine	A compound from black pepper, neither basic nor possessing any physiological activity, still it is included in the list of alkaloids.	Piperine
Colchicine	Neither basic nor it contains N-atom in heterocyclic ring but possesses distinct pharmacological activity.	Cochicine
Thiamine	It has heterocyclic nitrogenous base, but it is universally distributed in living matter.	Thiamine

Alkaloid distribution in the plant kingdom is uneven. They have been found to be absent in algae and in the lower groups of plants with the exception of one or two families of fungi, e.g. ergot alkaloids. The alkaloids are widely distributed in higher plants, particularly the dicotyledons families like Apocyanaceae, Rubiaceae, Rutaceae, Ranunculaceae, Papaveraceae, Solanaceae, Papilionaceae. But Labiateae and Rosaceae do not contain alkaloids. Alkaloids are less frequently found in monocotyledon families like Amaryllidaceae, Liliaceae. The concentration of alkaloids in plants depends upon the season, age and its locality.

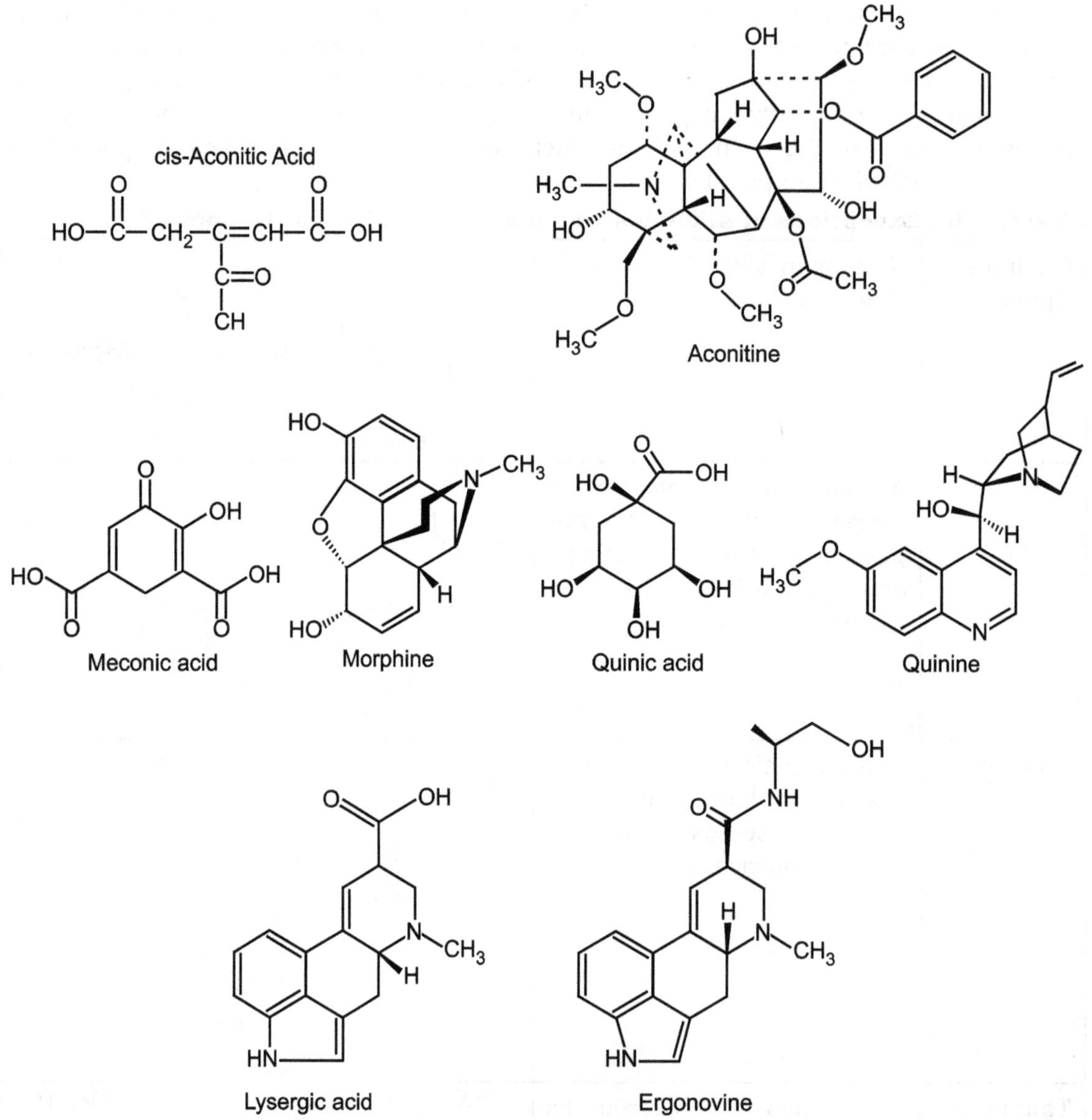

Fig. 1.13 : Alkaloids and associated Acids

It is also observed that different genera of the same family contain same or structurally related alkaloids. E.g. seven different genera of the family Solanaceae contain hyoscyamine. It is also found that simple alkaloids are often found in different plants where the complex alkaloids are in one species or genus of family.

In plants, alkaloids due to their basic nature, generally exist as salts of organic acid like acetic acid, oxalic acid, citric acid, malic acid, lactic acid, tartaric acid, tannic acid as shown in (Fig. 1.10). Example : (1) Opium alkaloids like morphine are found in the salt form of meconic acid. (2) Cinchona alkaloids are found with quinic acid. (3) Aconite alkaloids with aconitic acid. Some alkaloids like narceine and nicotine occur free in nature. A few alkaloids also occur as glycosides of sugars like glucose, rhamnose and galactose. E.g. alkaloids of *Solanum*.

Generally, all alkaloid's names must end with the suffix –ine. However, a few of them are named from the generic name of the plant producing them (e. g. Atropine from *A. belladonna*); from specific name of the plant yielding them (Belladonine from *A. belladonna*); from common name of the drug producing them (Ergotamine from *C. Purpurea*); from their specific physiological activity (Emetine from *Hedera helix*, Morphine from *P. somniferum*) and from the name of the discoverer (Pelletierine).

Alkaloidal salts are soluble in polar solvents and insoluble in organic solvents while all alkaloidal bases are soluble in the organic solvents and insoluble in the polar solvents.

Most alkaloids are generally colourless, crystalline solid compounds; however, some alkaloids are liquid in nature such as nicotine, coniine, sparteine and a few alkaloids are coloured, e.g. (1) Berberine is yellow in colour, (2) Betainidin is red in colour, (3) Salts of sanguinarine (bloodroot, *Sanguinaria canadensis*), are copper red in colour. Most alkaloids contain one or more N atoms usually in the tertiary state in a ring system. They are generally bitter to taste. Alkaloids are optically active and a majority being levorotatory, there is considerable difference in pharmacological activities of different isomers of alkaloids. E.g. (–) ephedrine is more active than (+) ephedrine, similar in case of ergotamine, (–) and (+) quinine both are pharmacologically active, while the exception is that (+) tubocurarine is more potent than (–) tubocurarine.

Alkaloids may act as reserve substances which supply nitrogen for protein synthesis. They may be end-products of the detoxification mechanism. They act as defense compounds to afford plants safety from herbivores and insects. They may function as plant's stimulants or regulators similar to the activities of hormones such as growth, metabolism and reproduction.

1.16 GLYCOSIDES

Glycosides can be defined as "organic compounds which on hydrolysis give one or more sugar moieties along with non-sugar moiety. The non-sugar component is known as the **aglycone** and the sugar component is called the *glycone*. The Aglycone part can be alcohol, anthraquinone, glycerol, sterol, phenol or terpens while the Glycone part can be glucose, galactose, mannose, rhamnose, digitoxoes, cymarose, xylose. Sugar moiety facilitates absorption of glycosides and helps in transportation of aglycone at the targeted site. Plants store important chemicals in the form of inactive glycosides. In animals (including humans), poisons are often bound to sugar molecules in order to remove them from the body. Glycone is attached by an acetal linkage to an aglycone (glycosidic linkage). An acetal has two ether functions at a single carbon atom. Thus, chemically glycosides are acetals or sugar ethers. Much of the chemistry of glycosides is explained in the section on 'glycosidic bonds'.

Glycosides readily undergo hydrolysis. The glycone and aglycone portions can be chemically separated by hydrolysis in the presence of acid and enzymes (plant glycoside hydrolases, synthetic glycosyltransferases). The mechanism by which aldehydes or ketones are interconverted to acetals or ketals is catalysed with aqueous acid but not aqueous base. Hence, glycosides can be hydrolysed with aqueous acid to give the component saccharides. Mutant enzymes glycosynthases have been developed that can form glycosidic bonds in excellent yield. There are a great many ways to chemically synthesize glycosidic bonds (Fischer glycosidation and Koenigs-Knorr reaction) by the reaction of unprotected monosaccharides or glycosyl halides with alcohols (usually as solvent) in the presence of metal salts or strong acid catalyst.

By elimination of a water molecule, linkage or a bridge is formed and the type of glycosides (Table 1.7) formed is named by putting the element as prefix like C-glycoside, N-glycoside, O-glycoside or S-glycoside. The interaction occurs between –OH group of glycone and –H coming through any of radicals like CH, –OH, –SH, and –NH present on glycone part.

Table 1.7 : Classification of Glycosides on the Basis of Linkage

Type	Structure
C-glycoside (Uncommon in higher plants) e.g. aloin from aloe, anthraquinone, cascacarosides from cascara Glycone –OH + HC-aglycone → glycone –c– glycone + H_2O	Aloin (barbaloin)
O-glycosides (Common in higher plants) e.g. Senna, rhubarb, fragula Glycone-OH + HO-aglycone → Glycone-O-aglycone + H_2O	Sennoside A
S-glycosides from sulfhydryl group e.g. Sinigrin from black mustard Glycone-OH + HS-glycone → glycone-S-aglycone + H_2O	

N-glycosides e.g. Nucleosides
Glycone-OH + N-glycone → glycone-N-aglycone + H_2O

Nicotinamide adenine dinucleotide (NAD^+)

1.16.1 Anthraquinone Glycosides

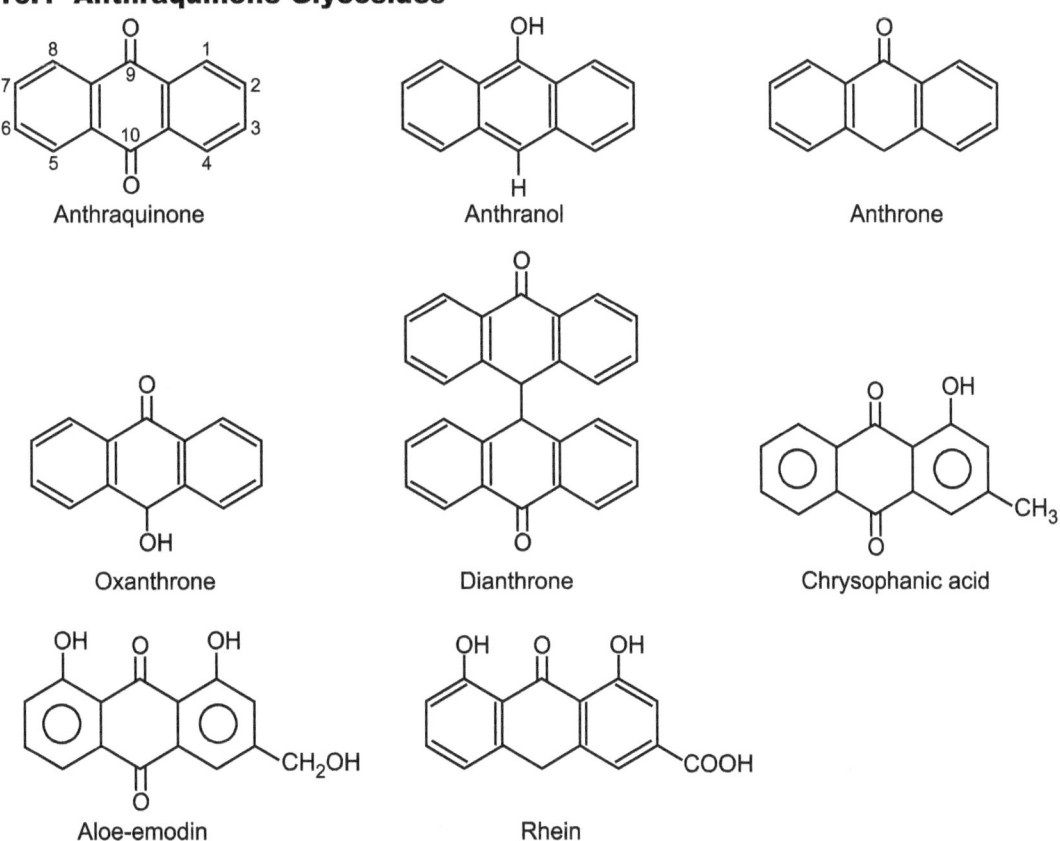

Fig. 1.14 : Reduced and Oxidised Forms of Anthraquinone

These glycosides contain an aglycone group that is a derivative of anthraquinone. Anthraquinone (9, 10-dioxoanthracene) is an aromatic organic compound. It is a derivative of anthracene. It is present in senna, rhubarb, cascara and aloes. Reduced forms (Fig. 1.11) of anthraquinone are anthrone, anthranol, oxanthrone. The Bimeric form is Dianthrone. Its oxidized form exhibits milder activity as compared to the reduced form. Anthraquinone naturally occurs in dicot plants and families like Leguminosae, Liliaceae, Rubiaceae, Rhamnaceae, Scrophulariaceae, Polygonaceae, but lower plants like bryophytes, pterodophytes and gymnosperms are devoid of such glycosides. In fungi, lichens and insects, these glycosides serve as a basic skeleton for their pigments. Natural anthraquinone derivatives from senna, cascara, rhubarb (Fig. 1.12) tend to have a laxative effect. They exert their action by increasing the tone of smooth muscle in the wall of colon and stimulate secretion of water and electrolytes into the large intestine.

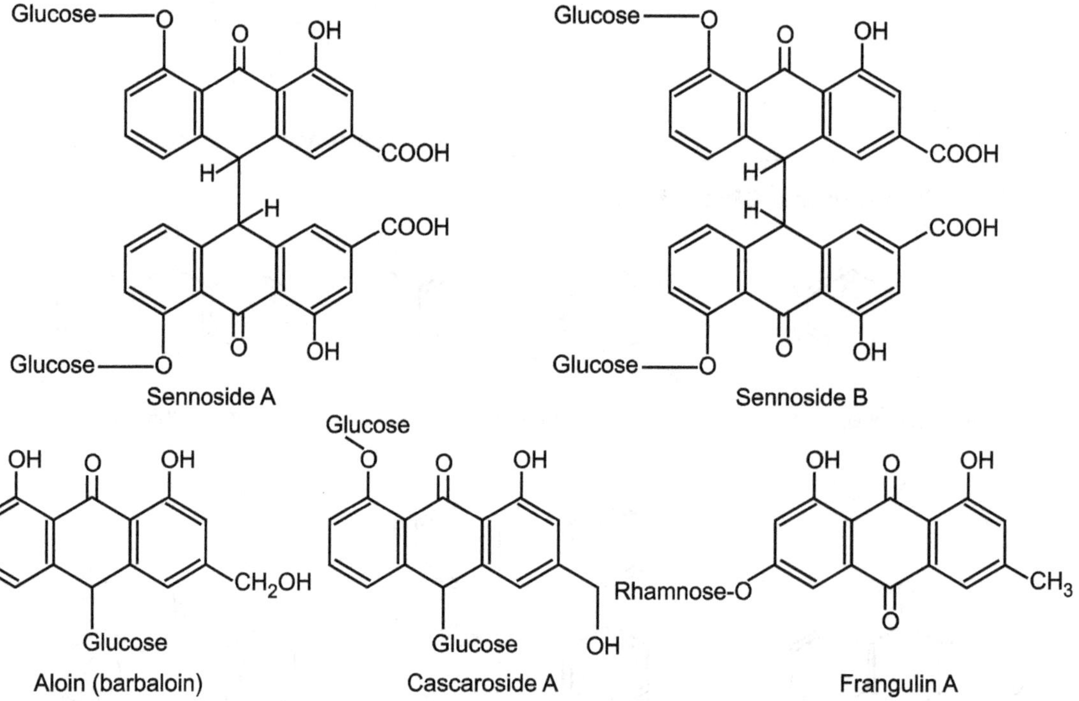

Fig. 1.15 : Anthraquinone Glycosides

1.16.2 Cardioactive Steroidal Glycosides

Cardioactive steroids have steroidal nucleus as an aglycone part along with rare sugars (digitoxose, cymarose, thevatose). Cardiac glycosides are used in the treatment of congestive heart failure and cardiac arrhythmia. In Africa these are used as arrow-poisons for hunting. These glycosides are restricted to angiosperms. Cardenoloides are generally found in Leguminoseae, Sterculaceae, Crucifereae, Scrophularaceae, Euphorbiaceae while Bufadienoloides are restricted to Liliaceae, Ranunculaceae. Cardenoloides are the C_{23} membered ring compounds containing a five membered lactone ring with single double bond. Examples : digitalis, stropanthus, thevetia.

Cardenolides　　　　　　Bufadienolides

Bufadienolides (the term derives from the toad genus Bufo) are C_{24} membered ring compounds containing six membered lactone ring with two double bonds in lactone moiety, Examples : squill, hellebore. Fig. 1.13 elaborates the aglycone moieties of cardioactive sterols.

Common features of cardio active steroids include,
- Steroidal nucleus must be present.
- 3b-OH group involved in glycosidic linkage.
- 14b-OH group at C-14.
- A/B ring junction *cis*
- B/C ring junction *trans*
- C/D ring junction *cis*
- Additional oH groups at C-5, C-11 and C-16 may be present.
- The presence of lactone ring

Beta linkage at C_3 position is necessary for activity. Presence of beta-hydroxyl group at C_3, C_{12}, C_{14}, or C_{16} modifies the activity and toxicity of the compounds. Lactone group should be beta oriented with at least one double bond.

According to the type of lactone ring Cardiac Glycosides are classified into:

Cardinolides : They are C-23 containing 5-membered unsaturated lactone ring, e.g. *Digitalis* & *Strophanthus*.

Bufadienolides : They are C-24 containing 6-membered unsaturated lactone ring, e.g. *Squill*.

Heart diseases can be primarily grouped into three major disorders : cardiac failure, ischemia and cardiac arrhythmia. Cardiac failure is actually the inability of the heart to pump blood effectively. So heart beats rapidly but weakly. Reduced contraction of heart leads to reduced heart output. But new blood keeps coming in, resulting in the increase in heart blood volume. Hence, the term congestive heart failure. Congested heart leads to lowered blood pressure and poor renal blood flow, edema in the lower extremities and the lung (pulmonary edema) as well as renal failure. The process of membrane depolarization / repolarization is controlled by the movement of three cations, Na^+, Ca^{+2}, and K^+, in and out of the cell. Cardioactive drugs act by inhibiting Na – K – ATPase enzyme which causes elevation in intracellular calcium concentration that ultimately results in an increase in the force of the myocardial contraction or a positive ionotropic effect.

	R¹	R²	R³	R⁴	R⁵
Digitoxigenin	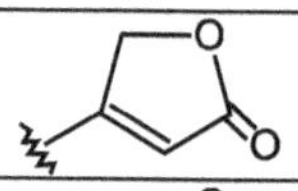 (cardenolide ring)	H	H	H	H
Digoxigenin	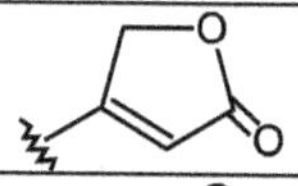 (cardenolide ring)	H	OH	H	H
Gitoxigenin	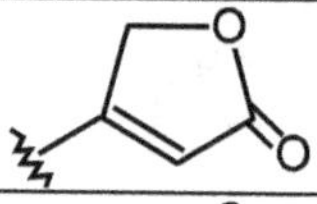 (cardenolide ring)	OH	H	H	H
Strophanthidin	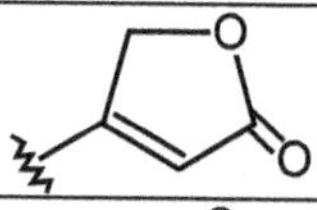 (cardenolide ring)	OH	H	=O	H
Ouabagenin	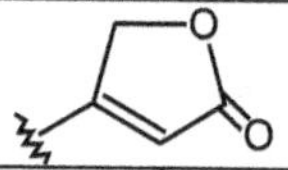 (cardenolide ring)	H	H	OH	H
Bufalin	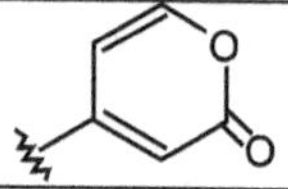 (butadienolide ring)	H	H	H	H
Hellebrigenin	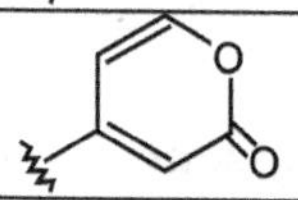 (butadienolide ring)	H	H	=O	OH

Fig. 1.16 : Cardenolides and Butadienolides

1.16.3 Flavonoid Glycosides

These are naturally occurring phenols comprising a large group of glycosides (o-glycosides and some are c-glycosides). About 2% of carbon photosynthesized by plants is converted to flavonoides or closely related compounds. It is biosynthesized from shikimic acid pathway and acetate pathway. Most flavonoids are found in the vacuole of the plant cell. Pteridophyta, dicots, monocots, gymnosperms shows presence of flavonoids. The prominent families like Leguminoseae, Polygonaceae, Rutaceae, Apiaceae contain flavonoids.

The basic moiety of this class is a 15 carbon skeleton where two phenyl rings are converted to a 3-carbon bridge. In case of chalcone and dihydrochalcone this 3-carbon bridge is open. The different classes of flavonoids include the chalcones, aurones, flavanones, flavanonols, flavones, anthocyanidins, flavonols, catechins, leucoanthocyanidins and isoflavones whose general structures are shown in Fig. 1.14. Examples are (shown in Fig. 1.15) Hesperidin (aglycone : Hesperetin, glycone : Rutinose), Naringin (aglycone : Naringenin, glycone : Rutinose), Rutin (aglycone : Quercetin, glycone : Rutinose), Quercitrin (aglycone : Quercetin, glycone : Rhamnose)

Flavonoids are very well-known for their properties which include antioxidant, antimicrobial, antiinflammatory, anticancer, antidiabetic, hypolipidemic and the like. The anthocyanins are the common red and rare blue pigments of flowers. The catechins and leucoanthocyanidins (Fig. 1.16) polymerize to form condensed tannins. Silymarin from Milk thistle *Silybum marianum* (Antihepatotoxic), Wedelolactone from *Eclipta alba* (Cirrhosis of liver), Genistin from *Glycin max* (antiulcer) are classic examples of flavonoids. Flavonoids are collectively also called as bioflavonoids i.e. vitamin P, known to decrease capillary fragility.

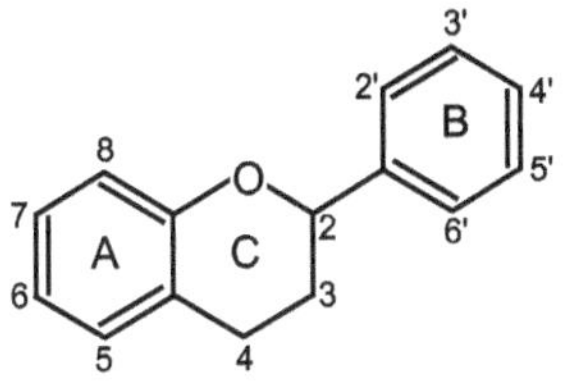

Flavan, 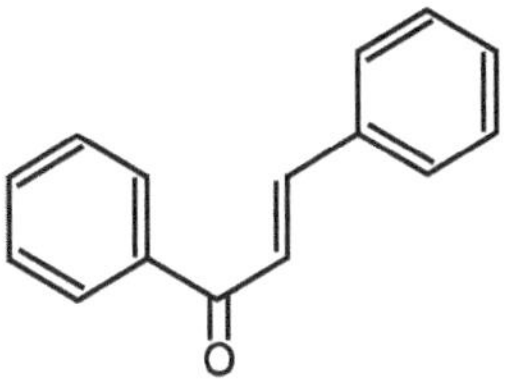 Chalcones, 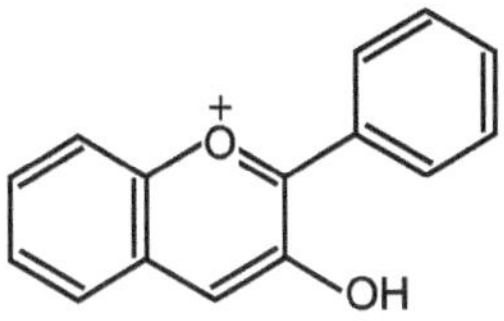 Anthocyanidins

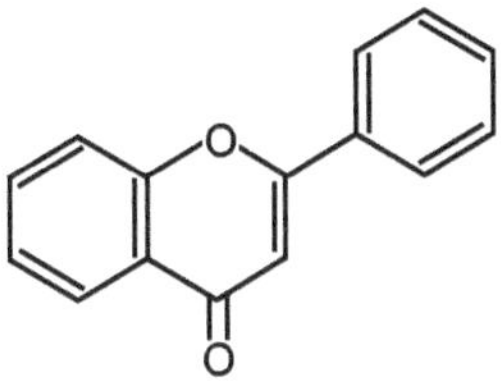

Flavone, 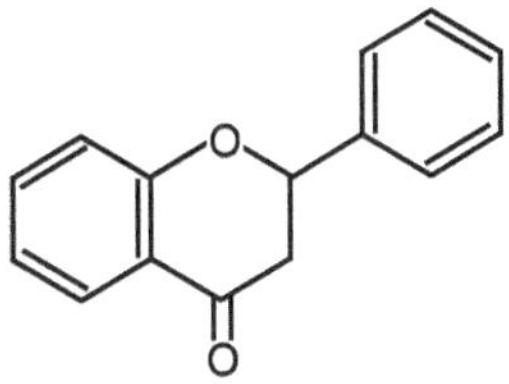 Flavanone, 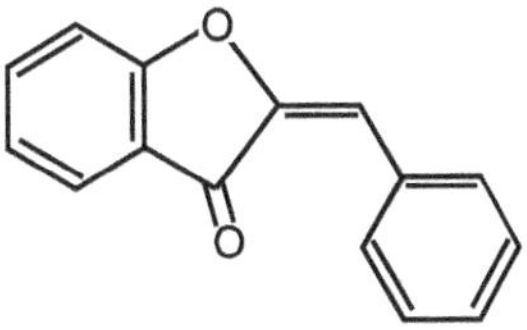 Aurone

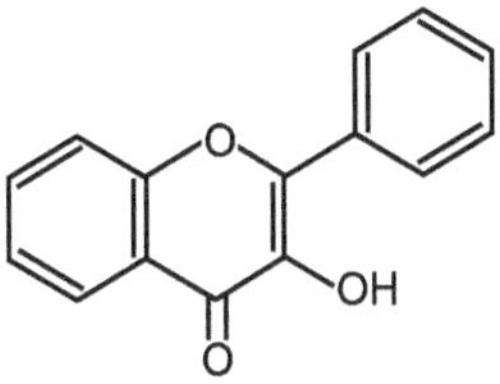

Flavonol, 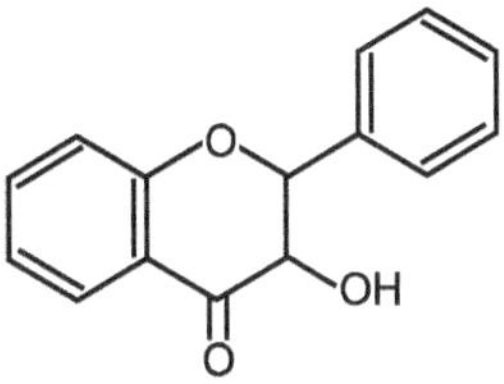 Dihydroflavonol, 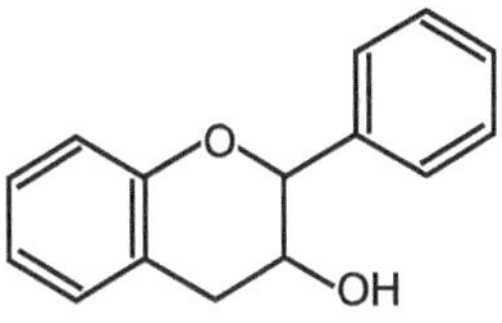 Flavan-3-ol

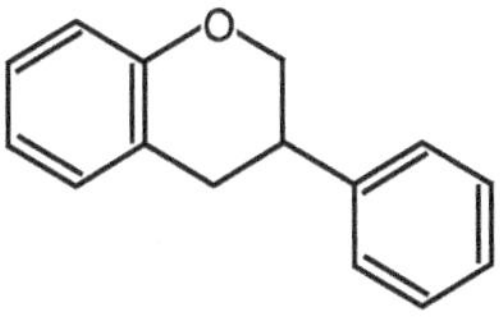

Isoflavan, 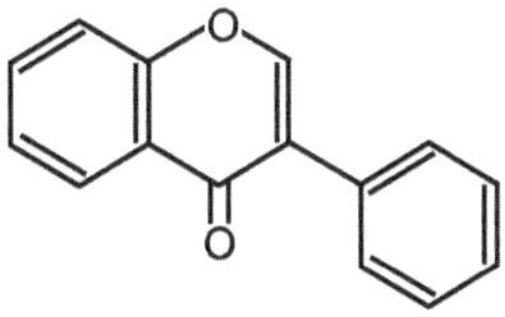 Isoflavone, 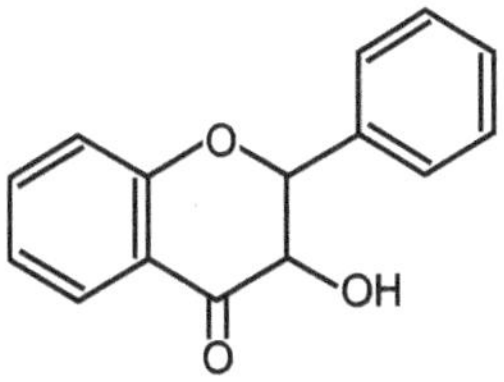 Flavanonols

Fig. 1.17 : Basic Nucleus and Derived Structures of Flavonoids

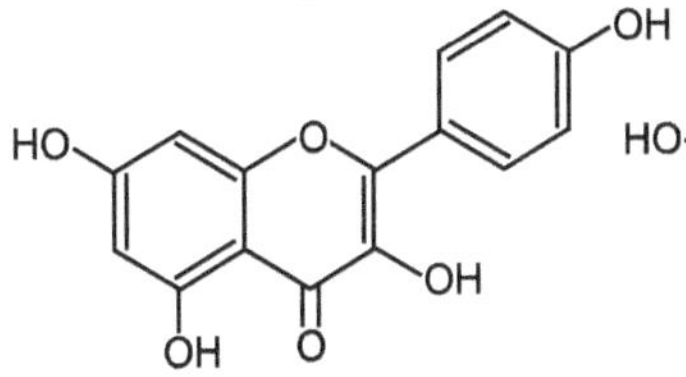

Kaempferol, 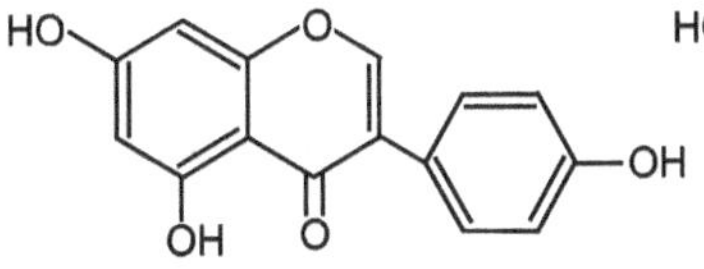 Daidzein, 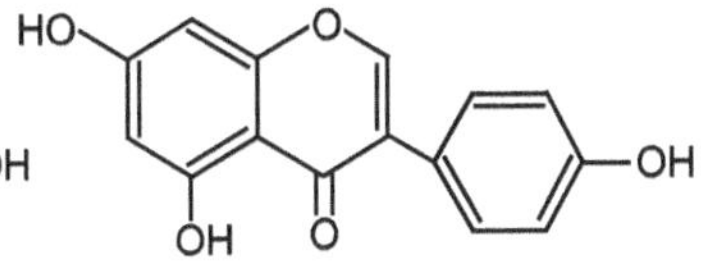 Genistein

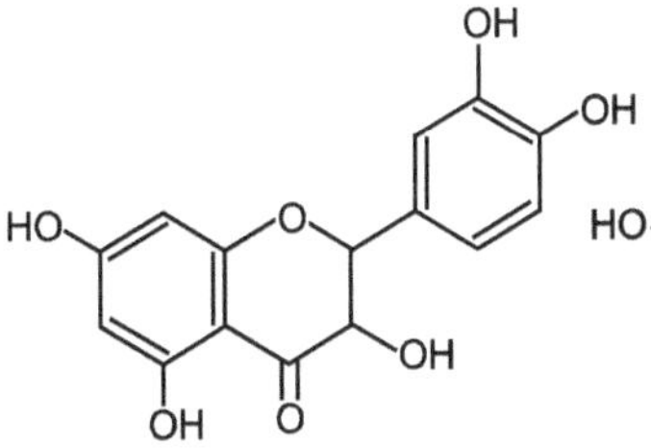

Taxifolin, 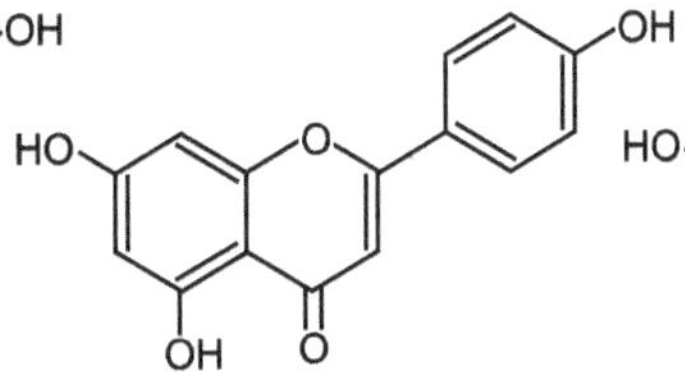 Apigenin, 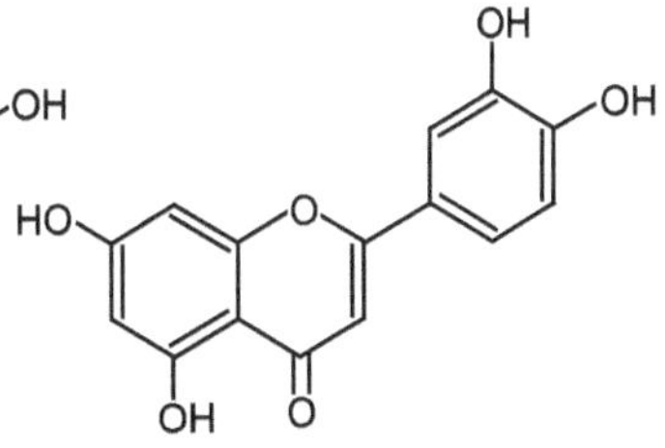 Luteolin

Contd. ...

Contd. ...

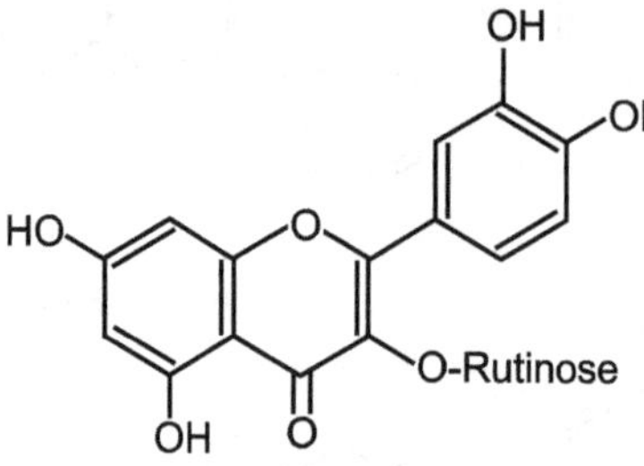

Fig. 1.18 : Flavonoids

Rutin, 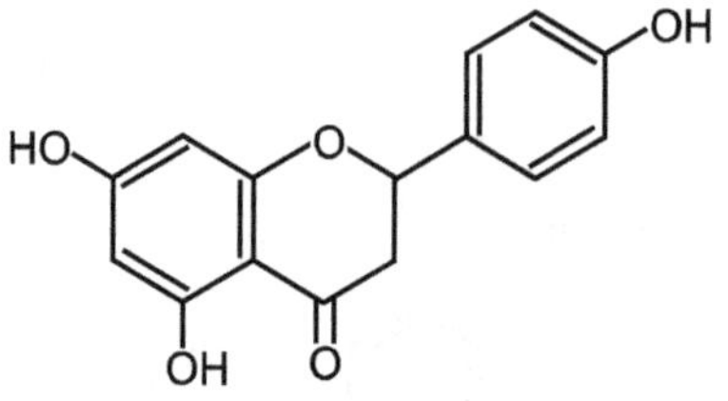 Naringenin, 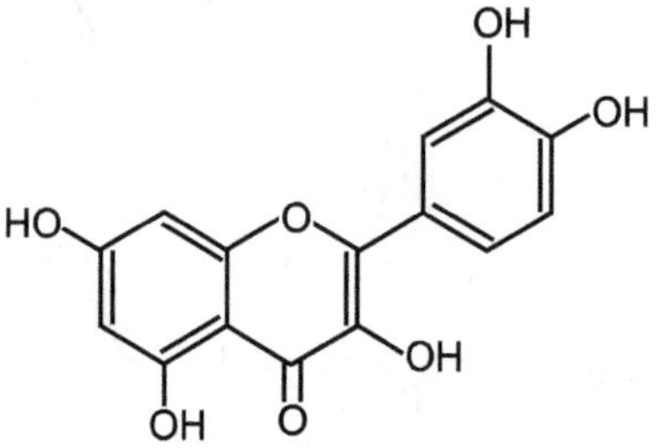 Quercetin, 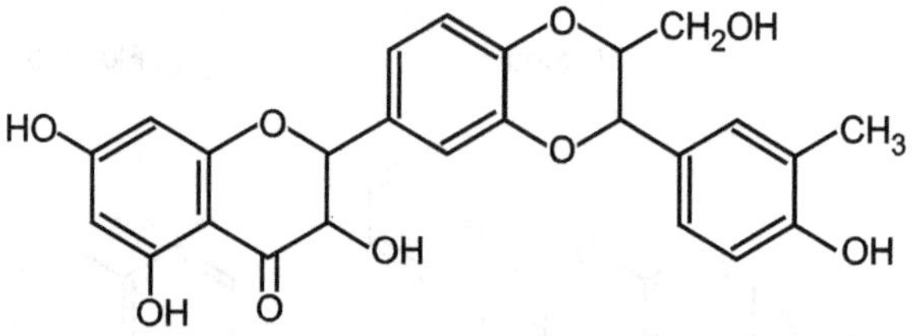 Silibinin

Fig. 1.19 : Anthocyanidins

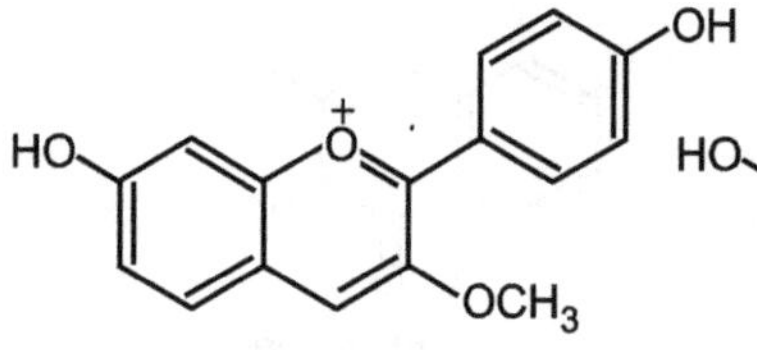

Anthocyanin, 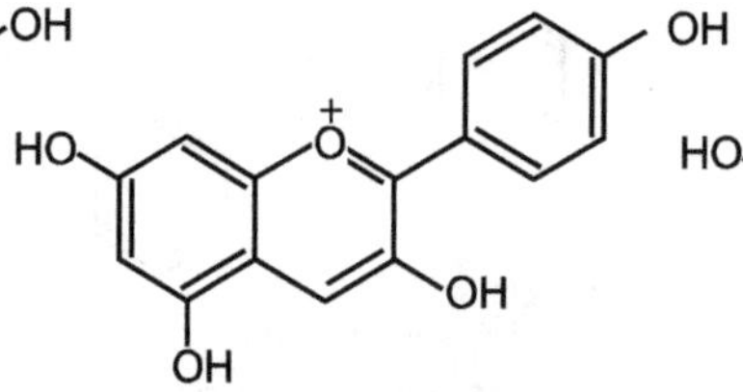 Pelargonidin, 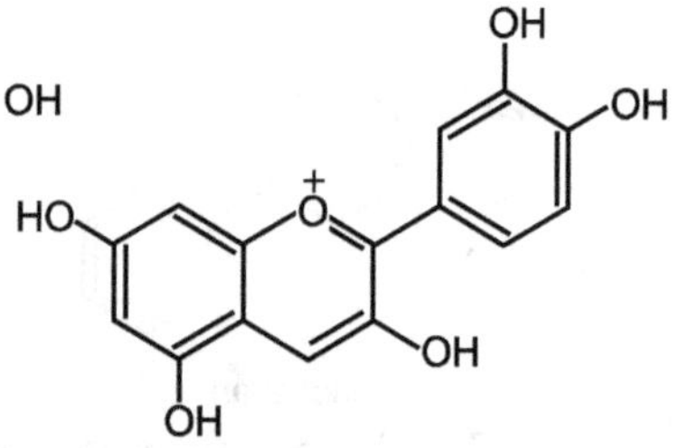 Cyanidin, 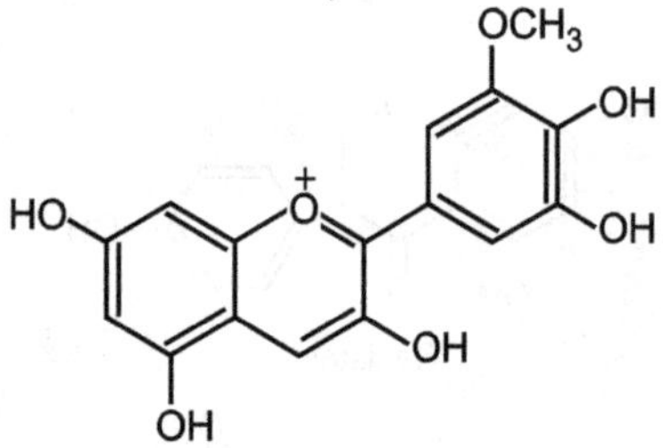 Petunidin, 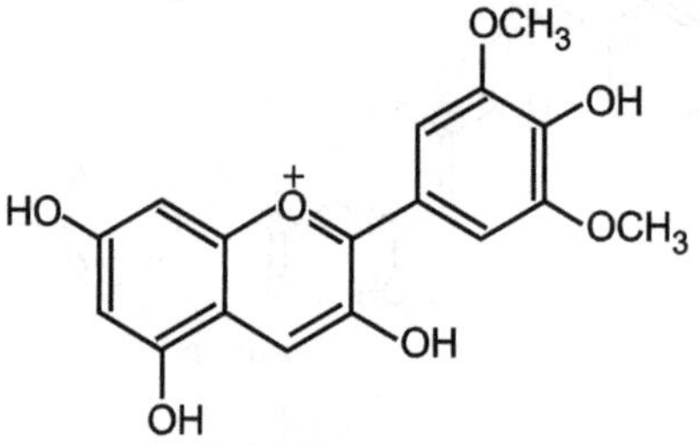 Malvidin, 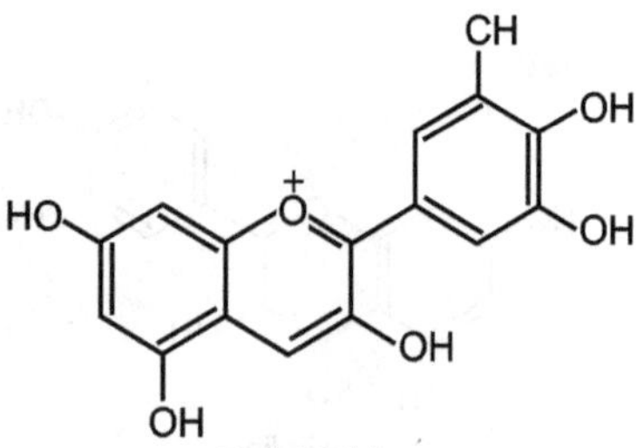 Delphinidin

1.16.4 Coumarin Glycosides

These glycosides consist of coumarin (alpha benzopyrone) as an aglycone moiety. Coumarins are mostly present in free form but sometimes occur as glycosides. They are considered to be derived from hydroxy cinnamic acid. These are distributed in families such as Leguminoseae, Solanaceae, Rubiaceae, Caprifoliaceae, Umbelifereae. Furanocoumarines forms by fusion of furan ring to coumarin at C_6 or C_7 position or $C_7 - C_8$ position. Example (Fig. 1.17) : Coumarin : umbelliferone, scopoletin, asculetin, aesculin. Furanocoumarines : psoralen , khellin, visnagin.

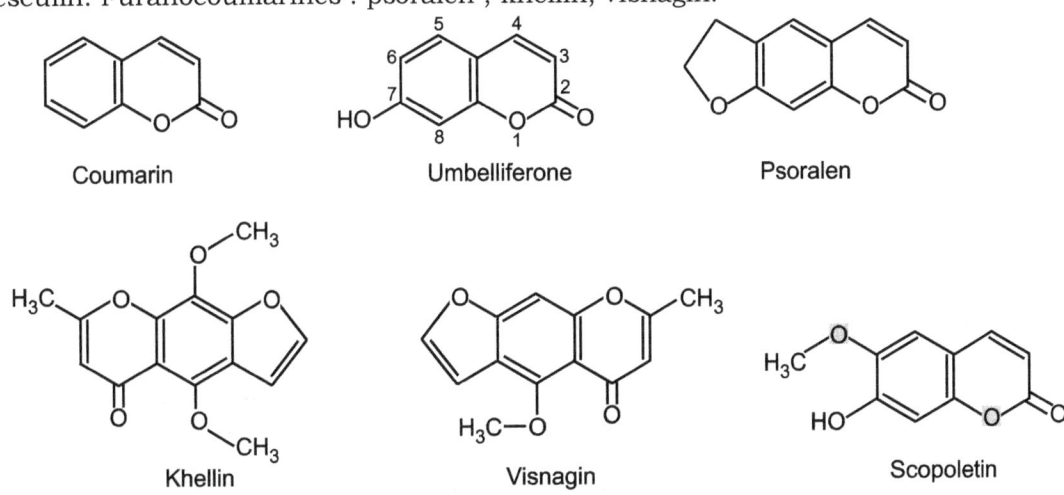

Fig. 1.20 : Coumarin Glycosides

1.16.5 Cyanogenic Glycosides

These are also called as cyanophore or aldehyde or mandelonitrile glycosides which contain hydrocyanic acid moiety as an aglycone part. These are actually derivatives of mandelonitrile (nitriles of mandelic acid) which on hydrolysis gives HCN and benzaldehyde. Example (Fig. 1.18) : Amygdalin from bitter almonds (*Prunus amygdalus*, rosaceae); Prunacin from Wild cherry bark (*Prunus serotina*, rosaceae). Cyanogenetic glycosides are distributed in about 110 families, among rosaceae is prominent.

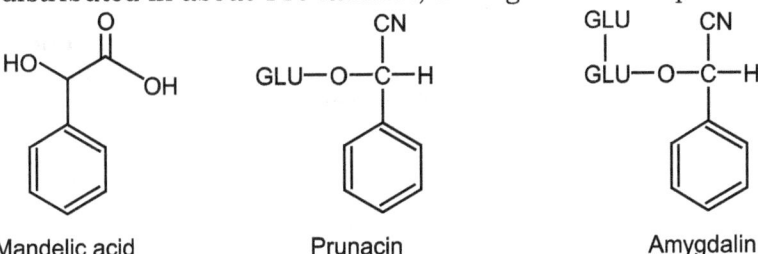

Fig. 1.21 : Cyanogenetic Glycosides

1.16.6 Isothiocyanate Glycosides

Glucosinolate compounds or S-Glycosides contain aglycone moiety isothiocyanate (sulphur along with nitrogen). There are distributed only in dicotyledons families like Crucifereae, Capparidaceae, Rosaceae. Chemically these compounds contain beta-D-1 glycopyranosyl residues i.e. glucosinolate. The general structure is given in Fig. 1.19. Examples : sinigrin from *Brassica nigra* (Black mustard) sinalbin from *Sinapis alba*

(White mustard). These are inactive in themselves but break down (either spontaneously in acid conditions or in hydrolytic reactions catalyzed by P-glycosidases) to liberate cyanide which is a potent inhibitor of cytochrome oxidase which is involved in the final transfer of electrons to molecular oxygen in the mitochondril respiratory chain. Biosynthetically cyanogenetic glycosides are derived from amino acids.

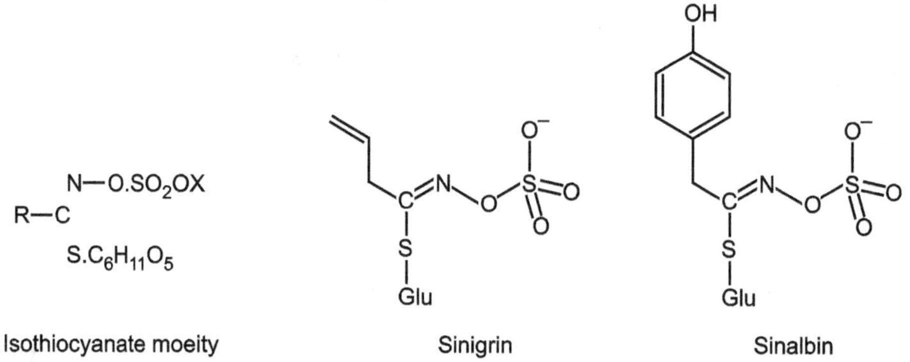

Isothiocyanate moeity — Sinigrin — Sinalbin

Fig. 1.22 : Isothiocyanate Glycosides

1.16.7 Saponin Glycosides

Saponin (Latin name which means "soap like") are high molecular weight compounds which possess specific characteristics such as foam formation in aqueous solution, bitter and acrid taste, haemolysis of RBC, irritation to mucosa. On the basis of aglycones, saponins can be steroidal saponins or tetracyclic triterpenoid saponins. Steroid saponins (Dioscorea, shatavari, sarsaparilla) are distributed in families Amarylliaceae, Dioscoreaceae, Liliaceae, Apocynaceae, Leguminoseae, Solanaceae and the like. Steroidal saponins are cyclopentano-phenanthrene derivatives (Fig. 1.20). These are useful in the synthesis of a number of medicinally potent steroids such as vitamin D, sex hormones like testosterone, progesterone, oestradiol and the like. Pentacyclic triterpenoid saponins (glychrrhiza, brahmi, ginseng, senega) are restricted to families Leguminoseae, Araliaceae etc. It is linked with either sugars or uronic acids. Triterpenoid saponins may be further classified into three major categories namely α-amyrin, β-amyrin and lupeol (Fig. 1.21).

Miscellaneous glycosides involve steviol glycosides (stevioside and rebaudioside A) which are sweeter than sucrose. Phenolic glycosides arbutin obtained from common Bearberry (*Arctostaphylos uva-ursi*) has a urinary antiseptic effect. Alcoholic β-glycoside like salicin which is found in the genus salix is an anti-inflammatory compound.

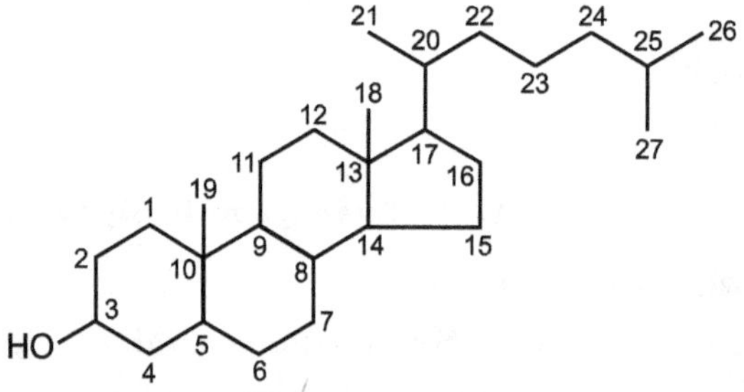

Steroid moeity

Contd. ...

Contd. ...

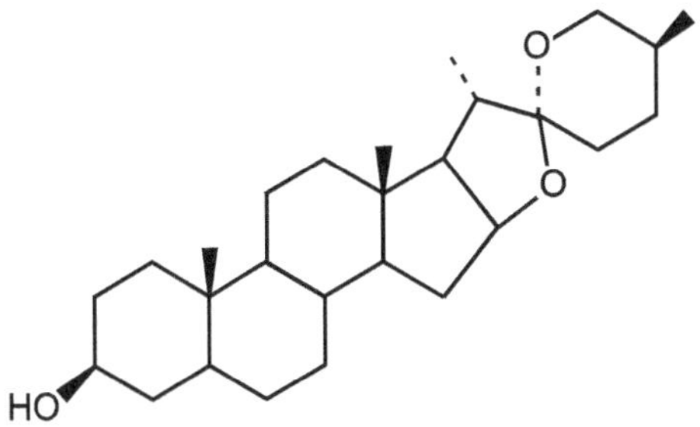

Fig. 1.23 : Steroidal Saponins

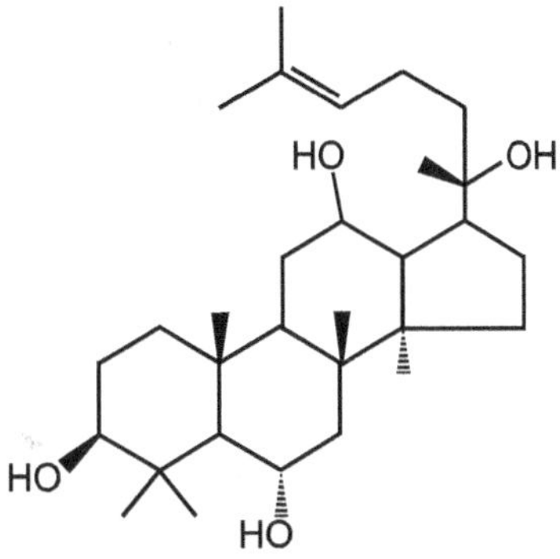

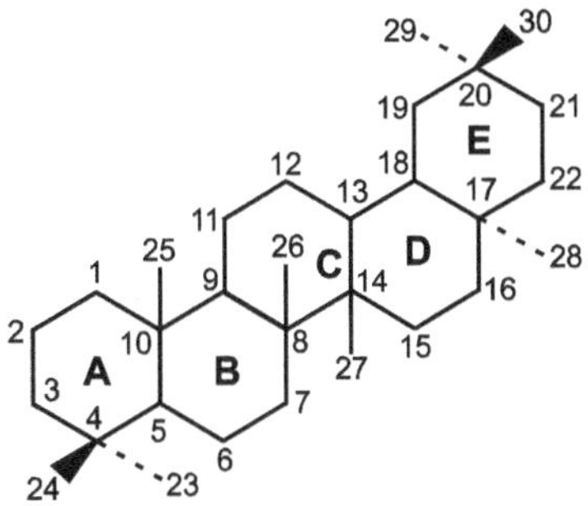

Sarsapogenin

Ginsenoside Rg1

Pentacyclic triterpenoid skeleton

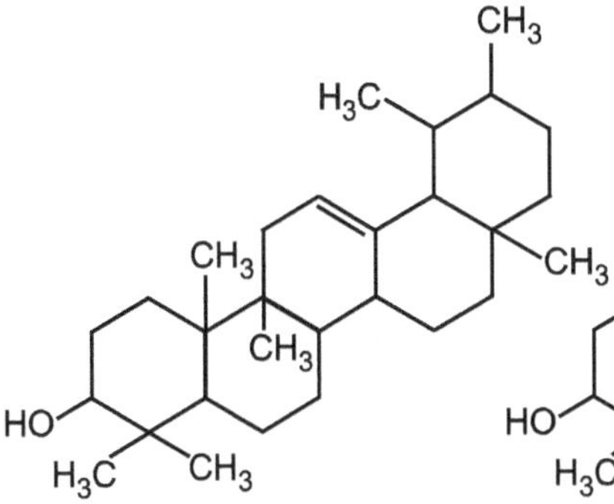

α - Amyrin

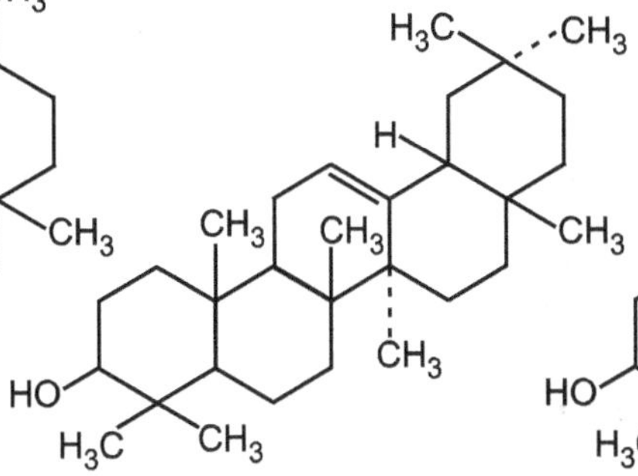

β - Amyrin

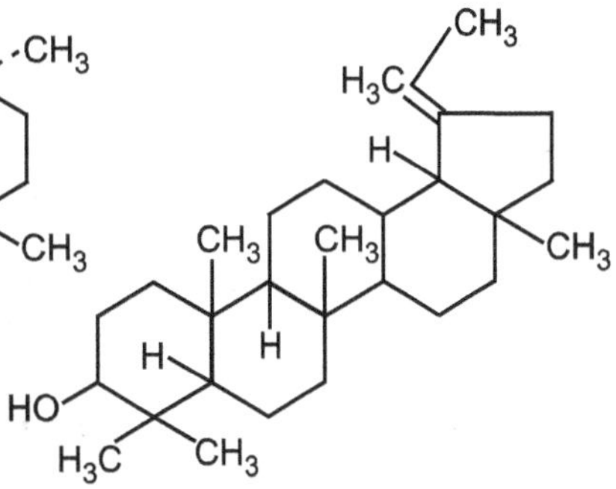

Lupeol

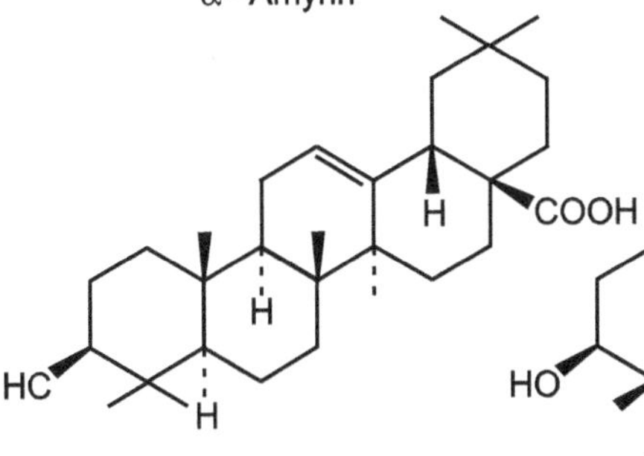

Oleonolic acid

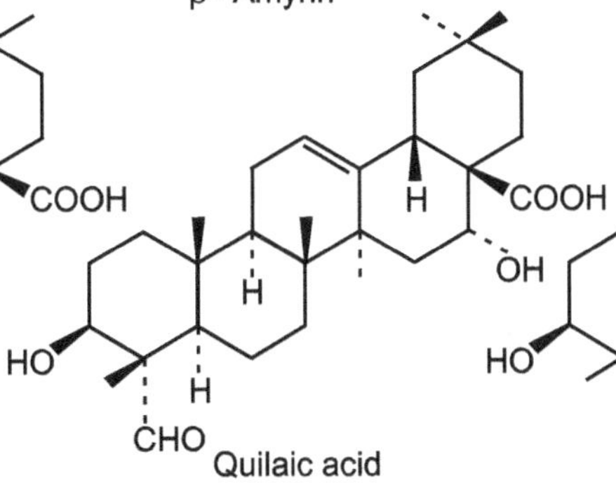

Quilaic acid

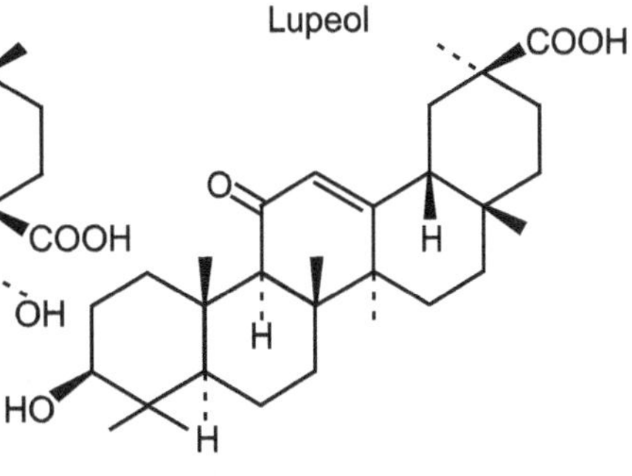

Glycyrrhzetic acid

Fig. 1.24 : Triterpenoid Saponins

1.17 TERPENOIDS

Terpenoids are most widespread chemically interesting compounds which provide structures of great diversity. Although majority of terpenoids occur in the plant kingdom more particularly among phanerograms, a few of them are also obtained from other sources. These are commonly found in Labiateae, Rutaceae, Piperaceae, Zinziberaceae, Umbelliferae, Myrtaceae, Lauraceae. The oils derived from carbon and hydrogen are called 'terpenes' and their oxygenated compounds are called 'terpenoids'. Terepnes are found to be involved in carotenoid biosynthesis, hormone regulation and flower colours.

Chemically these are derived from isoprene units and their oxygenated compounds. The simpler mono and sesquiterpenoids are the chief constituents of the essential oils.

Only mono and sesquiterpenoids are volatile in nature while higher terpenoids are non-volatile. "Odorous volatile principles of plant and animal origin are known as essential oils or etheral oils or volatile oils." Plants containing essential oils are known as aromatic plants. They produce characteristic flavours and/or odours due to the presence of compounds that are volatile in nature. These are called essential due to the fact that they represent the essence or active principle of the plant.

Most of them are colourless liquids particularly when they are fresh, but on long standing they may oxidize, and darken in colour. They are characterized by high refractive indices. Most of them are optically active and their specific rotation is often a valuable diagnostic property. Essential oils are immiscible with water. Density is generally lower than water and they are soluble in common organic solvents such as ether, alcohol etc.

They are unsaturated compounds having one or more double bonds. The structure can be open chain or cyclic, with one or more carbon atoms in the ring. Terpenoids undergo addition reactions with hydrogen, halogen etc. They also form characteristic addition products with NO_2, $NOCl$ and $NOBr$. These addition products are found to be useful in the identification of terpenoids. A number of addition products have antiseptic properties. They undergo polymerization and dehydrogenation. As they have olefin bonds they are very easily oxidized nearly by all oxidizing agent. On thermal decomposition terpenoids yield isoprene as one of the products. Thus, terpenes are classified (Table 1.8) by the number of isoprene units : Hemiterpenes C_5, Monoterpenes C_{10}, Sesquiterpenes C_{15}, Diterpenes C_{20}, Sesterterpenes C_{25} (very rare), Triterpenes C_{30}, Tetraterpenes C_{40}.

Table 1.8 Classification of terpenoids

Class	Number of Isoprene Unit	Molecular Formulae	Examples
Hemiterpene or isoprene	1	C_5H_8	Hemiterpene from *Hamamelis japonica* leaves.
Monoterpenes	2	$C_{10}H_{16}$	Limonene, Cineole, Menthol, Carvone.
Sesquiterpenes	3	$C_{15}H_{24}$	Zingiberine, Santonin, Bornyl acetate.

Class	Number of Isoprene Unit	Molecular Formulae	Examples
Diterpenes	4	$C_{20}H_{32}$	Taxol, Forskolin, Abietic acid.
Triterpenes	6	$C_{30}H_{48}$	Glycyrrhizin, amberin azadirachtin.
Tetraterpenes	8	$C_{40}H_{64}$	B-carotene, Crocetin, Bixin.
Polyterpenes	n	$(C_5H_8)n$	Rubber.

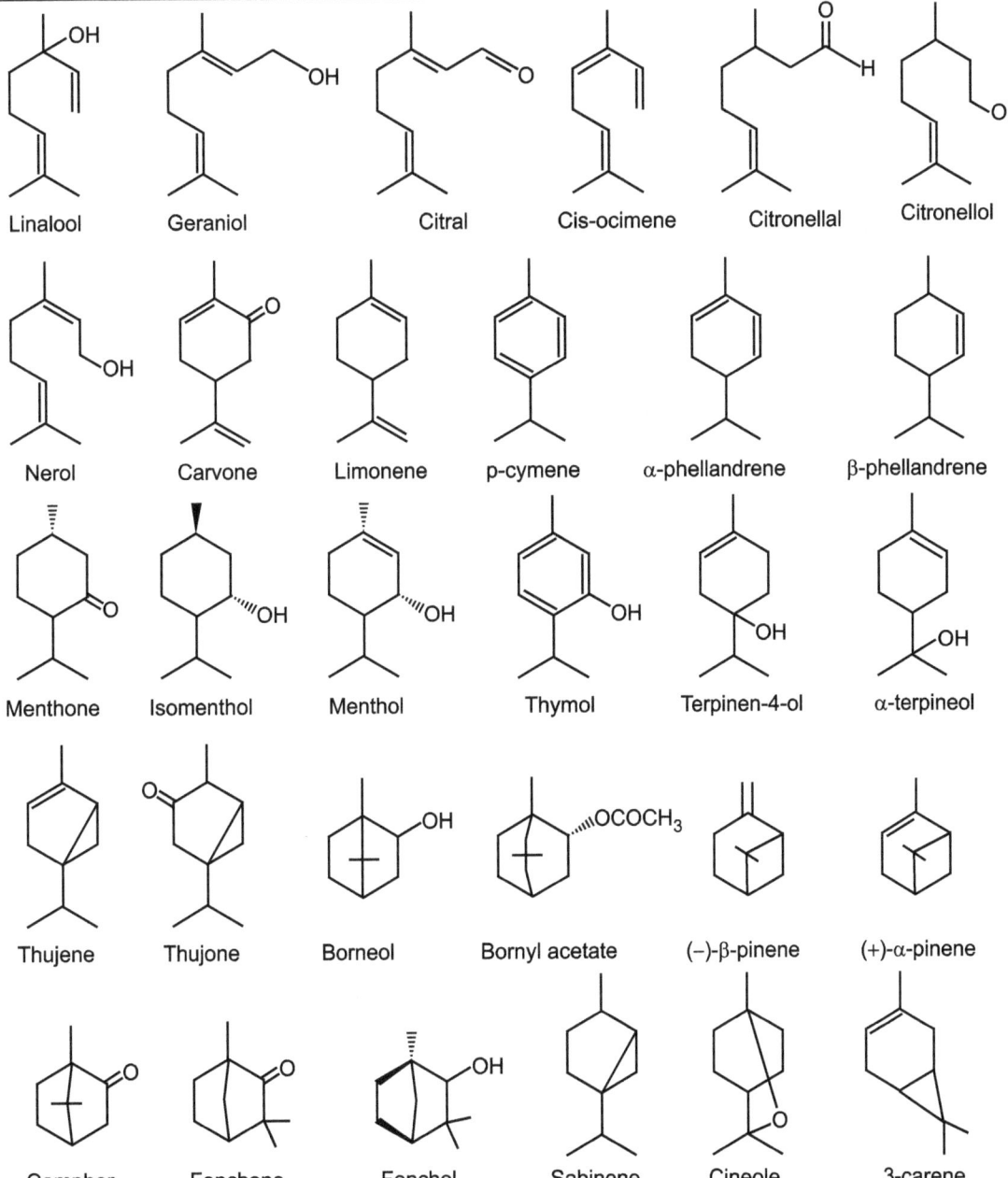

Fig. 1.25 : Monoterpenoids

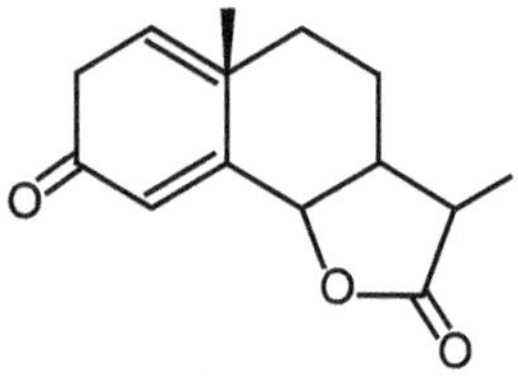

Santonin, 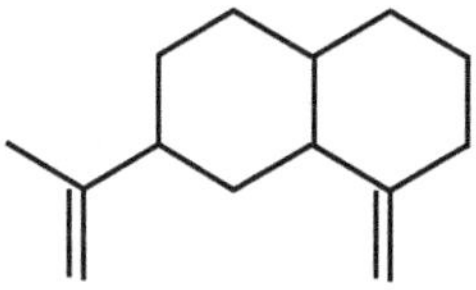 β-selinene, 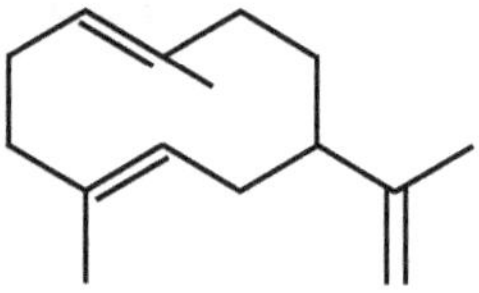 Germacrene A, 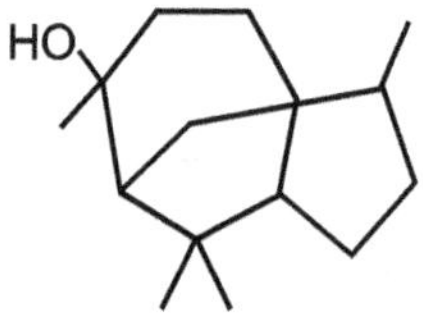 Cedrol

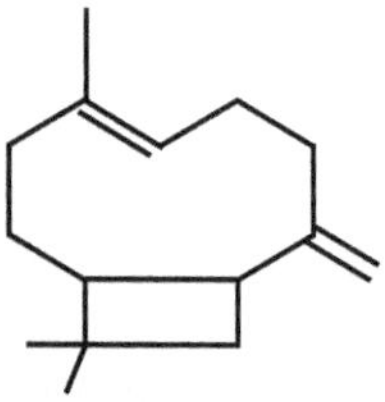

β-caryophyllene, 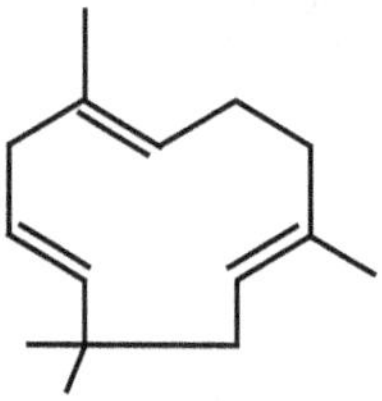 α-humulene, 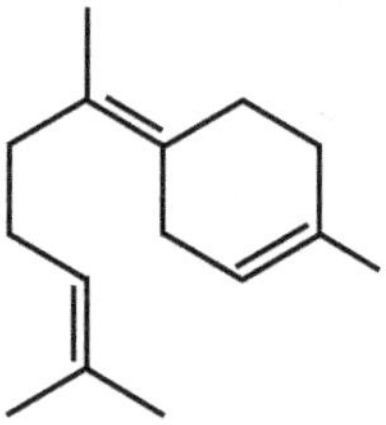 γ-bisabolene, 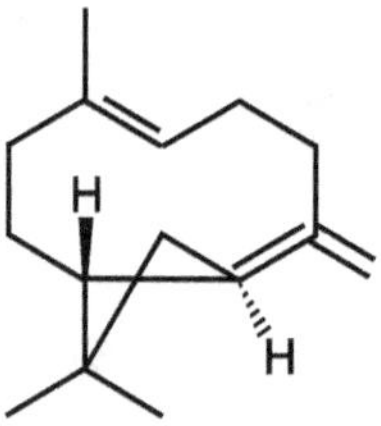 β-caryophyllene

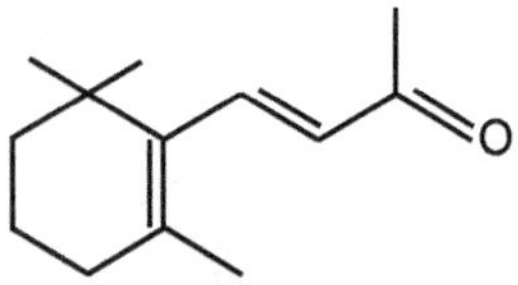

β-ionone, 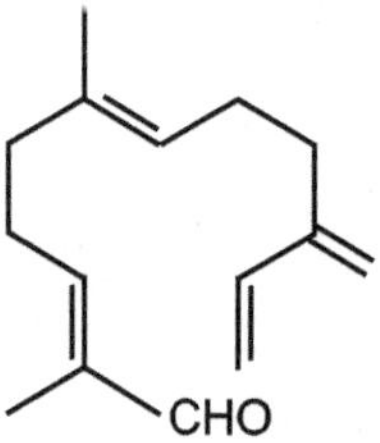 β-sinesal, 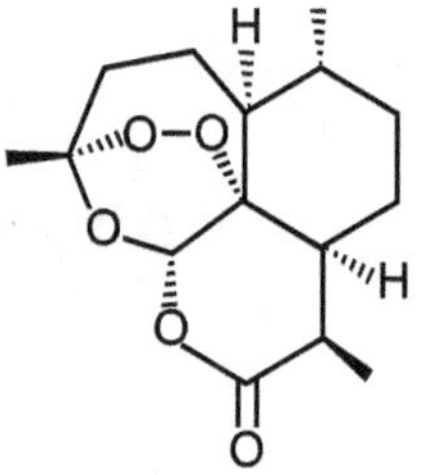 Artemisinin

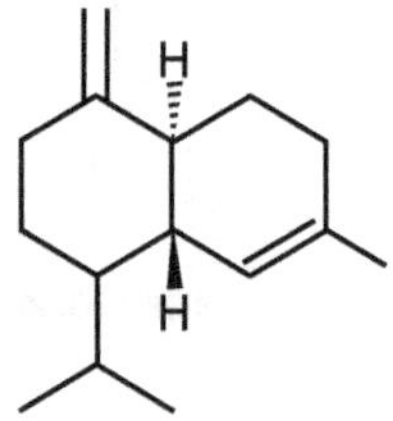

γ-cadinene, 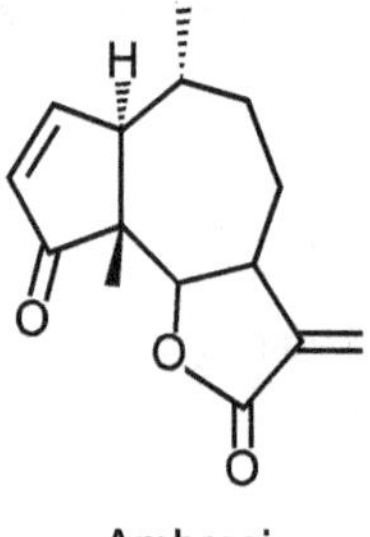 Ambrosin, 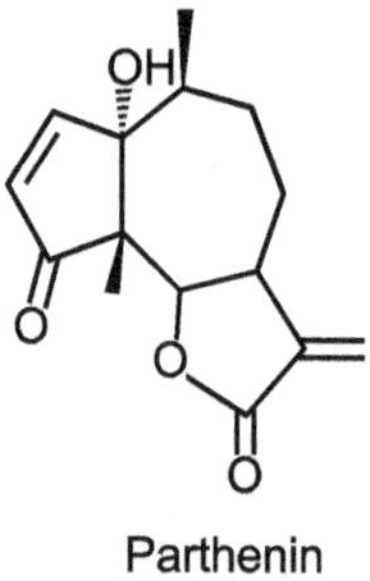 Parthenin

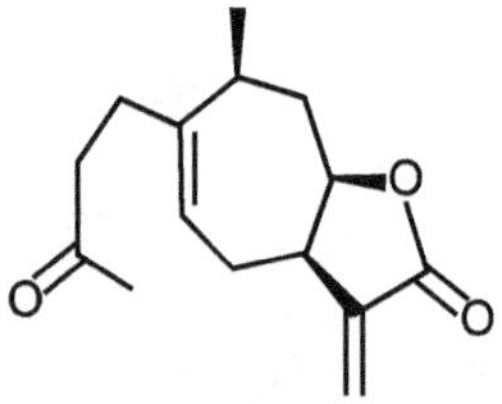

Tomentosin, 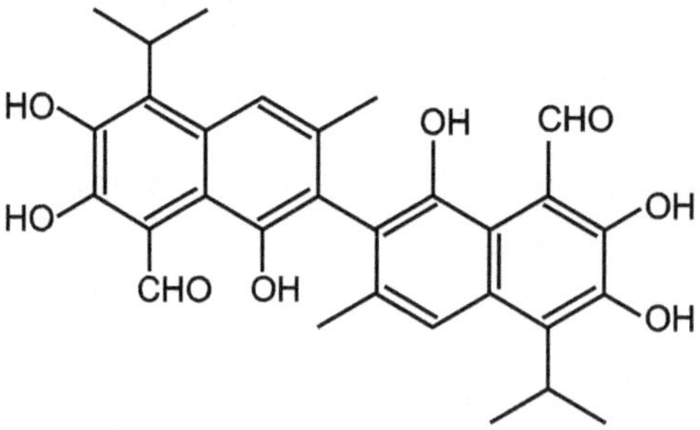 Gossypol

Fig. 1.26 : Sesquiterpenoids

It is further classified in the following subclasses on the basis of the ring present in the molecule. **Acyclic** – those having open ring structure, e.g. Myrcene; **Monocyclic** – those having one ring in their structure, e.g. Limonene; **Bicyclic** – those having two rings in their structure, e.g. Cadienene, pinene; **Tricyclic** – those having three rings in their structure, e.g. Abietic acid. Volatile oils (mono and sequiterpenoids) are classified on the basis of the functional group present which is elaborated in Table 1.9.

Table 1.9 : Classification of Volatile Oils

Functional Group		Phytoconstituent	Plant
Hydrocarbon	C_5H_8	Pinene	Turpentine
Alcohol volatile oil	C–OH	Linalool, menthol	Coriander, pepermint
Aldehyde volatile oil	CHO	Citronellal, cinnamic aldehyde	Citronella, cinnamon
Ester volatile oil	–HC=O	Borneol acetate, gualtherin	Lavender, gaultheria
Ketone volatile oil	C=O	Carvone, camphor, menthone	Caraway, camphor, spearmint
Ether	R–O–R'	Cineol, myristicin	Eucalyptus, jayphal
Peroxide volatile oil	R–O–O–R'	Ascaridole	Chenopodium
Phenol volatile oil	Ar–OH	Eugenol, thymol	Clove, cinnamon
Glycoside derived	R–Sugar	Allylisothiocynate, methyl salycilate	Wintergreen, mustard

All terpenoids biogenesis starts with mevalonic acid (see chapter 6). Monoterpenoids (Fig. 1.22) are derived from 2 isoprene units. Iridoids are monoterpenes which are typically bicyclic hemiacetals or lactones. In the seco-iridoids, the alicyclic C_5 ring is opened or expanded by oxygen insertion. Sesquiterpenes (Fig. 1.23) derived from farnesylpyrophosphate having three isoprene units include monocyclic, bicyclic and tricyclic compounds and the sesquiterpene lactones. Geranylgeranyl diphosphate (GGPP) derived diterpenoids (Fig. 1.24) involve the simplest form like phytol (part of chlorophyll and heamoglobin) as well as the most complex structure like taxol. Chlorophyll, a porphyrin molecule, is product of amino acids, magnesium and phytol molecule. Triterpenoids (Fig. 1.25) are derived from combination of two FPP molecules. Steroids, saponins, quassinoids and limonoids are actually the modified triterpenoids. Carotenoids and related products are the examples of tetraterpenoids (Fig. 1.26).

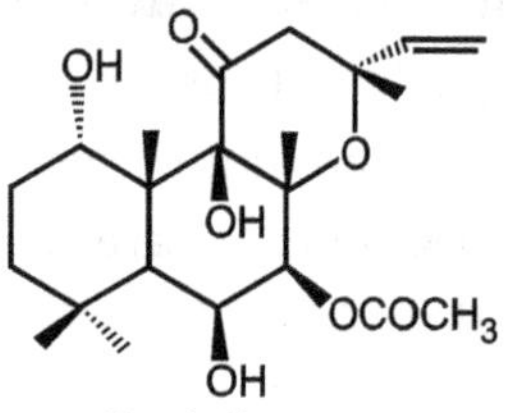
Forskolin

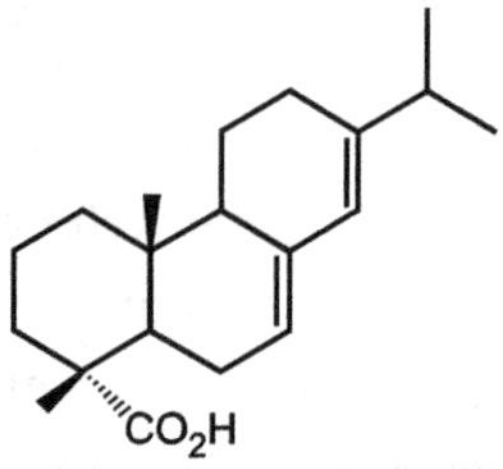
Abietic acd

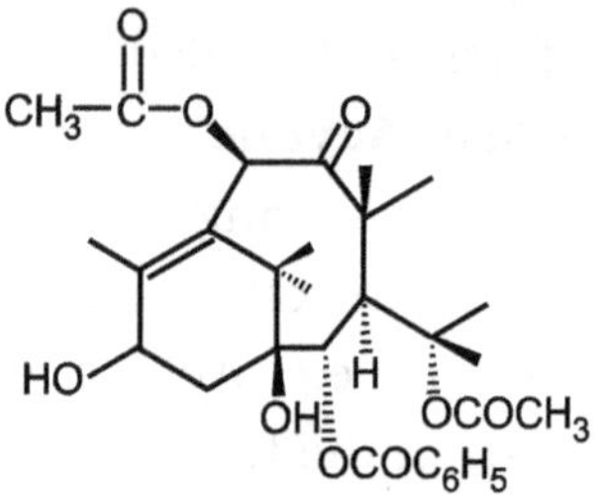
Baocatin III

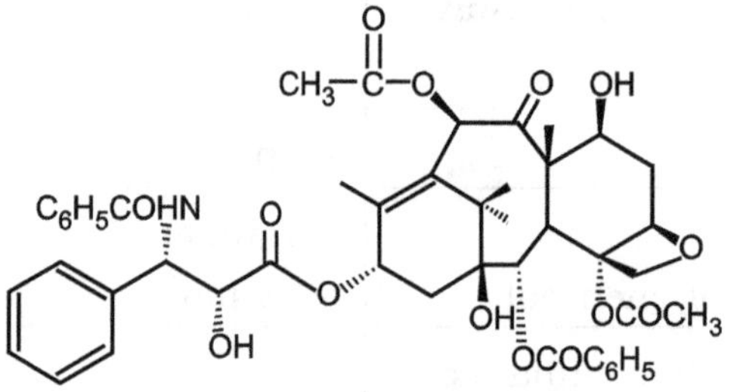
Taxol

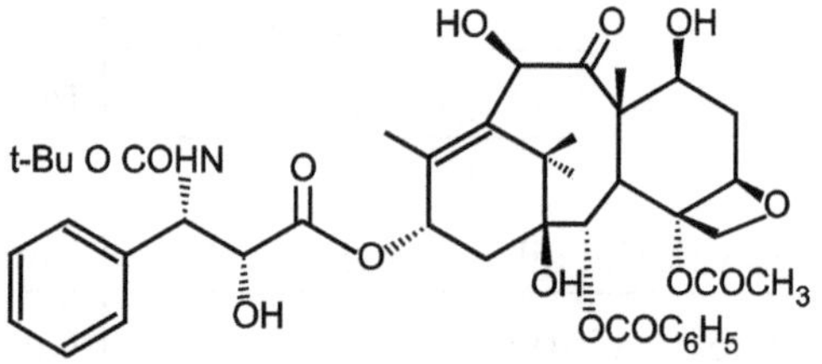
Taxotere

Fig. 1.27 : Diterpenoids

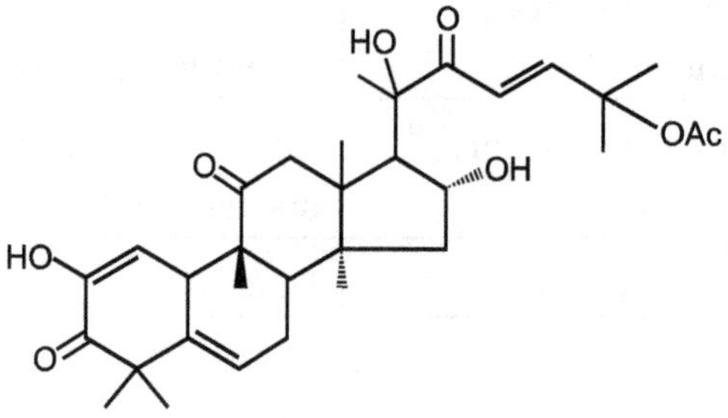
Cucurbitacin E

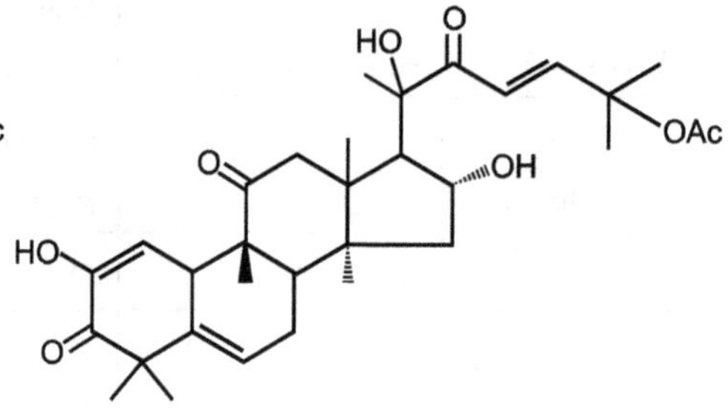
Cucurbitacin B

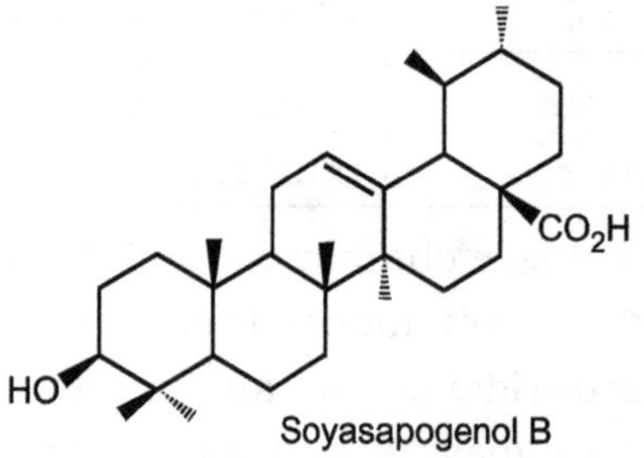
Soyasapogenol B

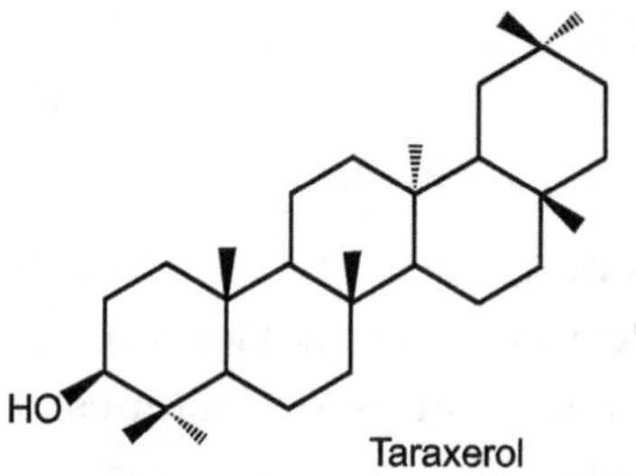
Taraxerol

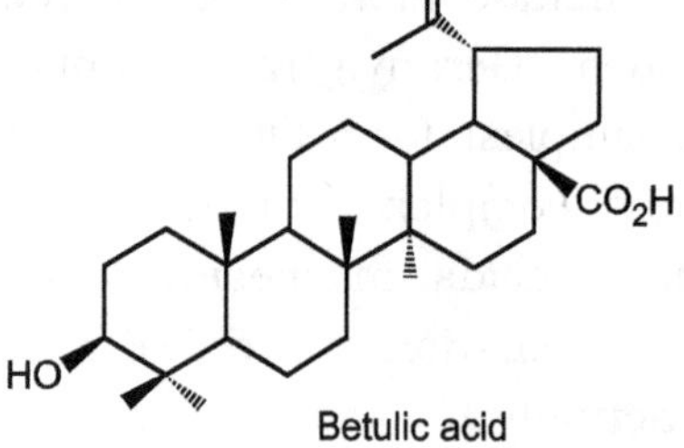
Betulic acid

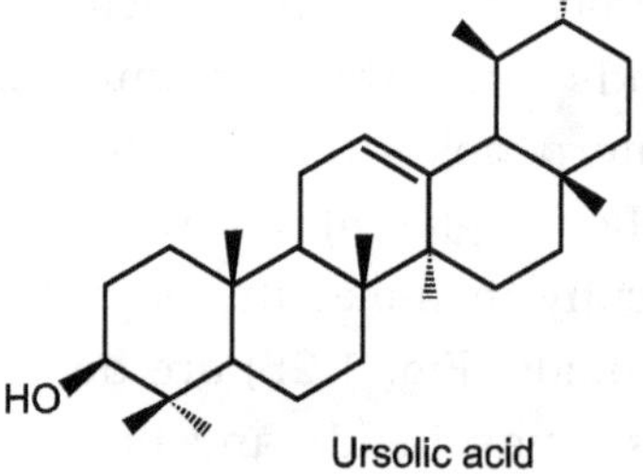
Ursolic acid

Fig. 1.28 : Triterpenoids

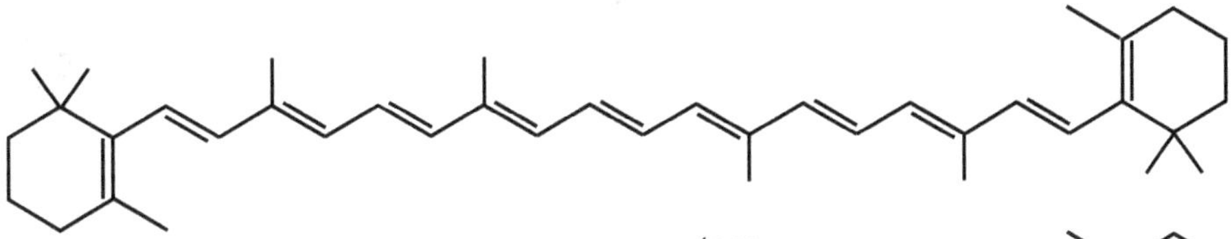

α-carotene

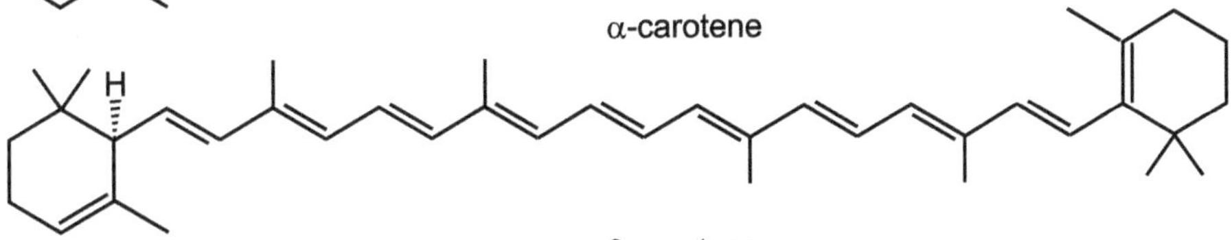

β-carotene

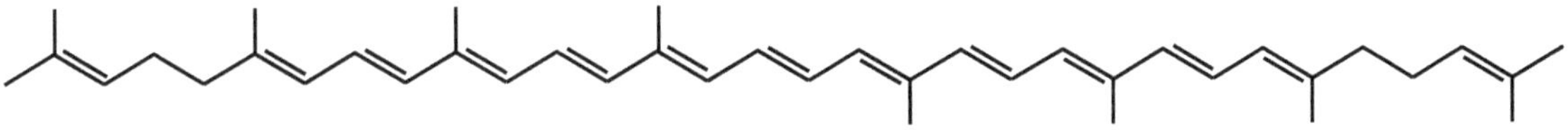

Lycopene

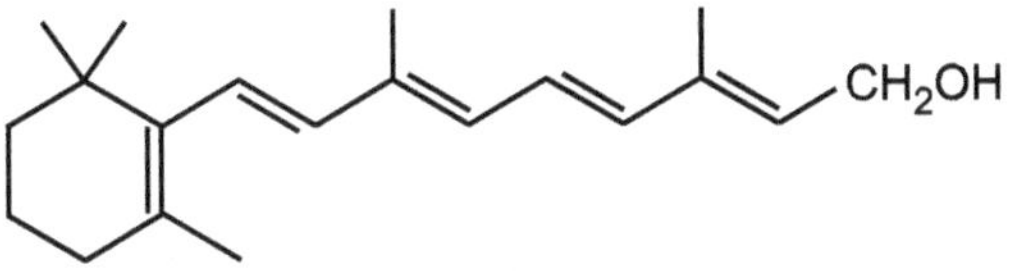

Retinol (vitamin A)

Fig. 1.29 : Tetraterpeneoids

CHAPTER 2

BIOGENESIS

- Introduction
- Photosynthesis: C_3, C_4, CAM
- Glycolysis
- Citric acid cycle (Kreb's Cycle)
- Pentose Phosphate Pathway

2.1 INTRODUCTION

Biogenesis or *in-vivo* synthesis of both primary and secondary metabolites starts with photosynthesis to produce sugar molecules which are metabolised to glycerates, pyruvates and finally acetyl CoA. This acetyl CoA is used in TCA cycle to generate a number of amino acids and excess is to synthesize fatty acids. A few of the acetyl CoA molecules are condensed to form mevalonic acid, precursor of synthesis of steroids and terpenoids. Amino acids give rise to alkaloids. The intermediates of glycolysis i.e. glyceraldehyde 3-phosphate and erythrose 4- phopshate from pentose phosphate pathway yields shikimic acid which is the main precursor for biosynthesis of a number of important aromatic chemicals such as phenylpropanoides, lignin, lignans, flavonoides and terpenoid quinones.

2.2 PHOTOSYNTHESIS

Photosynthesis means "putting together with light". Photosynthesis in green plants and specialized bacteria is the process of utilizing light energy to synthesize organic compounds from carbon dioxide and water. Plants absorb light primarily using the pigment chlorophyll, which is the reason that most plants are green in colour. Besides chlorophyll, plants also use pigments such as carotenes and xanthophylls. Carbon dioxide and oxygen enter and leave through tiny pores called *stomata*. It consists of the light dependent part (light reaction) and the light independent part (dark reaction, carbon fixation).

The general equation for photosynthesis is therefore :

$$2n\ CO_2 + 2n\ H_2O + Sunlight \rightarrow 2(CH_2O)n + n\ O_2 + 2n\ A$$

Carbon dioxide + Electron donor + Light energy → Carbohydrate + Oxygen + Oxidized electron donor

In the first stage, light-dependent reactions capture the energy of light and use it to make the energy-storage molecules ATP and NADPH via ATP synthase.

In the second stage, the light-independent reactions together known as *Calvin cycle* (Fig. 2.1) reduce carbon dioxide via enzyme RuBisCO (Ribulose-1, 5-bisphosphate carboxylase oxygenase). The product of the Calvin cycle is 3-carbon compound glyceraldehyde-3-phosphate and water. Two molecules of glyceraldehyde-3-phosphate combine to form one molecule of glucose and later diverse larger carbohydrates.

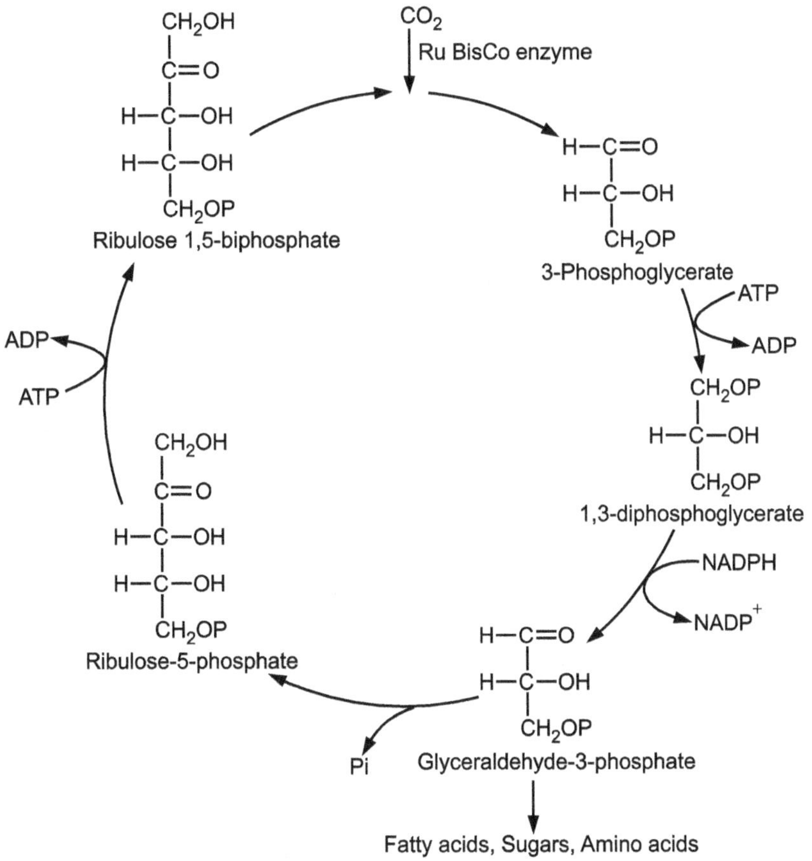

Fig. 2.1 : Calvin Cycle

The overall equation for the light-dependent reactions is :

$$2 H_2O + 2 NADP^+ + 2 ADP + 2 Pi + Light \rightarrow 2 NADPH + 2 H^+ + 2 ATP + O_2$$

The overall equation for the light-independent reactions is :

$$3 CO_2 + 9 ATP + 6 NADPH + 6 H^+ \rightarrow C_3H_6O_3\text{-phosphate} + 9 ADP + 8 Pi + 6 NADP^+ + 3H_2O$$

In the light independent part the carbon fixation refers to any process through which gaseous carbon dioxide is converted into a solid compound like sugar molecules. There are three types of Carbon fixation: C_3, C_4 and CAM. The difference between C_3

and C_4 photosynthesis depends on differences in the chemical compounds to which the incoming CO_2 is linked during the dark reactions (CAM photosynthesis differs from both C_3 and C_4 photosynthesis in that prior to fixation, CO_2 is an acid form known as carbonic acid).

C_3 Photosynthesis

C_3 plants use Calvin cycle (C_3 cycle or Calvin–Benson-Bassham cycle or reductive pentose phosphate cycle or CBB cycle). C_3 is the most well-known type of photosynthesis, is used by most plants, and indeed until recent decades was the only type of photosynthesis known to exist. In C3 photosynthesis, the compound to which CO_2 is integrated first is a 3-carbon compound. The "enzyme" necessary for this process is known as RuBisCO. C_3 photosynthesis is more efficient than C_4 or CAM photosynthesis when the environment is cool and moist and when light is plentiful. However, since C_3 uses more water than the other two types of photosynthesis, it is not as useful to organisms living in hot, arid environments.

C_4 Photosynthesis

The name "C4" comes from the fact that the first product of CO_2 fixation in these plants has four carbon atoms, rather than three, as is the case in C3 plants. C4 plants preface the Calvin cycle with reactions that incorporate CO_2 into a 4-carbon compound C4 carbon fixation is one of three biochemical mechanisms, along with C_3 and CAM photosynthesis, functioning in land plants to "fix" carbon dioxide (binding the gaseous molecules to dissolved compounds inside the plant) for sugar production through photosynthesis.

CAM Photosynthesis

Crassulacean Acid Metabolism, also known as CAM photosynthesis, is an elaborate carbon fixation pathway in some plants. These plants fix carbon dioxide (CO_2) during the night, storing it as the four carbon acid malate. The CO_2 is released during the day, where it is concentrated around the enzyme RuBisCO, increasing the efficiency of photosynthesis. The CAM pathway allows stomata to remain shut during the day; therefore it is especially common in plants adapted to arid conditions.

2.3 GLYCOLYSIS

Glycolysis (figure 2.2) is the process of enzymatic reactions that convert glucose into three-carbon compounds, (pyruvate and glycerates) small amounts of ATP (energy) and NADH (reducing power). The glycolytic pathway operates in both situations, in the presence (aerobic) and absence (anaerobic) of oxygen. Under anaerobic conditions, the metabolism of each glucose molecule yields only two ATPs. In contrast, the complete aerobic metabolism of glucose to carbon dioxide by glycolysis and Krebs cycle yields up to thirty-eight ATPs. It is a central pathway that produces important precursor metabolites : six-carbon compounds of glucose-6P and fructose-6P and three-carbon compounds of glycerone-P, glyceraldehyde-3P, glycerate-3P, phosphoenolpyruvate and pyruvate. Acetyl-CoA, another important precursor metabolite, is produced by oxidative decarboxylation of pyruvate in the presence of pyruvate dehydrogenase to form acetyl coenzyme A (acetyl CoA). Under conditions where energy is needed, acetyl CoA is metabolized by Krebs cycle to generate carbon dioxide and a large amount of ATP. When the cell does not need energy, acetyl CoA can be used to synthesize fats or amino acids.

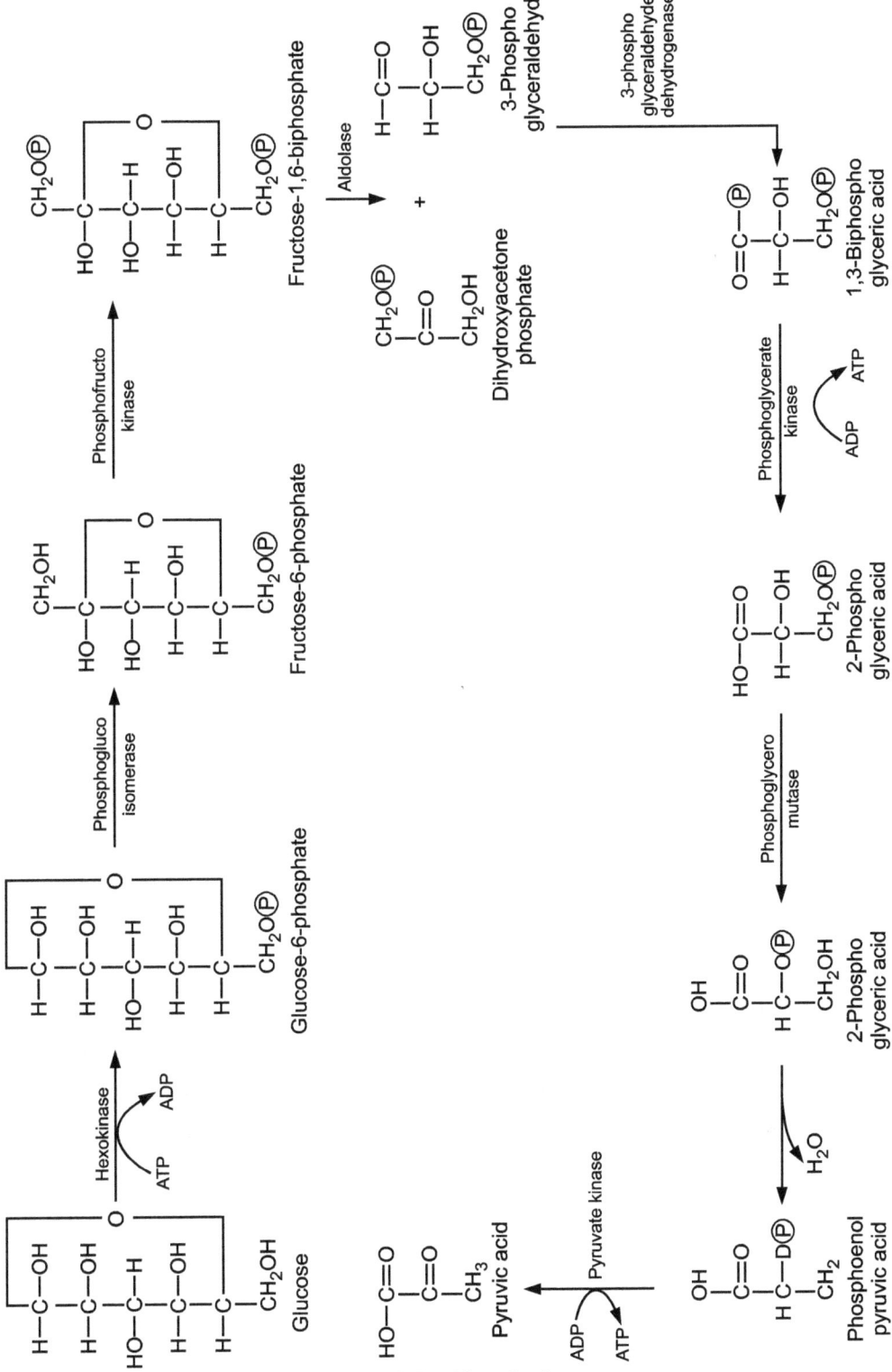

Fig. 2.2 : Glycolysis

As the glucose is oxidized by the glycolytic enzymes, the coenzyme nicotinamide adenine dinucleotide (NAD^+) is converted from it's oxidized to reduced form (NADH). When oxygen is available (aerobic conditions), NADH can reoxidize to NAD^+. However, if either oxygen levels are insufficient (anaerobic conditions) or mitochondrial activity is absent, NADH must be reoxidized by the cell using some other mechanism. In animal cells, the reoxidation of NADH is accomplished by reducing pyruvate, the end-product of glycolysis, to form lactic acid. This process is known as *anaerobic glycolysis*. During vigorous exercise, skeletal muscles rely heavily on it. In yeast, anaerobic conditions result in the production of carbon dioxide and ethanol from pyruvate rather than lactic acid. This process, known as *alcoholic fermentation*, is the basis of wine production and the reason why bread dough rises.

Although some cells are highly dependent on glycolysis for the generation of ATP, the amount of ATP generated per glucose molecule is actually quite small. Therefore, in the majority of cells the most important function of glycolysis is to metabolize glucose to generate three-carbon compounds that can be utilized by other pathways. The final product of aerobic glycolysis is pyruvate.

2.4 CITRIC ACID CYCLE

Citric acid cycle also known as the tricarboxylic acid (TCA) cycle or the Krebs cycle (figure 2.3) is the common mode of oxidative degradation of carbohydrates, fatty acids and amino acids. The cycle starts with acetyl-CoA, the activated form of acetate, derived from glycolysis and pyruvate oxidation of carbohydrates and from beta oxidation of fatty acids. The two-carbon acetyl group in acetyl-CoA is transferred to the four-carbon compound of oxaloacetate to form the six-carbon compound of citrate. In a series of reactions two carbons in citrate are oxidized to CO_2 and the reaction pathway supplies NADH for use in the oxidative phosphorylation and other metabolic processes. The pathway also supplies important precursor metabolites including 2-oxoglutarate. At the end of the cycle the remaining four-carbon part is transformed back to oxaloacetate. Because two acetyl-CoA molecules are produced from each glucose molecule, two cycles are required per glucose molecule. Therefore, at the end of two cycles, the products are : 6 molecules of NADH, two molecules of $FADH_2$, two molecules of ATP, and four molecules of CO_2.

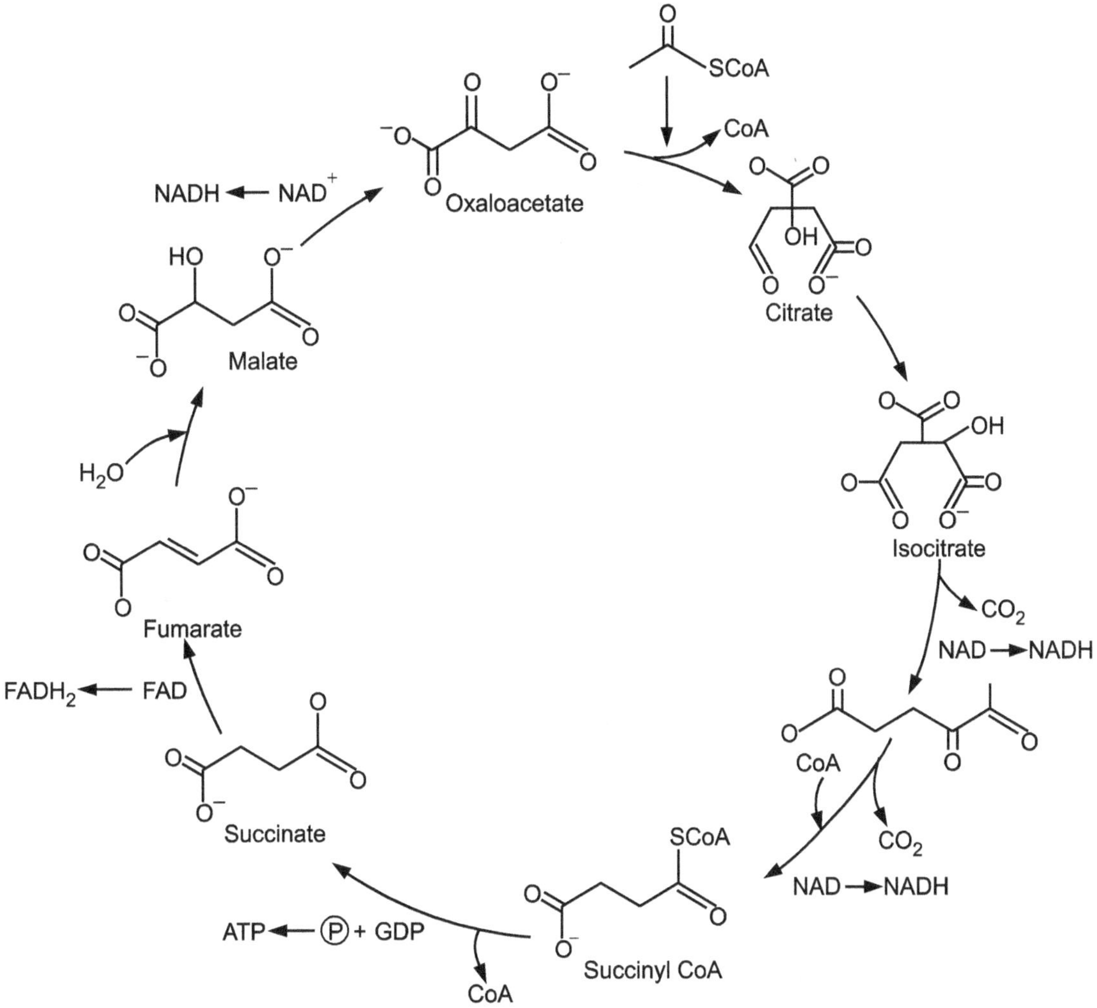

Fig. 2.3 : TCA Cycle

2.5 PENTOSE PHOSPHATE PATHWAY

The pentose phosphate pathway (Figure 2.4), also called the phosphogluconate pathway or hexose monophosphate shunt, is a process that generates NADPH and 5-carbon sugars, pentoses. This pathway is an alternative to glycolysis. There are two distinct phases in the pathway. The first is the oxidative phase, in which NADPH is generated, and the second is the non-oxidative synthesis of pentoses. The role of this pathway can be summarized as :

- Production of NADPH,
- Production of ribose-5-phosphate used in the synthesis of nucleotides and nucleic acids.
- Production of erythrose-4-phosphate used in the Shikimic acid pathway, synthesis of aromatic amino acids.

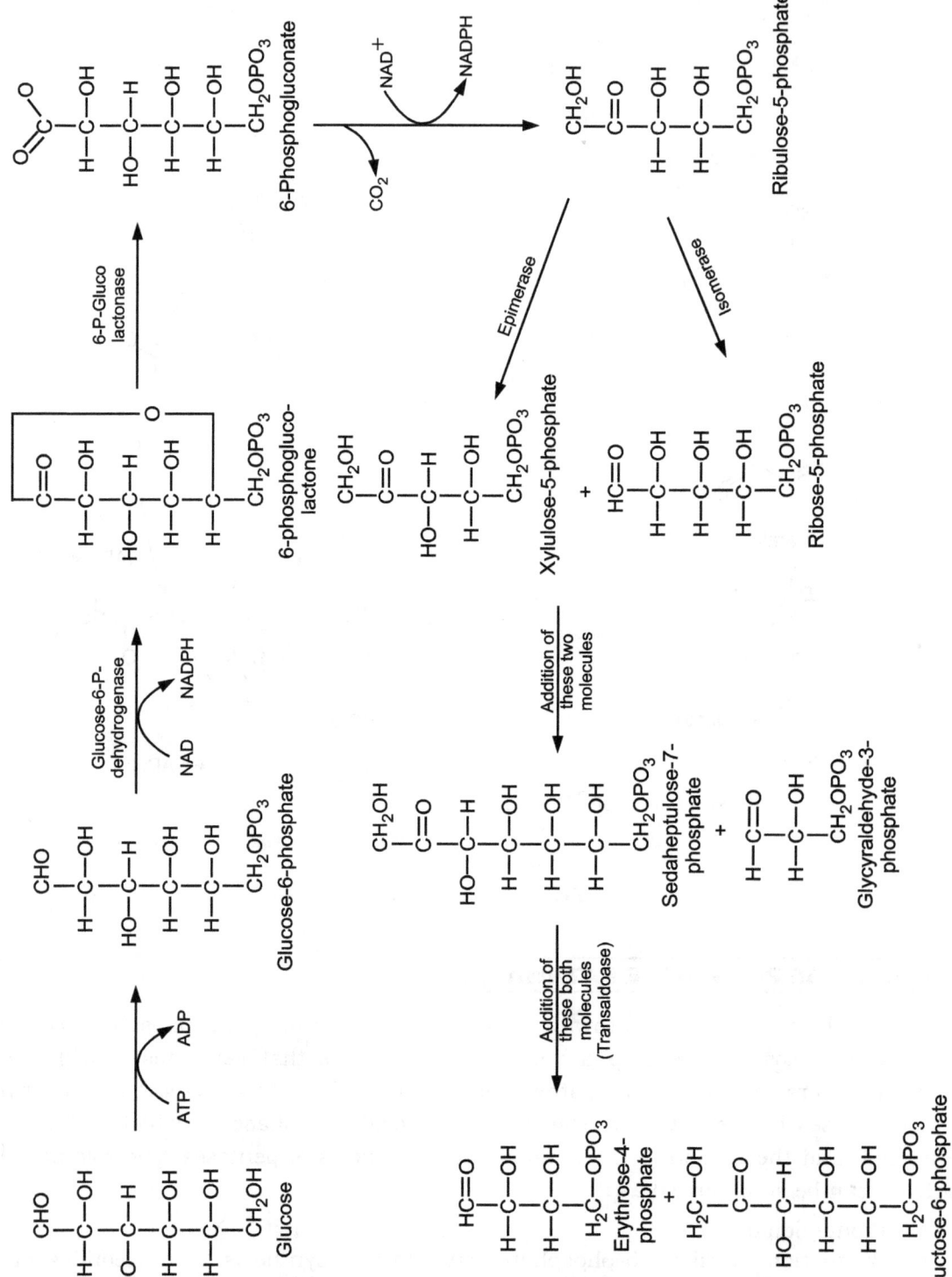

Fig. 2.4 : Pentose Phosphate Pathway

CARBOHYDRATES

- ✍ Introduction: Classification, Glycosidic Linkage, Anomerisation
- ✍ Biosynthesis of Sugars
- ✍ Oligosaccharides
- − Polysaccharides: Starch
- − Vitamin C Biosynthesis

3.1 INTRODUCTION

The carbohydrates are the more common of natural compounds with numerous functions in living things, such as storage and transport of energy (e.g., starch, glycogen) and formation of structural components (e.g., cellulose in plants and chitin in arthropods).

Carbohydrates (Fig. 3.1) can be classified into two groups, simple sugars and complex carbohydrates. Simple sugars are the monosachharides (glucose, mannose, galactose). Complex carbohydrates, according to the different number of monosaccharide units, can be classified into oligosaccharides [e.g. disaccharides (sucrose, lactose, maltose), trisaccharides (raffinose, maltotriose), tetrasaccharides (acarbose, stachyose)] and polysachharides (starch, cellulose, dextrin, inulin, mannan).

Anomerization is one of the common parts of carbohydrate chemistry. Anomerization is the process of conversion of a structure from one anomer to the other. An anomer is a special type of epimer (Fig. 3.5). It is a stereoisomer (diastereomer, more exactly) of cyclic sugars that differs only in its configuration at the hemiacetal or hemiketal carbon, also called the *anomeric carbon.*

3.2 GENERAL BIOSYNTHESIS OF SUGARS

All the monosaccharides are produced by photosynthesis. 3-phosphoglyceraldehyde which is a first sugar of photosynthesis containing 3-carbons produces pentoses (ribose, ribulose and xylulose) via Calvin cycle. (Fig. 2.1) Two moles of 3-phosphoglyceraldehyde combine to form hexose moiety glucose-6-phosphate. Glucose can be synthesized from non-carbohydrate precursors, such as pyruvate and lactic acid, by the process of gluconeogenesis.

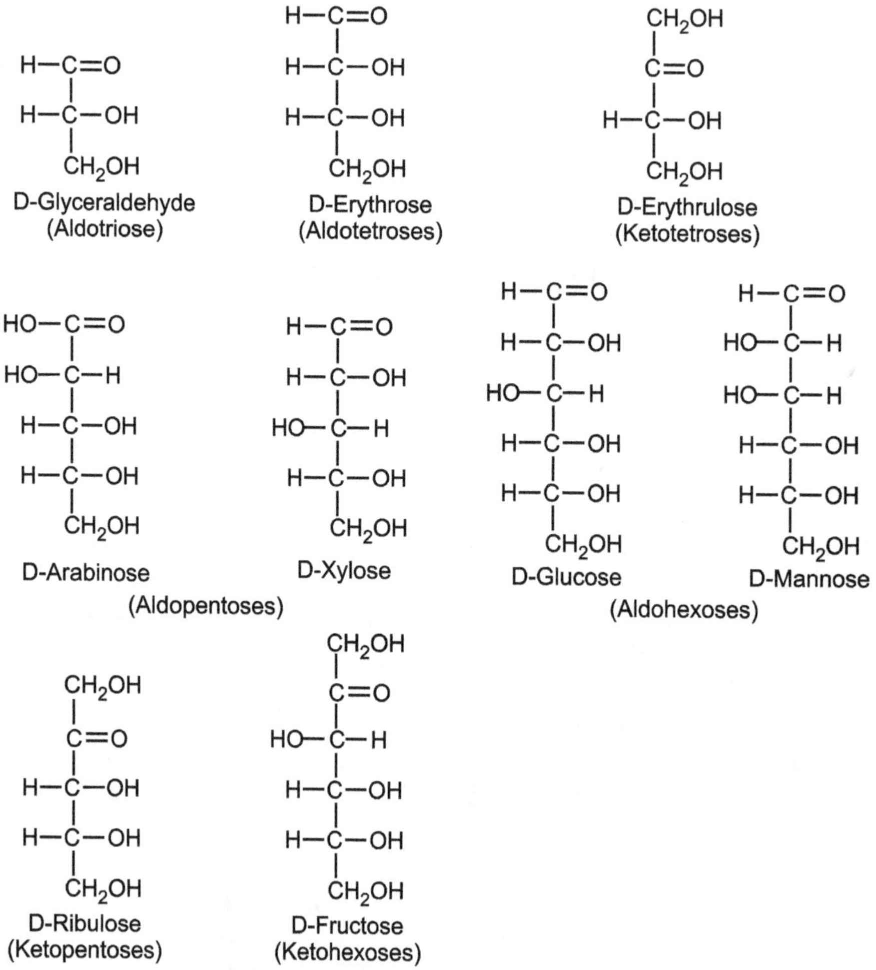

Fig. 3.1

Carbohydrate biosynthesis normally consists of preparation of glycosyl donors, preparation of glycosyl acceptors with a single unprotected hydroxyl group, coupling them, and the deprotection process. Condensation of monosaccharides via glycosidic linkage with elimination of one, two or three water molecule yields di-, tri- or tetrasaccharides respectively. The glycosidic bond or linkage (Fig. 3.2) is formed from a glycosyl donor and a glycosyl acceptor.

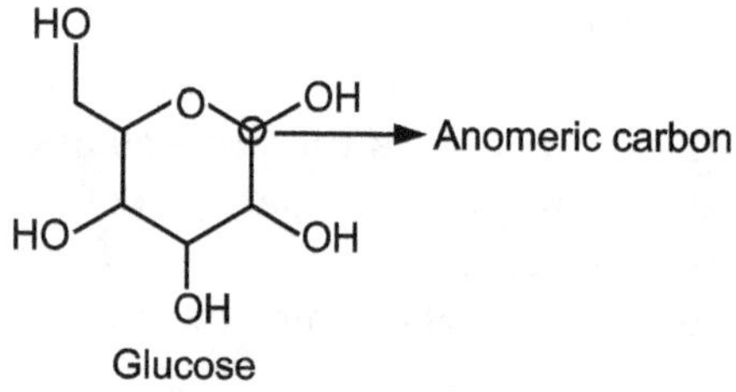

Fig. 3.2

3.3 OLIGOSACCHARIDES

Oligosaccharides (Fig. 3.3) usually contain two to nine monosaccharide units i.e. di-, tri- or tetrasaccharides. They are generally found either O- or N-linked to compatible amino acid side chains in proteins or to lipid moieties. Fructo-oligosaccharides, galacto-oligosaccharides and mannan-oligosaccharides are a few types of oligosaccharides.

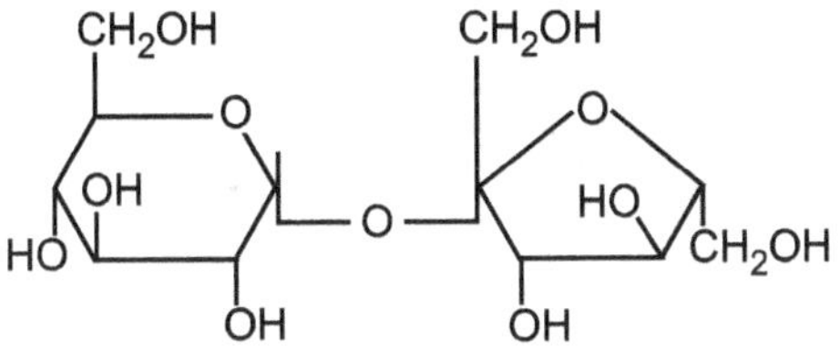

Sucrose

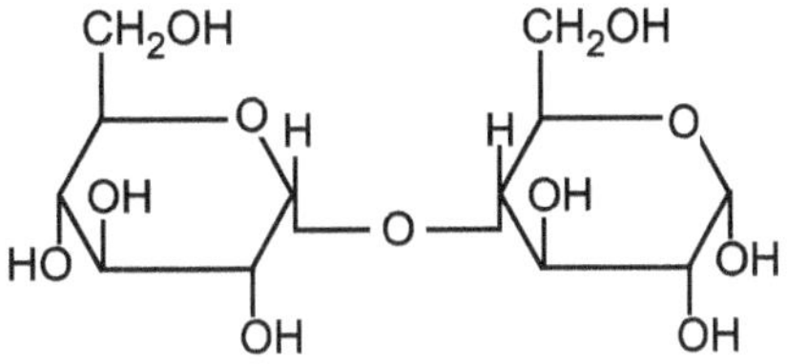

Maltose

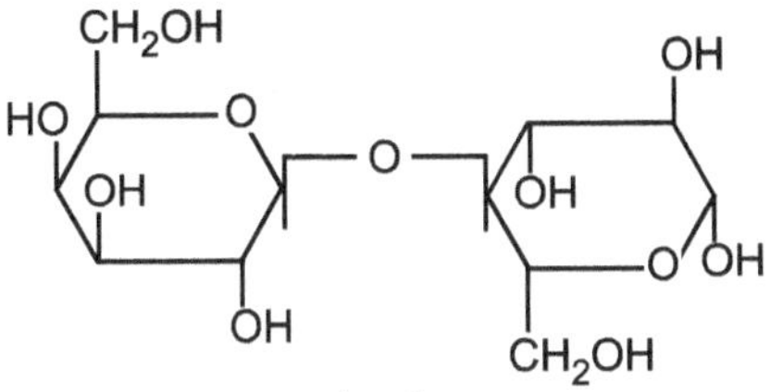

Lactose

Fig. 3.3

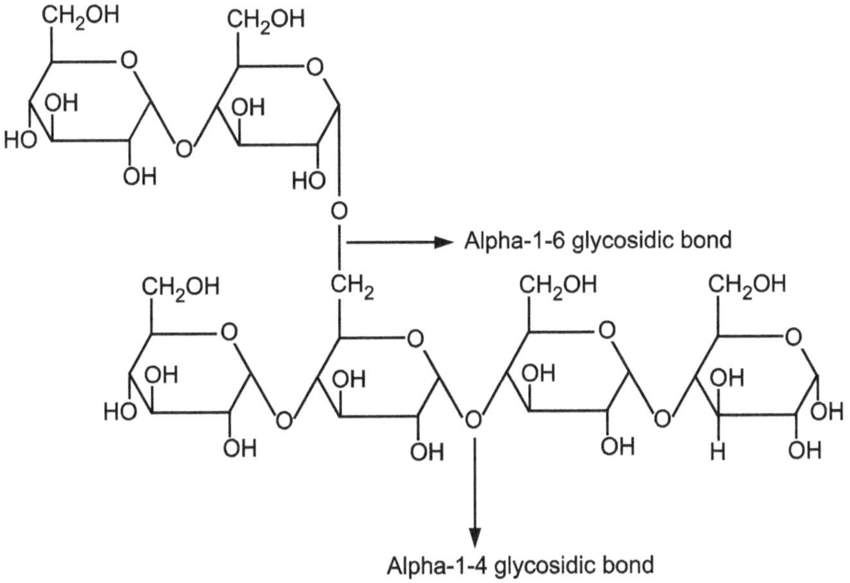

Starch

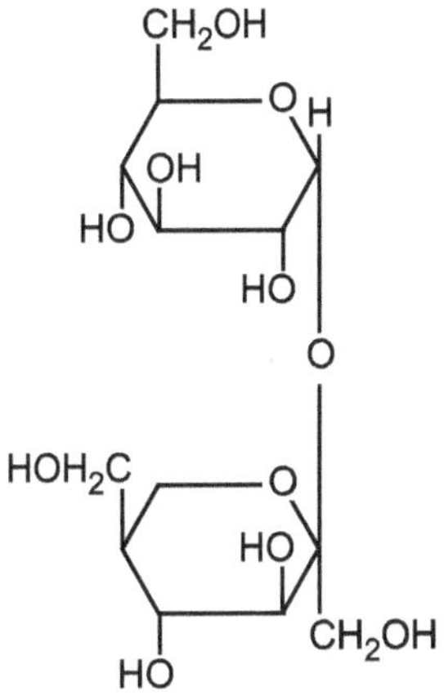

Inulin

Fig. 3.4

3.4 POLYSACCHARIDES : STARCH

Polysaccharides (Fig. 3.4) are also derived like other sachharides but the number of sugar units is approximately known. Polysachharides are broadly grouped into homoglycans and heteroglycans. Starch, cellulose, inulin, dextrin are examples of homoglycans. Heteroglycans which are acidic substances are mostly present in gums and mucilages. Pectin, pectosan, glucoronic acid, agar and alginic acid are a few popular examples of heteroglycans. The latter two are obtained from marine sources.

Starch is the most common polysaccharide found abundantly in endosperm of the seeds. Amylose and amylopectin are the components of starch. Amylose, α-1, 4 linked glucan, is unbranched while amylopectin is a branched chain starch.

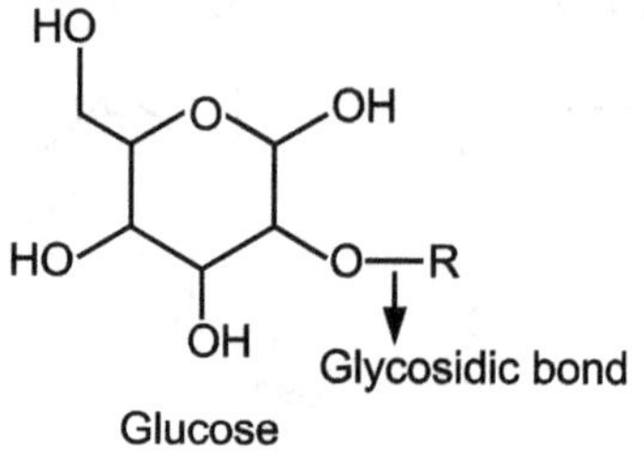

Fig. 3.5

Hence, short grain rice contains high amount of amylopectin and long grain rice contains a large amount of amylose.

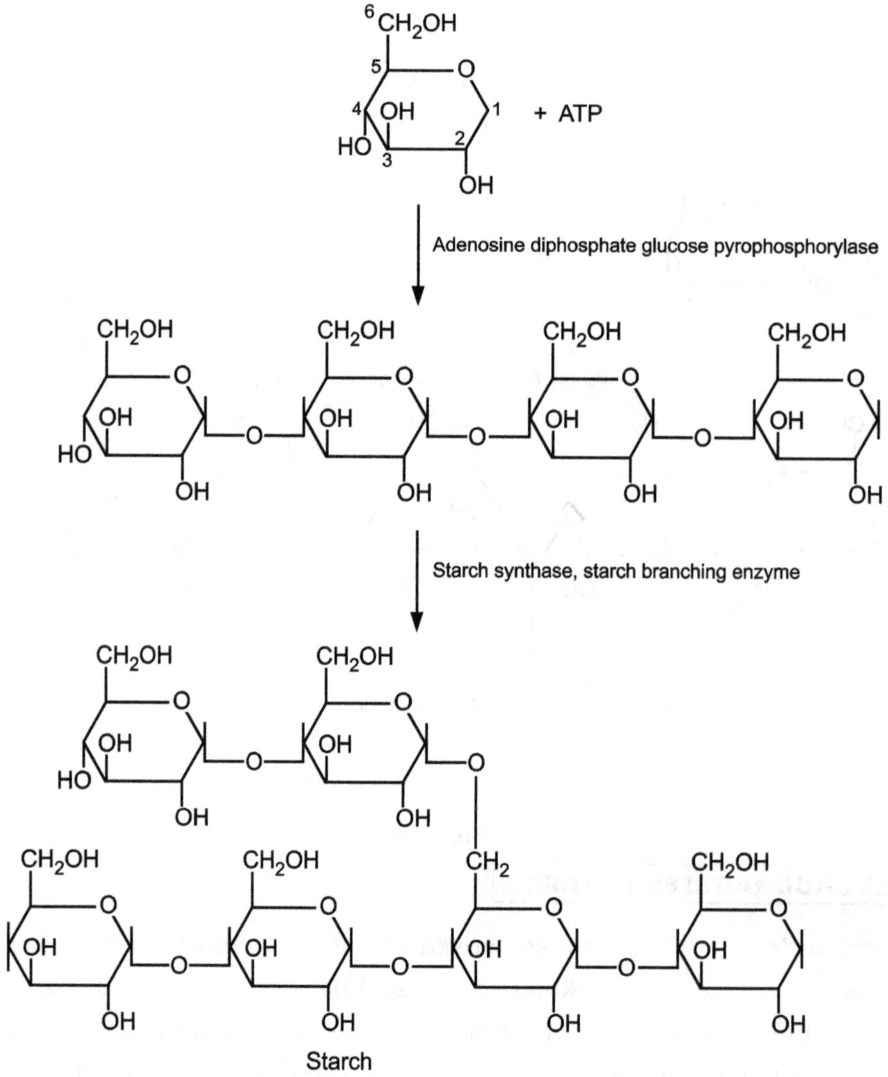

Fig. 3.6 : Starch Biosynthesis

3.5 VITAMIN C BIOSYNTHESIS

One of the important metabolites in carbohydrate biosynthesis is ascorbicic acid commonly called as vitamin C.

Vitamin C is not synthesized by man and hence he depends on external supplements. In plants, vitamin C is biosynthesized from glucose or galactose as shown in Fig. 3.7.

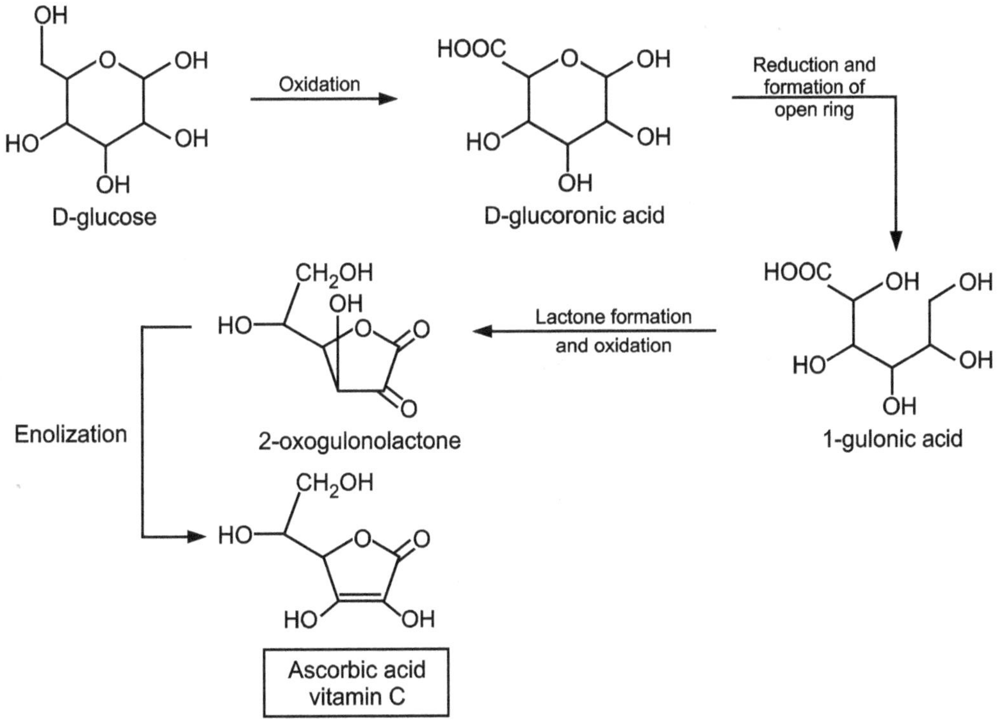

Fig. 3.7

ACETATE PATHWAY

- Introduction: Fatty Acids, Saturated Fatty Acids, Unsaturated Fatty Acids
- Saturated Fatty Acids Biosynthesis
- Unsaturated Fatty Acids (UFA) Biosynthesis
- Aromatic Polyketides Biosynthesis: Anthraquinones - Emodin, Aloe emodin, Rhein, Sennoside, Frangulin Cascaroside, Hypercin, Khelin, Visnagin

4.1 INTRODUCTION

Acetate pathway is the pathway where the acetate unit is the precursor for the biosynthesis of fatty acids and anthracene glycosides. In a few compounds mevalonic acid or shikimic acid pathway intermediates are associated with acetate which further produces modified isoprenoid or flavonoid like compounds respectively.

Fatty acids are carboxylic acids with long hydrocarbon chains. The hydrocarbon chain length may vary from 10-30 carbons (most usual is 12-18). Fatty acids, also called as *aliphatic acids,* are important sources of energy stored in the form of triglycerides and act as intermediates in the biosynthesis of polyketides and hormones. Commercially, fatty acids and their derivatives are useful in the manufacturing of food, cosmetics and toiletries such as soaps, papers, plastic, varnishes, paints and insecticides.

Fatty acids can be saturated (Table 4.2) and unsaturated (Table 4.3), depending on double bonds. Saturated fatty acids are long-chain carboxylic acids that usually contain 12 and 24 carbon atoms with no double bonds. Unsaturated fatty acids which may be mono- or poly-unsaturated, are similar to saturated fatty acids, except that one or more alkenyl functional groups exist along the chain. Monounsaturated fatty acids (MUFAs) have only one double bond. Polyunsaturated fatty acids (PUFAs) have more than one double bond. Fatty acids are frequently represented by a notation such as C18:2 that indicate that the fatty acid consists of an 18-carbon chain and 2 double bonds.

Table 4.1: Fatty Acid Containing Plants

Plant	Biological Source	Constituents	Uses
Almond	Seeds of *Prunus amygdalus*, Rosaceae	Oleic, linoleic, palmitic, stearic.	Adjuvant, emollient base,
Arachis	Seeds of *Arachis hypogaea*, Leguminosae	Arachidic, oleic, linoleic, palmitic, stearic	Emollient base
Bees wax	Honey comb of *Apis mellifeca*, Apidae	Myristic, palmitic, cerotic	Ointment base
Carnauba	Leaves of *Copernicia prunifera*, Palmae	Carnaubic, cerotic, melissyl	Opharmaceutical base
Castor	Seeds of *Ricinus communis*, Euphorbiaceae	Ricinoleic, oleic, linoleic, palmitic, stearic.	Purgative, emollient base
Chaulmoogra	Seeds of *Hydnocarpus heterophylla*, Flacourtricaceae	Chaulmoogric acid, hydnocarpic acid	Anti T. B., anilprotic
Coconut	Seeds kernel of *Cocos nucifera*, Arecaceae	Lauric, myristic, oleic, palmitic, stearic	Cosmetic preparation
Cod-liver	Fresh liver of *Gadus morrhua*, Gadidae	Oleic, myristic, palmitic, stearic, DHA	Nutritive supplement
Corn	Grains of *Zea mays*, Gramineae	Oleic, linoleic, palmitic, stearic, arachidic, linolenic	Solvent for injection, cosmetic preparation
Cotton seed	Seeds of *Gossypium hirsutum*, Malvaceae	Oleic, linoleic, palmitic, stearic	Cosmetic preparation
Evening primrose	Seeds of *Oenothera biennis*, Onagraceae	Oleic, linoleic, palmitic, gamma linolenic.	Nutritive supplement
Jojoba	Seeds of *Simmondsia chinensis*, Buxaceae	Eicosenoic. Docosenoic, oleic acid	Cosmetic preparation
Karanja	Seeds of *Pongamia glabra*, Papilionaceae	Oleic, linoleic, palmitic, stearic, arachidic, linolenic	Skin diseases
Kokum butter	Seeds of *Garcinia indica*, Guttiferae	Oleic, linoleic, palmitic, stearic, capric	Demulcent, emollient
Lard	Adnominal fat of *Sus scrofa*, Suideae	Oleic, linoleic, palmitic, stearic.	Nutritive supplement
Linseed	Seeds of *Linum usitatissimum*, Linaceae	Oleic, linoleic, palmitic, stearic.	Edible oil, demulcent
Mustard	Seeds of *Brassica nigra*, Cruciferae	Arachidic, linolenic, linoleic, oleic, myristic	Counter irritant, rubefacient.
Olive	Fruits of *Olea europaea*, Oleaceae	Oleic, linoleic, palmitic, stearic	Edible oil, emollient base

Palm kernel	Kernel of *Elaeis guineensis*, Arecaceae	Oleic, linoleic, palmitic, stearic, lauric, myristic	Cosmetic toiliteries preparation
Rapeseed	Seeds of *Brassica napus*, Cruciferae	Oleic, linoleic, palmitic, stearic, erucic, alpha linolenic	Edible oil
Rice bran	Seeds of *Oryza sativa*, Gramineae	Oleic, linoleic, palmitic, stearic	Edible oil
Safflower	Seeds of *Carthamus tinctorius*, Compositae	Oleic, linoleic, palmitic, stearic, arachidic, linolenic	Edible oil
Sesame	Seeds of *Sesamum indicum*, Pedaliaceae	Oleic, linoleic, palmitic, stearic	Edible oil, cosmetic toiliteries preparation
Shark liver	Fresh liver of *Hypoprion brevirostris*,	DHA (docosahexaeonic acid) and EPA (eicosapentaenoic acid).	Antixeropthalmic factor
Soya bean	Seeds of *Glycine max*, Leguminosae	Oleic, linoleic, palmitic, stearic, alpha linolenic	Edible oil
Spermaceti	Head of *Physeter macrocephalus*, Physeteridae	Lauric, myristic, stearic, cetyl palmitate	Ointment base
Suet	Abdominal fat from *Ovies aries*, Bovidae	Oleic, myristic, palmitic, stearic	Nutritive supplement
Theobroma	Kernels of *Theobroma cacao*, Sterculiaceae	Oleic, linoleic, palmitic, stearic	Suppository base
Wheat germ	Wheat germs of *Triticum aestivum*, Gramineae	Oleic, linoleic, linolenic	Nutritive supplement
Sunflower	Seeds of *Helianthus annuus*, Compositae	Oleic, linoleic, palmitic, stearic	Edible oil

Table 4.2 : Examples of Saturated Fatty Acids

Common Name	Structural Formula
Propionic acid	CH_3CH_2COOH
Butyric acid	$CH_3(CH_2)_2COOH$
Valeric acid	$CH_3(CH_2)_3COOH$
Enanthic acid	$CH_3(CH_2)_5COOH$
Caprylic acid	$CH_3(CH_2)_6COOH$
Capric acid	$CH_3(CH_2)_8COOH$
Lauric acid	$CH_3(CH_2)_{10}COOH$
Myristic acid	$CH_3(CH_2)_{12}COOH$
Palmitic acid	$CH_3(CH_2)_{14}COOH$

Common Name	Structural Formula
Margaric acid	$CH_3(CH_2)_{15}COOH$
Stearic acid	$CH_3(CH_2)_{16}COOH$
Arachidic acid	$CH_3(CH_2)_{18}COOH$
Behenic acid	$CH_3(CH_2)_{20}COOH$
Tricosylic acid	$CH_3(CH_2)_{21}COOH$

Table 4.3 : Examples of Unsaturated Fatty Acids

Common Name	Chemical Structure
Myristoleic acid	$CH_3(CH_2)_3CH=CH(CH_2)_7COOH$
Palmitoleic acid	$CH_3(CH_2)_5CH=CH(CH_2)_7COOH$
Oleic acid	$CH_3(CH_2)_7CH=CH(CH_2)_7COOH$
Linoleic acid	$CH_3(CH_2)_4CH=CHCH_2CH=CH(CH_2)_7COOH$
α-Linolenic acid	$CH_3CH_2CH=CHCH_2CH=CHCH_2CH=CH(CH_2)_7COOH$
Arachidonic acid	$CH_3(CH_2)_4CH=CHCH_2CH=CHCH_2CH=CHCH_2CH=CH(CH_2)_3COOH$
Eicosapentaenoic acid	$CH_3CH_2CH=CHCH_2CH=CHCH_2CH=CHCH_2CH=CHCH_2CH=CH(CH_2)_3COOH$
Erucic acid	$CH_3(CH_2)_7CH=CH(CH_2)_{11}COOH$
Docosahexaenoic acid	$CH_3CH_2CH=CHCH_2CH=CHCH_2CH=CHCH_2CH=CHCH_2CH=CHCH_2CH=CH(CH_2)_2COOH$

4.2 SATURATED FATTY ACIDS BIOSYNTHESIS

Saturated fatty acids are synthesized by a series of decarboxylative Claisen condensation reactions from acetyl-CoA and malonyl-CoA in the presence of enzyme fatty acid synthase. Enzyme synthase contains ACP as part of its structure. Following each step of elongation the β-keto group is reduced to the fully saturated carbon chain by the sequential action of enzymes – ketoreductase, dehydratase and enol reductase. Fatty acid synthesis (Fig. 4.1) starts with acetyl CoA which is the two carbon containing precursor. This is used to add two carbons to growing a fatty acid chain stepwise. This explains why fatty acids always have an even number of carbons. This process occurs in cytosol.

During biosynthesis, the growing fatty acid chain gets attached covalently to the phosphopantethiene prosthetic group of ACP (acyl carrier protein) which allows intermediates to remain covalently linked to the synthases and access this intermediates to the right enzyme-active sites. Acyl Carrier Protein (ACP), converts malonyl CoA to malonyl ACP. ACP synthase is an enzyme that holds the growing fatty acid chain. Acyl enzyme thioester releases C_2 unit to malonyl ACP to form fatty acyl ACP through sequence of reduction, dehydration reactions. This fatty acyl ACP on attack of water generates fatty acids. Triglycerides (esters of glycerol containing same or different 3 fatty acids) are biosynthesized from glycerol 3-P (product of Calvin cycle) and first fatty acyl CoA esterification process which is elaborated in Fig. 4.2.

Acetate Pathway

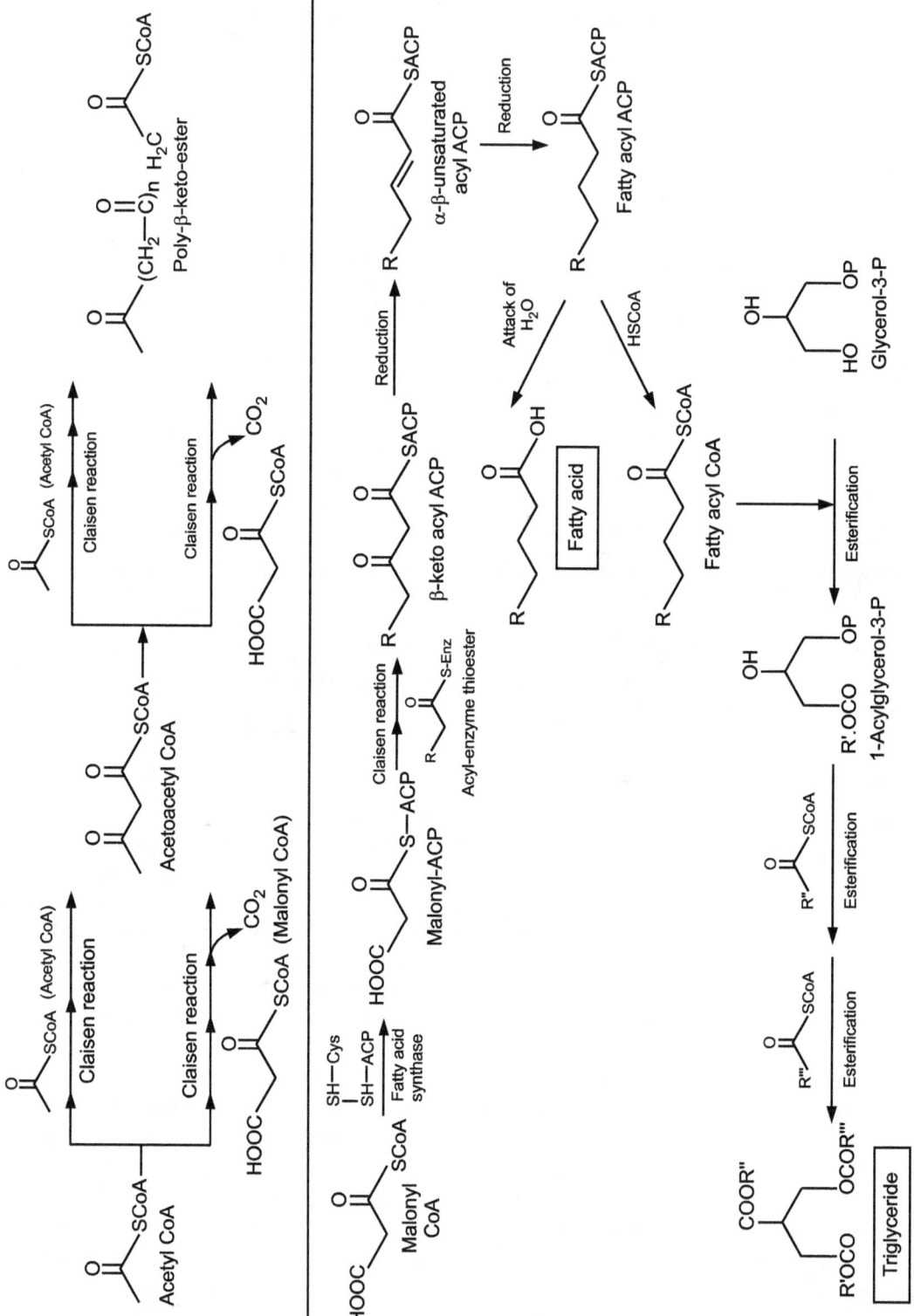

Fig. 4.1

Fig. 4.2

Fatty acid synthesis is simply a linear combination of acetate units facilitated by enzyme fatty acid synthase. ACP allows growing the fatty acid chain to react with thio group of enzyme fatty acid synthase and thus head-to-tail condensation followed by reduction gives rise to a long chain of saturated fatty acid. Mostly even numbers of carbon containing fatty acids are common in nature. But when the starting compound is other than acetate (e.g. propionic acid), odd number of C-containing fatty acids can also be synthesized by plants. C_{16} and C_{18} (Palmitic and stearic acids respectively) are the most common saturated fatty acids.

In fatty acid biosynthesis, acetate is the starter group and malonate is a chain extender. But in a few compounds there may be change in the starter or chain extender group. Cinnamoyl CoA obtained from shikimic acid pathway acts as a starter group in the synthesis of flavonoid and stilbenes. Anthranilolyl CoA obtained from anthranilic acid is used in the synthesis of quinoline and acridine alkaloids. Hexanoate is the starter group in the formation of aflatoxins and cannabinoides. Incorporation of propionate as a chain extender other than mevalonate from propionyl CoA or methyl malonyl CoA leads to the formation of macrolide antibiotics.

4.3 UNSATURATED FATTY ACIDS (UFA) BIOSYNTHESIS

UFAs are synthesized by sequential desaturation mechanism. Double bond is introduced by enzyme desaturase, oxidation and NADPH or NADH. Stearic acid is the common starting material to give various UFAs.

Essential fatty acids belong to the class of PUFAs. There are two types of essential fatty acids; omega-6 and omega-3 fatty acids which can be short chain (omega-3α linolenic acid, omega-6 eicosapentaenoic acid or EPA, docosahexaenoic acid DHA) or long-chain polyunsaturated fatty acids (omega-3α Linoleic acid, omega-6α gamma-linolenic acid or GLA, dihomo-gamma-linolenic acid or DGLA, arachidonic acid or AA). Linoleic acid and isomers of linolenic acid are EFA. As its derivative linolenate blocks synthesis of prostaglandins and hence useful in the treatment of various ailments especially cardiovascular diseases. Linoleic acid found to be the important compound in the prevention of hair loss, cancer, cystic fibrosis and dermatitis. DHA is present in mothers's milk and constituent of brain and retina. The consumption of alpha linolenic acid can be converted to DHA by animals which is used to prevent brain related diseases, colon cancer and cardiovascular risks.

In animals, EFA are obtained from diet which act as precursors for synthesis of DHA, which is (Figure 4.3) important (component) for normal functioning of brain. Dihomolinoleic acid (PGE_1), arachdinoic acid (PGE_2) and EPA (PGE_3) are important precursors for biosynthesis of prostaglandins. PGH_2 synthesizes thromboxanes and arachidonic acid syntehsizes leukotrienes. Eicosanoid is the collective term for oxygenated derivatives of three different 20-carbon essential fatty acids i.e. eicosapentaenoic acid (EPA), arachidonic acid (AA) and dihomo-gamma-linolenic acid (DGLA). There are four types of eicosanoids i.e. prostaglandins, prostacyclins, thromboxanes and leukotrienes.

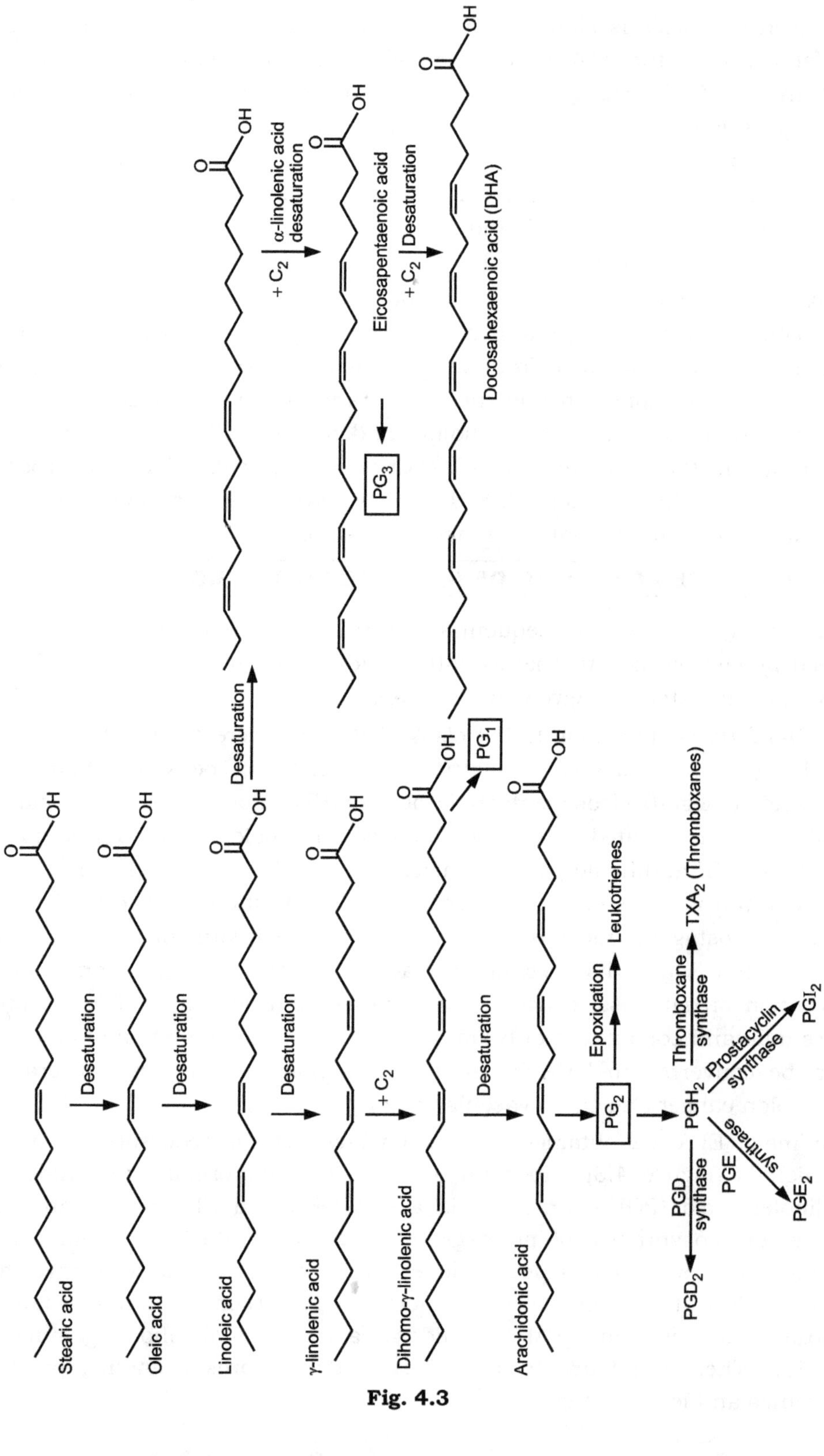

Fig. 4.3

Various branched chain fatty acids are biosynthesized by various mechanisms. Sterculi, malvalic acid and chaulmoogric acid are some of the important branched chain fatty acids obtained from stearic acid by alkylation, desaturation (sterculic) oxidation (malvalic). 2-cyclopentenyl carboxyl CoA as a starter unit and malonyl CoA as an extender unit gives chaulmoogric acid.

4.4 AROMATIC POLYKETIDES BIOSYNTHESIS

Polyketides also called as acetogenins or ketides are found in bacteria, fungi and plants. These are highly reactive compounds since they contain alternating carbonyl and methylene groups derived from repeated condensation of acetyl coenzyme A or malonyl coenzyme A.

Structurally these are classified into four major groups i.e. aromatic (flavonoides, stilbenes, doxorubicin, tetracycline), macrolides (erythromycin), polyethers (monesin, salinomycin) and polyenes (amphoterecin and candicidin).

There is a close relationship between the biosynthesis of fatty acids and polyketides, since in both cases, the formation of linear chains proceeds by the addition of C_2 units. In fatty acid biosynthesis every C_2 unit is added to the growing chain only after reduction of the previous carbonyl unit to a methylene group. The growth of a polyketide chain does not usually require such prior reduction but leads to formation of aromatic ring via poly-beta-ketoacids.

Polyketide biosynthesis starts with condensation of short fatty acids like acetates, propionates and butyrates via enzyme polyketide synthase. Chalcone synthases, stilbene synthases are plant polyketide synthases (PKSs) those catalyse biosynthesis of flavonoides, stilbenes respectively. ACP is type of PKSs and which forms ACP thioester of the starting unit, extender units and poly-β-ketone intermediates.

As seen in fatty acid synthesis, condensation followed by reduction gives long fatty acid chain. In the absence of reduction reaction, poly-β-keto-esters undergo intramolecular aldol/claisen reaction which causes cyclization of fatty acid chain. Poly β-keto ester folding occurs either by claisen and enolization reaction or aldol and enolization hydrolysis. The folded cyclic form of eight C_2 units is a starting component which through sequence of decarboxylation, O-methylation and oxidation reactions forms various anthraquinone derivatives as shown in figure 4.4 and 4.5. Aloe emodin anthrone on O and C-glycosilation gives cascorosides. Enodin anthrone on radical coupling forms emodin dianthrone which on sequential oxidation gives hypercin. Hypericin is a naphtodianthrone, a red-coloured principal and active constituent of *Hypericum perforatum*, family : Guttiferae. It is well known drug with a variety of therapeutic effects like antitumor, antiviral and antidepressant. It is also very popular photosensitizing agent useful in the treatment of many skin diseases along with photodyanamic therapy.

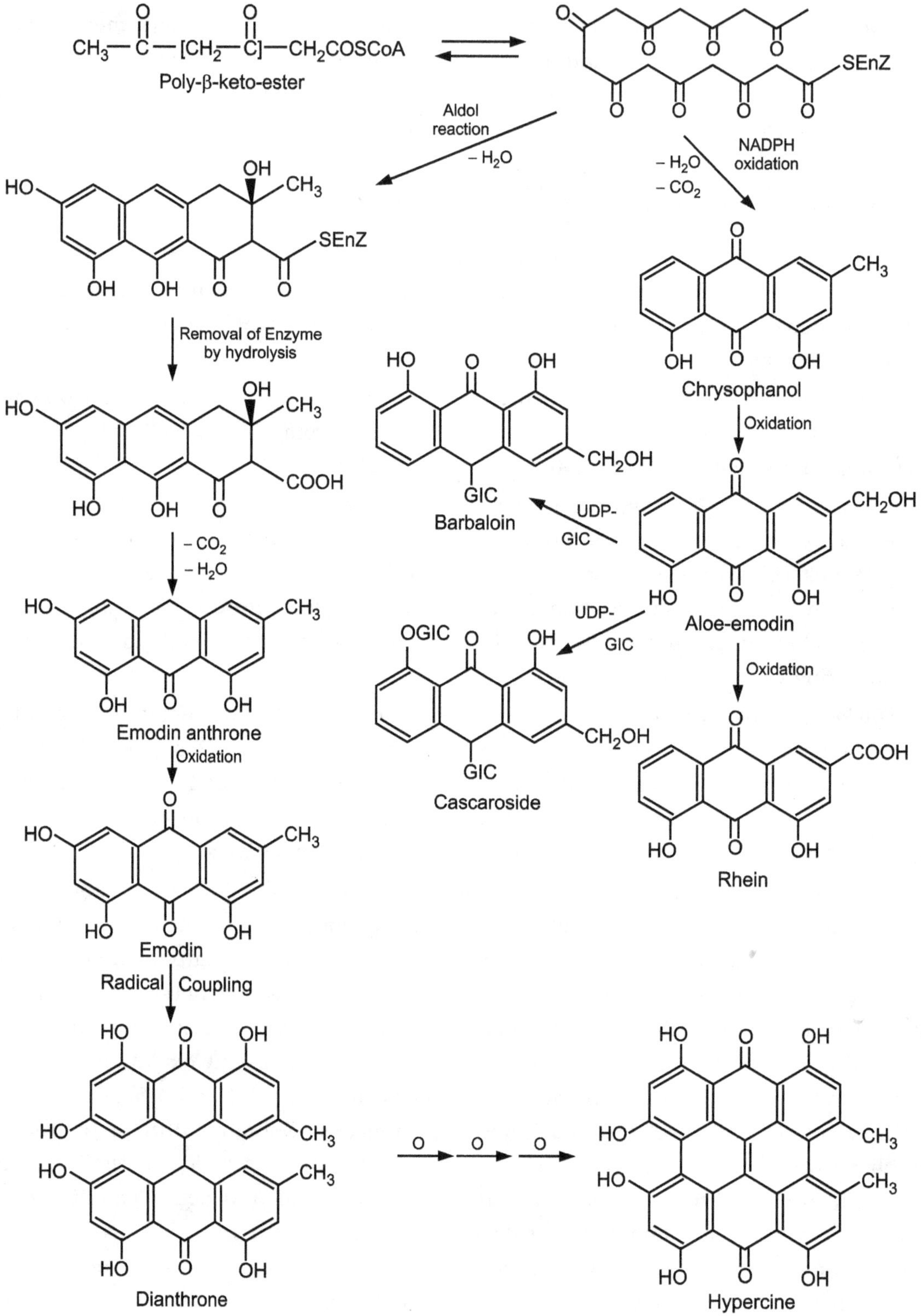

CH3—C—[CH2—C]—CH2COSCoA
Poly-β-keto-ester
SEnZ
Aldol reaction
– H2O
NADPH oxidation
– H2O
– CO2
HO
OH
CH3
SEnZ
OH
OH
Removal of Enzyme by hydrolysis
COOH
– CO2
– H2O
Emodin anthrone
Oxidation
Emodin
Radical Coupling
Dianthrone
Hypercine
Chrysophanol
Oxidation
Aloe-emodin
CH2OH
UDP-GIC
Barbaloin
GIC
OGIC
Cascaroside
Oxidation
Rhein

Fig. 4.4

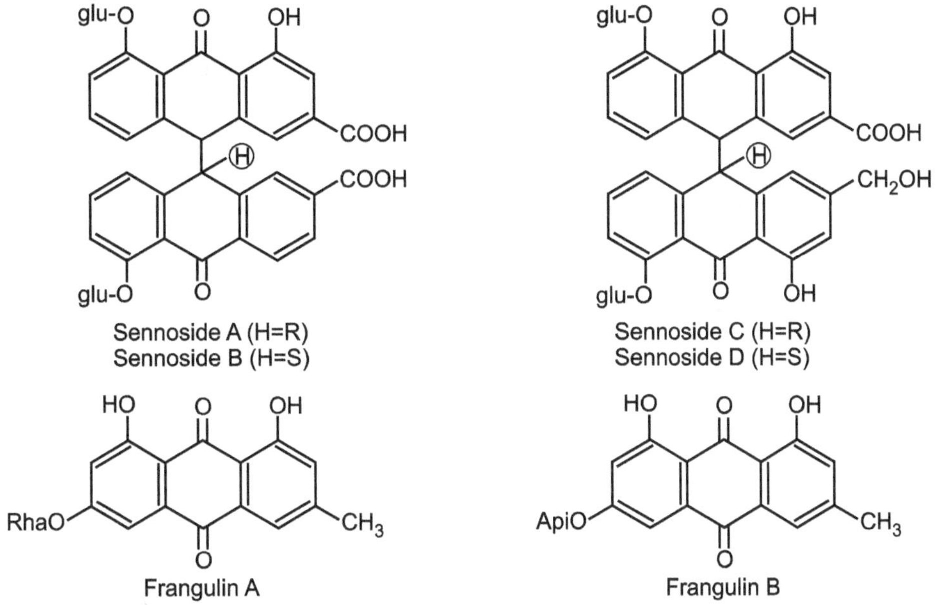

Fig. 4.5

SAM and DMAPP mediated O- or a C-alkylation reaction gives furanocoumarine derivatives like khellin and visnagin (Fig. 4.6). Khellin and closely related compound desmethoxykhellin (visnagin) are obtained from *Ammi visnaga*, family : Umbelliferae. Khellin is strong vasodilator and hence useful in angina pectoris and as a bronchodilator.

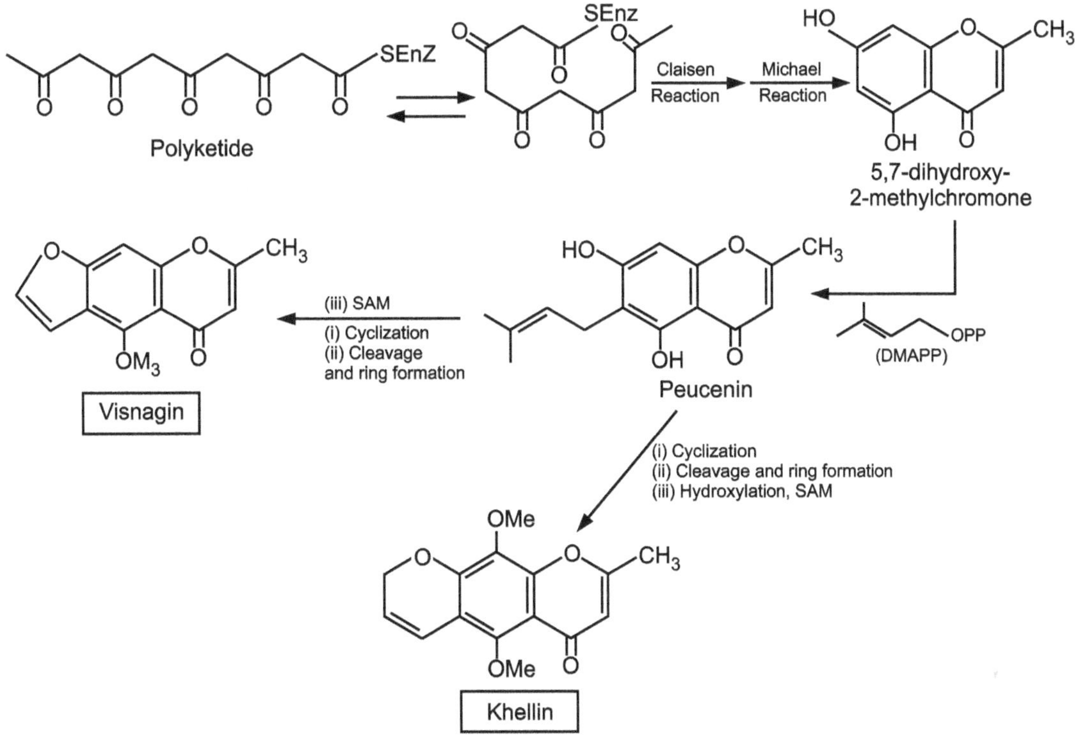

Fig. 4.6

Wax is the polymeric ester of Ω-hydroxyacids linkage. Sabinic acid, $HOCH_2(CH_2)_{10}COOH$, known as suberin and juniperic acid, $HOCH_2(CH_2)_{14}COOH$, known as cutin are the most common acid-waxes found in cork and cuticles of plant.

Fatty acid configuration shows cis or trans isomers. The trans fats which are always unsaturated found to be associated with coronary heart diseases.

CHAPTER 5

SHIKIMIC ACID PATHWAY

- Shikimic Acid Biosynthesis
- Phenylpropanoides
- Coumarin Biosynthesis: Furanocaumarins, Vanillin, Psoralen, Angelicin, Bergapten, Umbeliferon, Scopoletin, Scopolin.
- Lignans and Lignins Biosynthesis: Podophylotoxin
- Volatile Oils Biosynthesis: Anethole, Eugenol, Myristicin,
- Flavonoid Biosynthesis: Naringin, Resveratrol, Daidzein, Hesperidin, Genistein, Kaemferol, Quercetin, Pelargonidin, Silybin
- Miscellaneous: Lawsone, Alizarin, Aloe emodin, Vitamin K, Vitamin E

5.1 SHIKIMIC ACID BIOSYNTHESIS

Shikimic acid pathway is considerably important as it leads to formation of almost all aromatic compounds present in nature like phenylpropanoides (lignans, lignnins), coumarin, flavonoids and isoflavonoids and terpenoid quinones.

Shikimate pathway (Fig. 5.1) starts with erythrose 4-phospate (obtained from the pentose phosphate pathway) and phosphoenolpyruvate (obtained from glycolysis pathway) coupling to yield phosphorylated 7-carbon keto sugar, 3-deoxy-D-arabino-heptulosonic acid-7-phosphate, (DHAP). DHAP on removal of phosphoric acid cyclizes to 3-dehydroquinic acid which on reduction yields quinic acid. By dehydration 3-dehydroquinic acid forms 3 dehydroshikimic acid which forms shikimic acid followed by reduction.

3-dehydroshikimic acid on dehydration and enolisation forms protocatechuic acid and on dehydrogenation and enolisation forms gallic acid which is the component of many types of tannins.

Shikimic acid through phosphorylation and elimination reactions forms very important intermediate chorismic acid. Chorismic acid via simple rearrangement gives prephenic acid. Chorismic acid on another branch by glutamine mediated amination at C_2 gives anthranilic acid while amination at C_4 position (Fig. 5.2) gives P-aminobenzoic acid (PABA). PABA is a part of folic acid structure. Prephenic acid on dehydration and decarboxylation yields precursor of phenylalanine i.e. phenylpyruvic acid. On dehydrogenation and decarboxylation, prephenic acid yields p-hydroxy phenylpyruvic acid which is direct precursor of tyrosine.

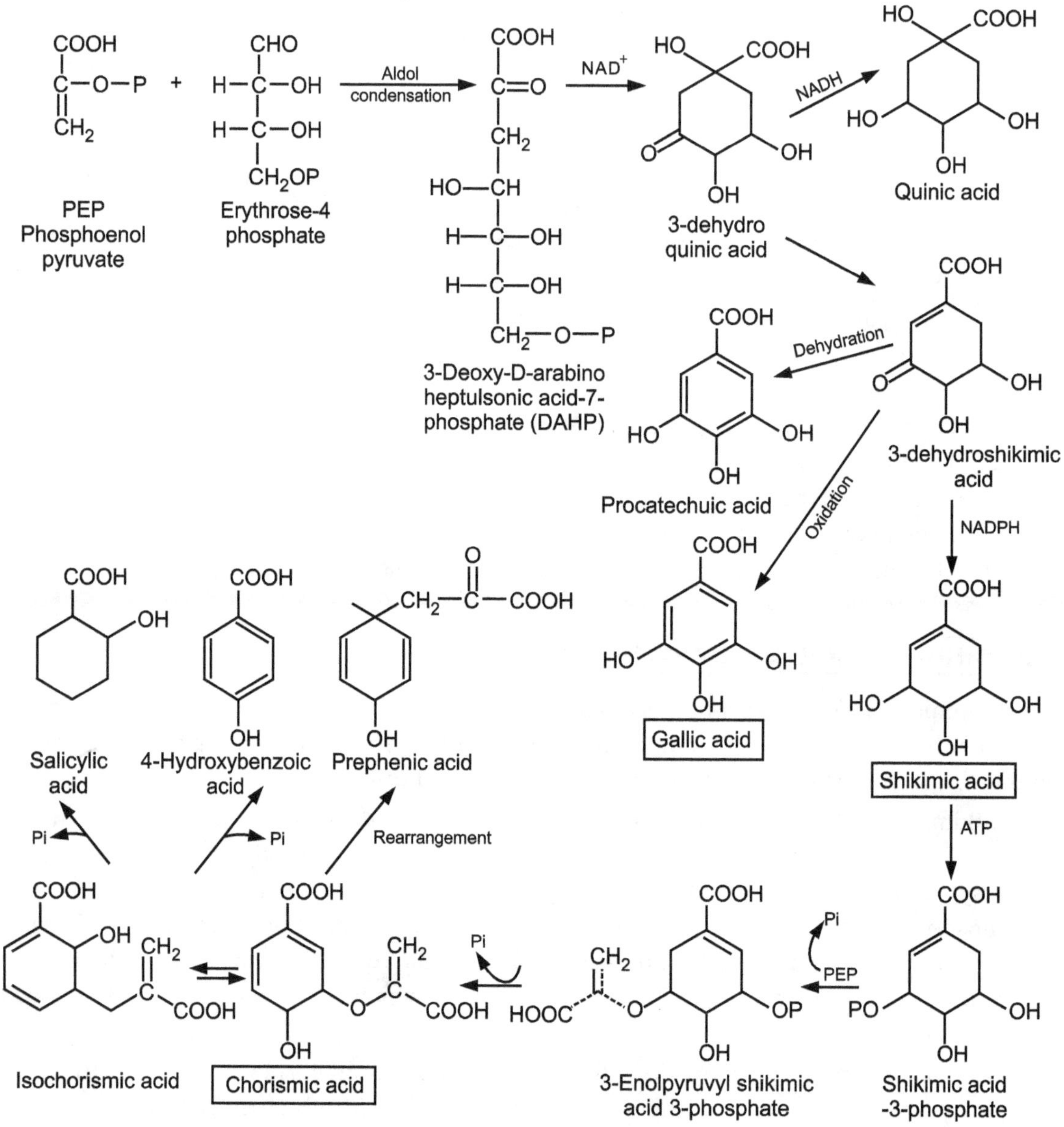

Fig. 5.1

Isochorismic acid, isomer of chorismic acid, on pyruvic acid elimination forms salicylic acid known as phenolic phytohormone present in *Salix alba*, Salicaceae and *Filipendula ulmaria*, Rosaceae. (Fig. 5.2).

Phenylalanine on enzymatic deamination forms cinnamic acid which is the starting material for biosynthesis of various phenylpropanoids. Phenylpropanoid compounds are so named because of the basic structure of a three-carbon side chain on an aromatic ring, which is derived from L-phenylalanine.

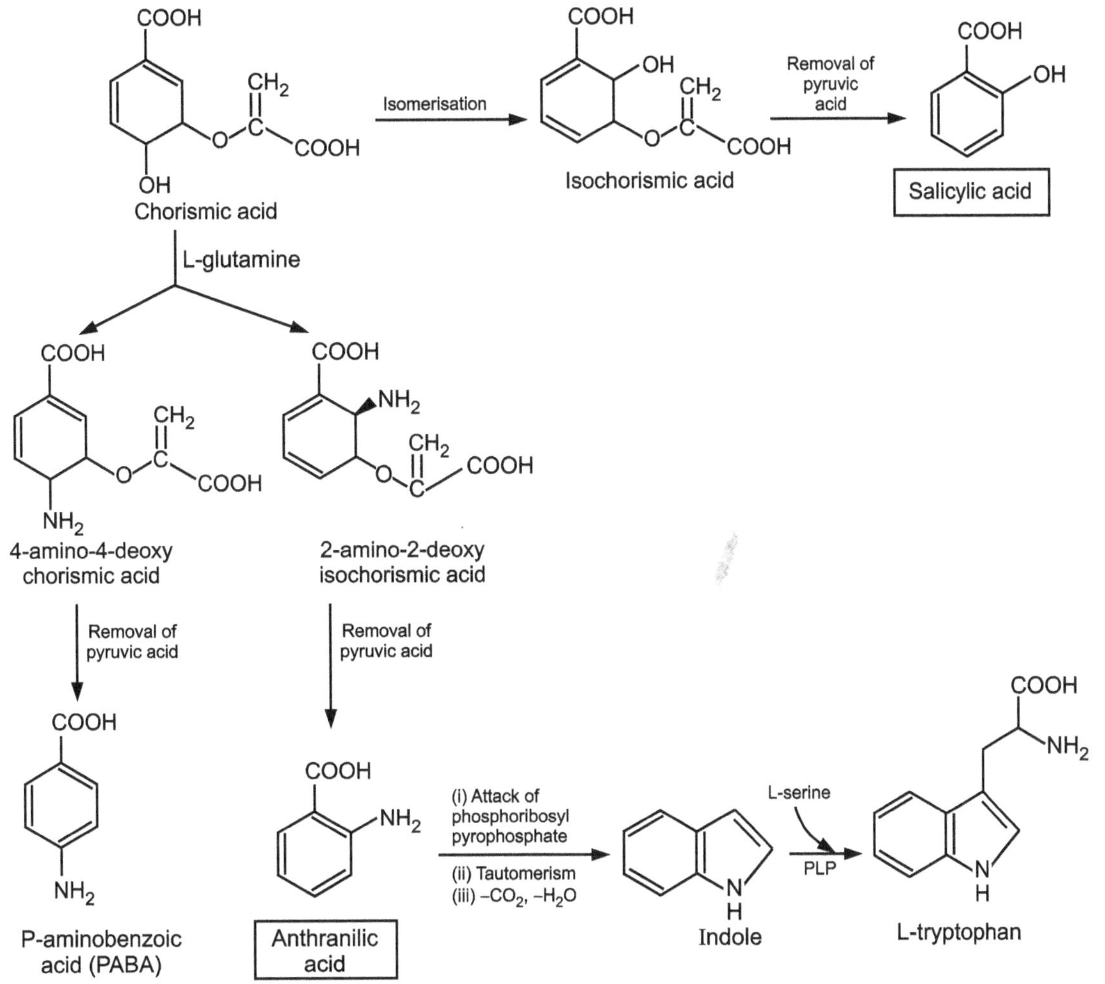

Fig. 5.2

5.2 PHENYLPROPANOIDES

Lignin and several other major classes of phenylpropene derivatives including flavonoids, coumarins, stilbenes, and benzoic acid derivatives are derived from shikimic acid pathway.

5.3 COUMARIN BIOSYNTHESIS

Coumarins (1, 2-benzopyrones) essentially found to be present in many plants of family Umbelliferae and Rutaceae playing roles such as defense against phytopathogens, response to abiotic stresses, regulation of oxidative stress, and probably hormonal regulation. The biosynthesis of coumarin in plants is via hydroxylation, glycolysis and cyclization of cinnamic acid.

Hydroxylation of meta and ortho position of cinnamic acid produces umbelliferone, aesculetin, scopolin and scopoletin (Fig. 5.5). P-coumaric acid is the precursor for 4-hydroxybenzoic acid and ferulic acid. Ferulic acid, abundantly present in seeds of many plants such as rice, wheat, pineapple and orange, is an important precursor for preparation of synthetic vanillin and being strong antioxidant can be useful as a good anticancer agent. Ferulic acid on hydroxylation and reverse aldol reaction generates vanillin, which can be naturally obtained from *Ananas comosus*, Bromeliaceae, *Ferula asafoetida*, Apiaceae and *Vanilla lanifolia*, Orchidaceae, is strong flavouring agent for pharmaceutical and food products (Fig. 5.3). Umbelliferone and aesculetin are ingredients of many sunscreen formulations but aesculetin also acts as a photosensitizer. Scopolin and its hydrolysed derivative scopoletin are well known coumarins with antimicrobial properties.

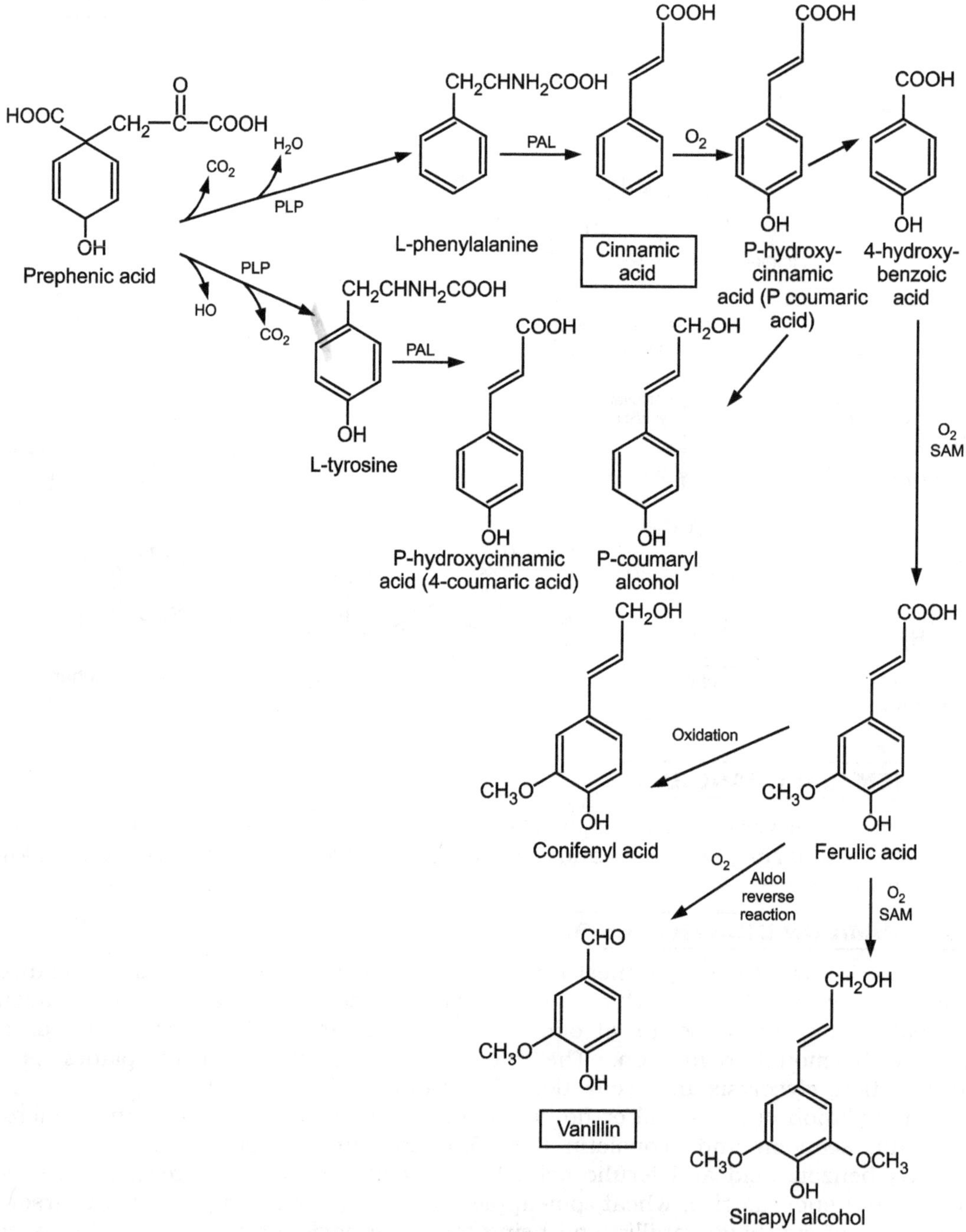

Fig. 5.3

Furanocoumarins (Fig. 5.4) is a major class of phytoalexins derived from umbelliferone. The attack of alkylating agent i.e. dimethyl allyl phosphate, cyclization and epoxide ring formation are mediated by cytochrome P_{450} dependent monooxygenase enzymes. Furanocoumarins can be classified as linear furanocoumarins (e.g. psoralen, bergapten), substituted furanocoumarins (e.g. bergapten, xanthoroxin and isopimpinellin) and angular furanocoumarins (e.g. angelicin). Furanocoumarins which get activated in the presence of ultraviolet radiation act as photosensitizing compounds for the treatment of vitiligo, psoriasis, and a number of other related skin diseases.

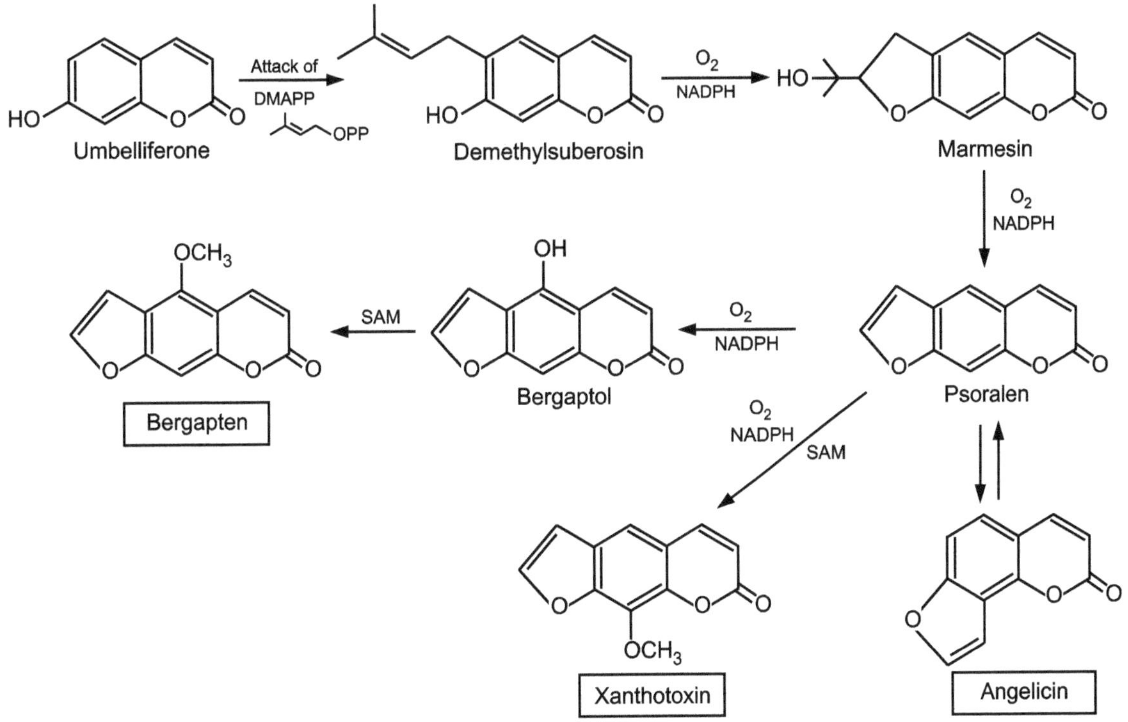

Fig. 5.4 : Coumarin Biosynthesis

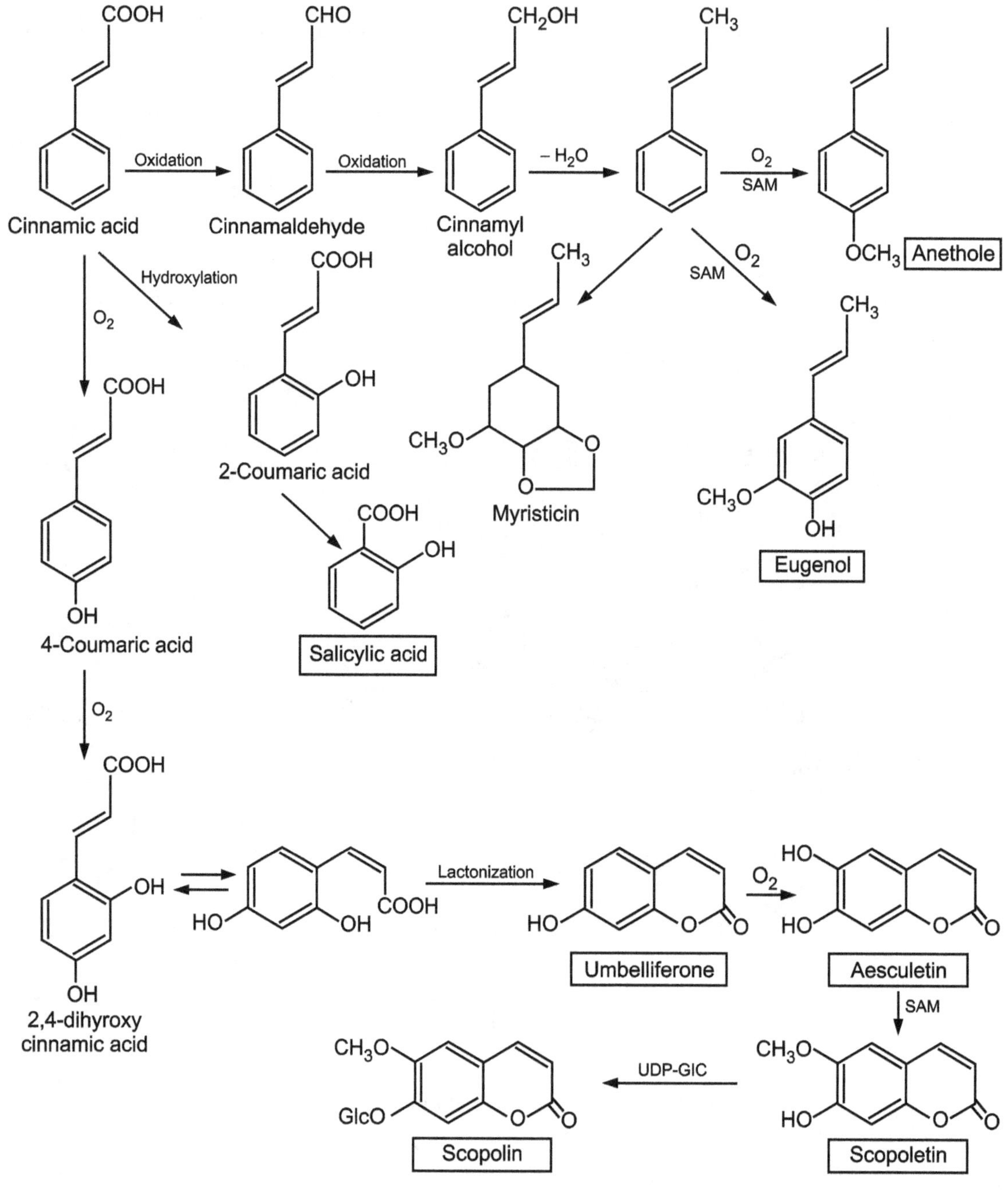

Fig. 5.5

5.4 LIGNANS AND LIGNINS BIOSYNTHESIS

Lignans and lignins are phenylpropene derivatives. Lignin is one of the world's most abundant natural polymers, found in vessels, tracheids and fibers. It serves as a matrix around the polysaccharide components of some plant cell walls, providing additional rigidity and compressive strength as well as rendering the walls hydrophobic and water impermeable. Lignans are dimers of hydroxyl cinnamic alcohols, e.g. podophylotoxins. Unlike lignin, lignans are optically active and formed by reductive coupling of monomers.

The initial steps in the biosynthesis of all these compounds are shared through the general phenylpropanoid pathway.

Cinnamic acid, the intermediate compound of shikimic acid pathway, gives P-coumanyl alcohol, coniferyl alcohol and sinapyl alcohol through a series of hydroxylation and methylation reactions. The order in which hydroxylation, methylation, thioactivation, and reduction reactions occur during monolignol synthesis may vary at some or all of these levels as well, although the extent and physiological significance of this variation are not clear.

Resonance forms of coniferyl alcohol on radical coupling gives pinoresinol, dehydrodiconiferyl alcohol and B-coniferyl ether. All these dimers are precursors for biosynthesis of lignan and lignins, viz. podophyllotoxin as given in Fig. 5.6.

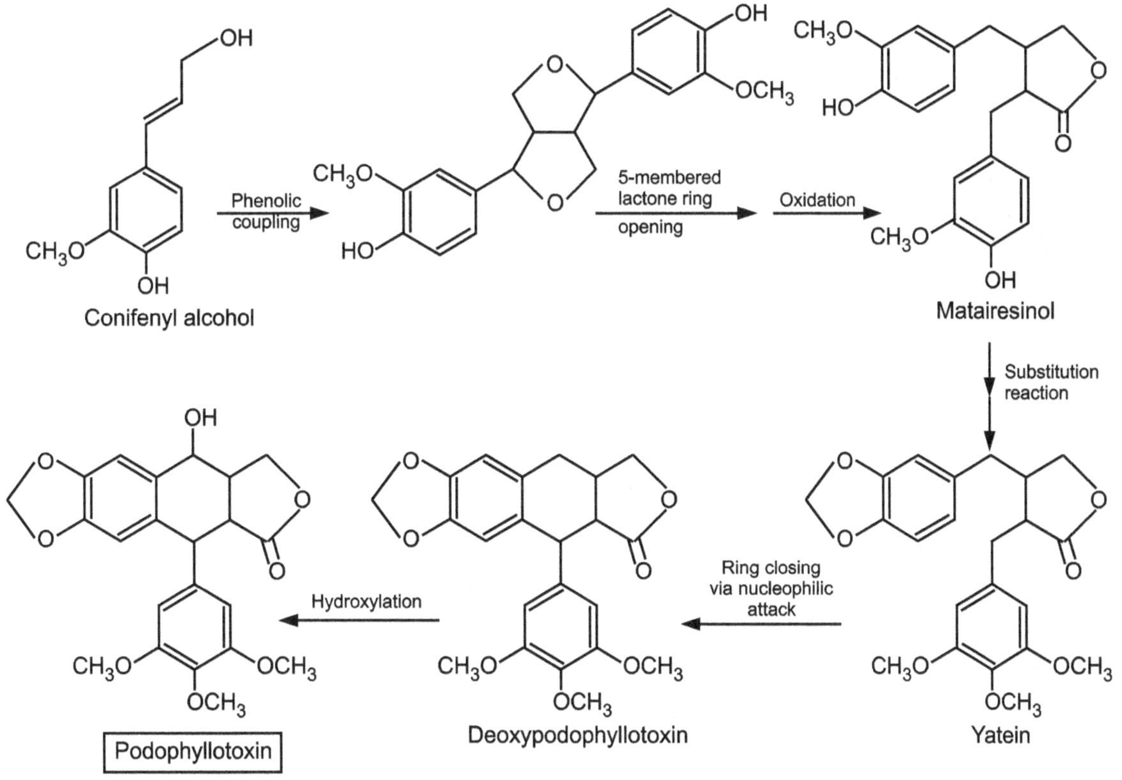

Fig. 5.6

Pinoresinol obtained from coniferyl alcohol yields matairesinol due to reductive opening of the furan ring followed by oxidation and then lactonization. Aromatic substitution of matairesinol yields yatein which on cyclization gives deoxypodophyllotoxin and podophyllotoxin followed by hydroxylation. Podophyllotoxin is a potent anti-cancer agent and also acts as a precursor for the synthesis of etoposide.

5.5 VOLATILE OILS BIOSYNTHESIS

Most of the volatile oils have their biosynthetic origin in mevalonate pathway but a few of the terpenoids (viz. anethole from aniseed, fennel; cinnamaldehyde from cinnamon, and myristicin from nutmeg) are generated from the shikimate pathway. Cinnamyl alcohol on reduction generates phenylpropenes (Fig. 5.5) such as allylphenols (e.g. cinnamaldehyde, eugenol, myristicin) and propenyl phenol (e.g. anethole).

Sometimes, the shikimate pathway intermediates combine with the acetate pathway to give pharmacologically significant compounds such as styrylpyrones, flavonoids, stilbenes, flavonolignans, and isoflavonoids.

First we will discuss biosynthesis of styrylpyrones i.e. yangogenin. Cinnamoyl Co-A as a starter unit and one or two C_2 units from malonyl CoA combine to form lactone derivative like yangogenin (Fig. 5.7) which is one of the six major kavalactones found in the kava plant *Piper methysticum* which has anxiolytic activity.

5.6 FLAVONOID BIOSYNTHESIS

Flavonoids collectively called as Vitamin P, polyphenols of plant origin, are a major class of plant secondary metabolites that serve a multitude of functions including colour pigments, anti-oxidant, anti-inflammatory, anti-cancer and anti-diabetic activity. Dicot families like Compositae, Leguminosae, Polygonaceae, Rutaceae, Umbelliferae etc. contain a large number of flavonoids. Flavonoids have been also reported from some green algae.

Flavonoids which are chemically considered as Benzo –γ-pyrone derivatives are synthesized from phenylpropanoid derivatives by condensation with malonyl-CoA. For example, condensation of p-coumaryl-CoA (C_6-C_3) with three malonyl-CoA (C_3) molecules results in naringenin-chalcone with a diphenylpropane (C_6-C_3-C_6) unit, which is converted to flavanone moiety, naringenin, by conjugate ring closure. Further modifications yield a variety of structural forms such as flavones (basic flavonoid structure), flavanone (lacking the double bond in the 2, 3 position), flavanols (having a 3 hydroxyl substituent), dihydroflavanols, isoflavononoids (having the B ring attached at the 3 position instead of the 2 position with reduced 2, 3-double bond), flavolignans, anthocyanidins (as a aglycone of naturally occurring glycosides) and catechins.

Three molecules of malonyl CoA combine with cinnamoyl CoA (Fig. 5.8) in the presence of enzyme stilbene synthase or chalcone synthase giving rise to stilbenes (viz. resveratrol potent anti-inflammatory and anti-apoptoic agent obtained from grapes, black and green teas, berries) – or chalcones (viz. naringenin, isoliquiritigenin) respectively. An aldol-claisen reaction occurs to form aromatic rings from open ring structures as shown in Fig. 5.8.

Chalcone is the main precursor moiety for biosynthesis of structurally different flavonoid like compounds. Flavanone (e.g. Narigin) moiety on series of hydroxylations followed by reduction or dehydration reactions (Fig. 5.9) gives rise to a variety of compounds like flavones (e.g. apigenin, tangeritin, luteolin), dihydroflavonols (e.g. dihydrokaempferol, dihydroquercetin or taxifolin), flavonols (e.g. kaemferol, fisetin, quercetin), catechins (e.g. afzalechin, catechin), flavanone (e.g. hesperetin, naringenin, eriodictyol, homoeriodictyol) and anthocyanidins (e.g. pelargonidin, cyanidin).

Isoflavones are isomeric with flavones, having the B ring attached at the 3 position instead of the 2 position. Isoflavonoids have the 2, 3-double bond reduced, so that they are related to isoflavones in the same way that flavanones are related to flavones. Isoflavonoid is the rare type of subclass of flavonoids restricted to family Fabaceae. Isoflavonoid biosynthesis involves aromatic ring migration through rearrangement reaction mediated by cytochrome P_{450} dependent enzyme, NADPH and oxidation. Hydroxylation, alkylation, oxidation or formation of additional rings gives to varied number of isoflavonoids viz. delphinidin, malvidin, daidzein, genistein medicarpin, coumestrol, rotenone and pisatin

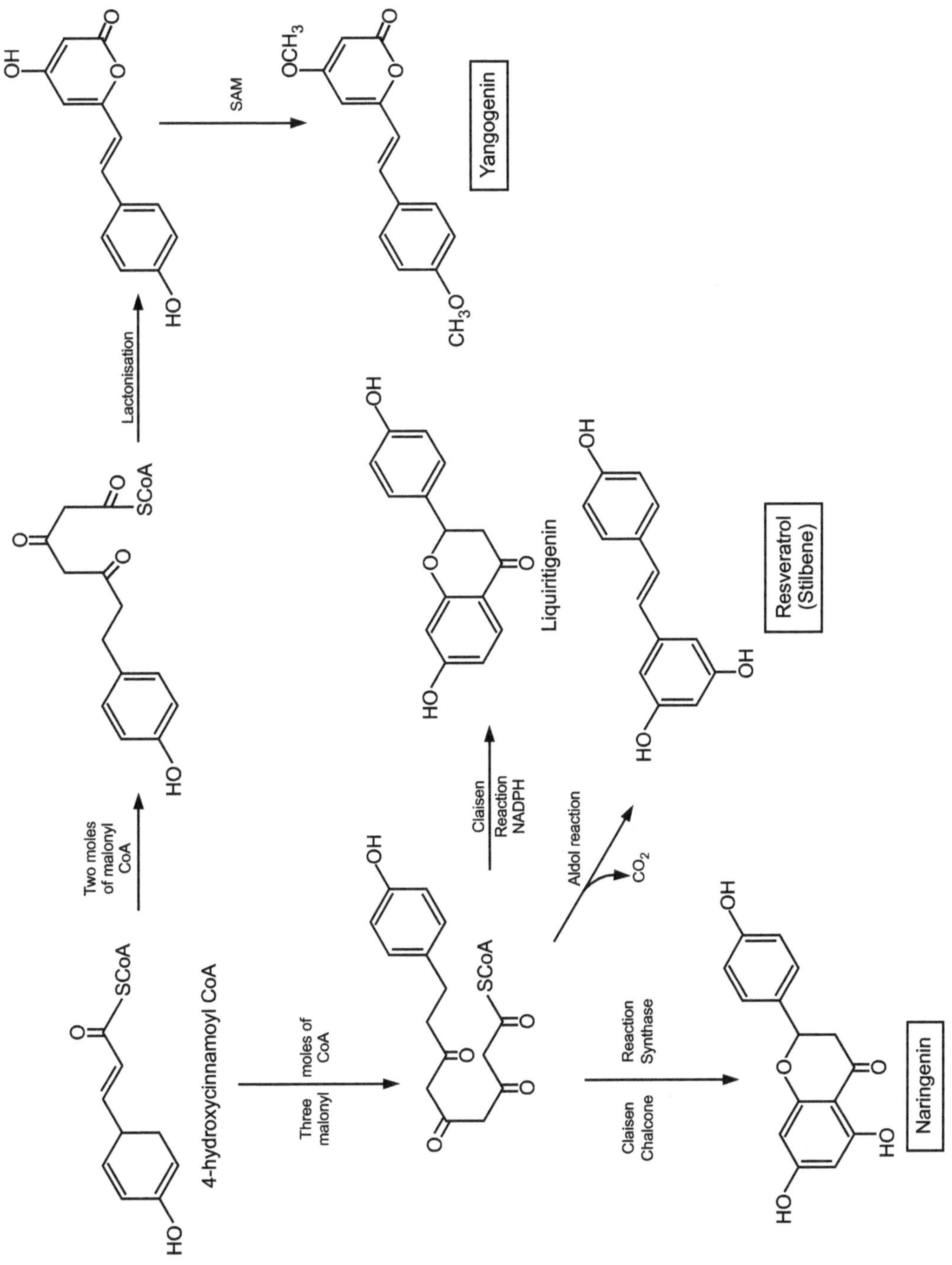

Fig. 5.7

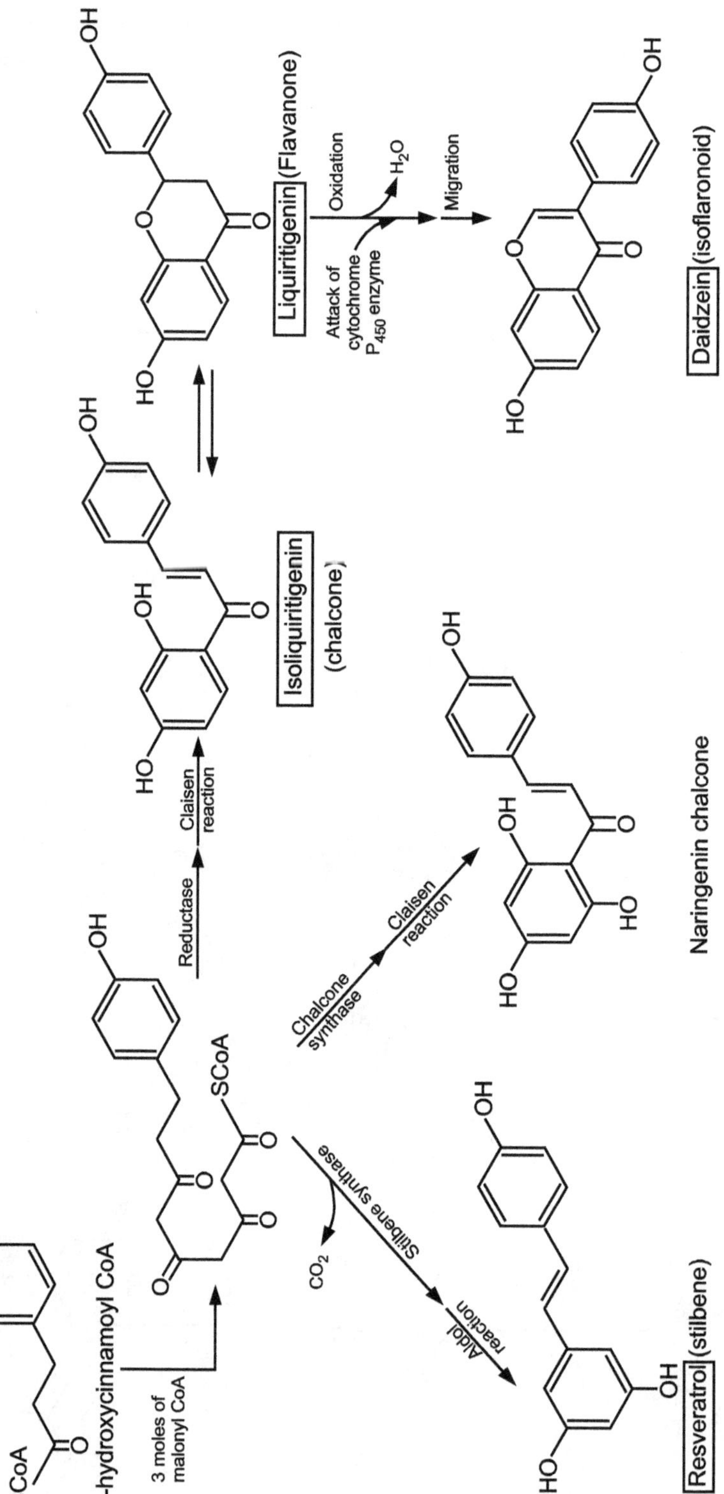
4-hydroxycinnamoyl CoA
3 moles of malonyl CoA
SCoA
Reductase
Claisen reaction
Isoliquiritigenin
(chalcone)
Liquiritigenin (Flavanone)
Oxidation
H_2O
Attack of cytochrome P_{450} enzyme
Migration
Daidzein (isoflaronoid)
Chalcone synthase
Claisen reaction
Naringenin chalcone
Stilbene synthase
CO_2
Aldol reaction
Resveratrol (stilbene)

Fig. 5.8

Shikimic Acid Pathway

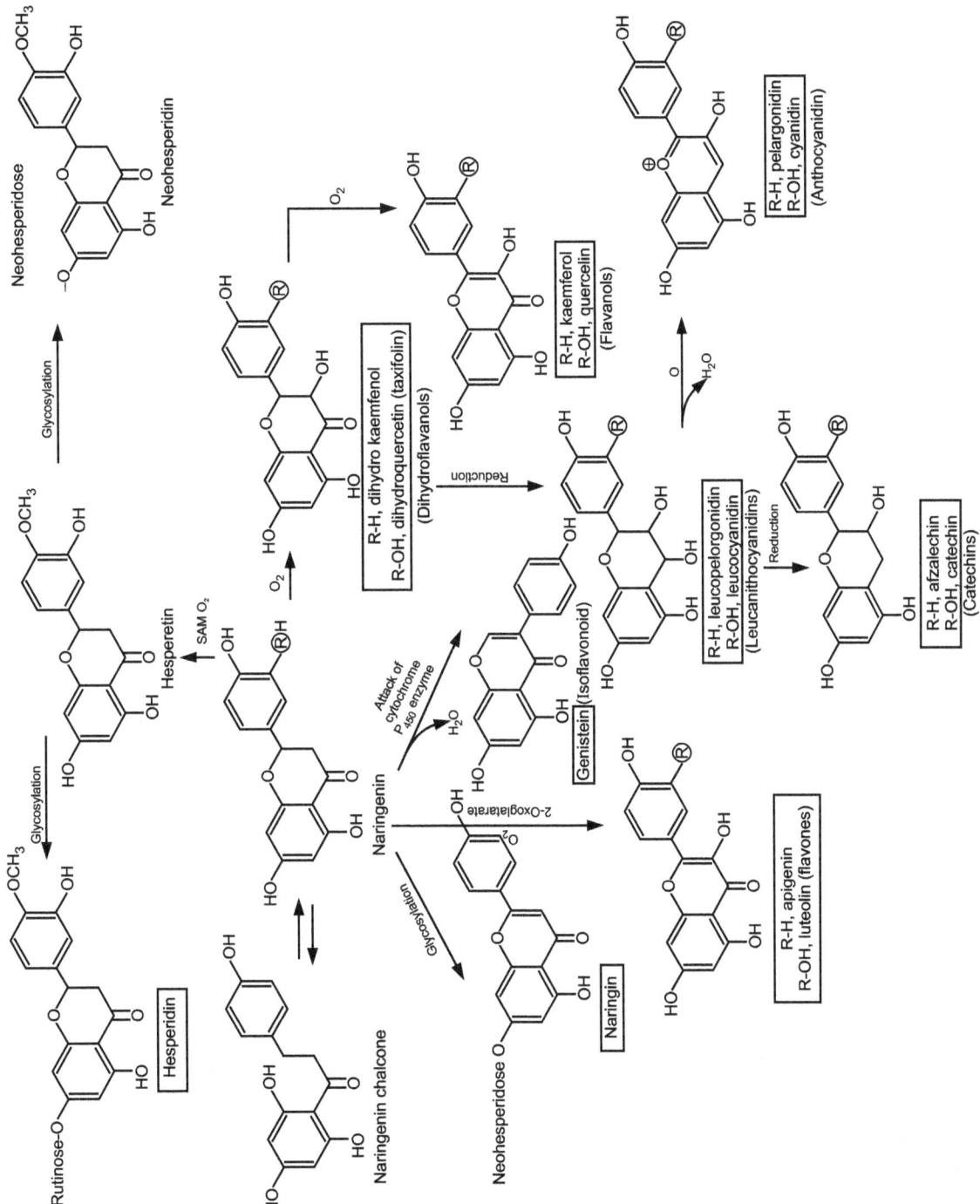

Fig. 5.9

Flavolignans are a combination of flavonoids and lignans. One of the very important examples of this class is hepatoprotective agent silybin (Fig. 5.10) which is obtained through the radical coupling of taxifolin and coniferyl alcohol followed by nucleophilic attack. Silybin is the mixture of flavonolignans extracted from milk thistle (*Silybum marianum*) consisting of silibinin A and B, isosibilinin A and B, silicristin and silidianin. Silymarin is potent hepatoprotective agent which acts by altering the structure of the outer membrane of the hepatocytes in such a way as to prevent penetration of the liver toxins into the interior of the cell. It also stimulates the action of nucleolar polymerase A, resulting in ribosomal protein synthesis and, thus stimulates the regenerative ability of the liver and formation of new hepatocytes. Recently it is also found to be having anticancer properties.

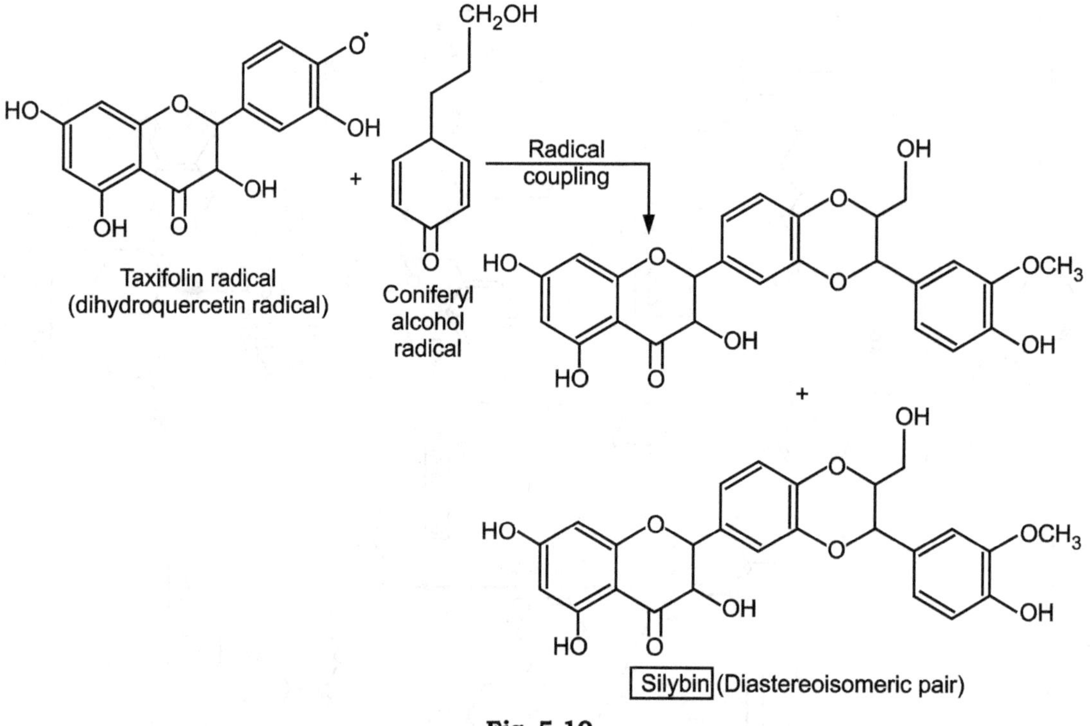

Fig. 5.10

5.7 MISCELLANEOUS PRODUCT

Combination of shikimate pathway intermediates with malonate pathway terpenoid fragments give rise to important phytoconstituent class i.e. terpenoid quinone as shown in Fig. 5.11.

Terpenoid quinones are actually the higher terpenoids, for example, ubiquinoes containing C_{40-50} isoprene units, plastoquinones containing C_{45} unit and menaquinones containing upto C_{65} units. Ubiquionones (Coenzyme Q), plastoquinones, tocopherol, napthoquinones or anthraquine derivatives (Fig. 5.12) which are widely distributed in nature play important roles in photosynthesis and respiration. Anthraquinone derivatives, the aromatic polyketide discussed in the previous chapter, has its origin in

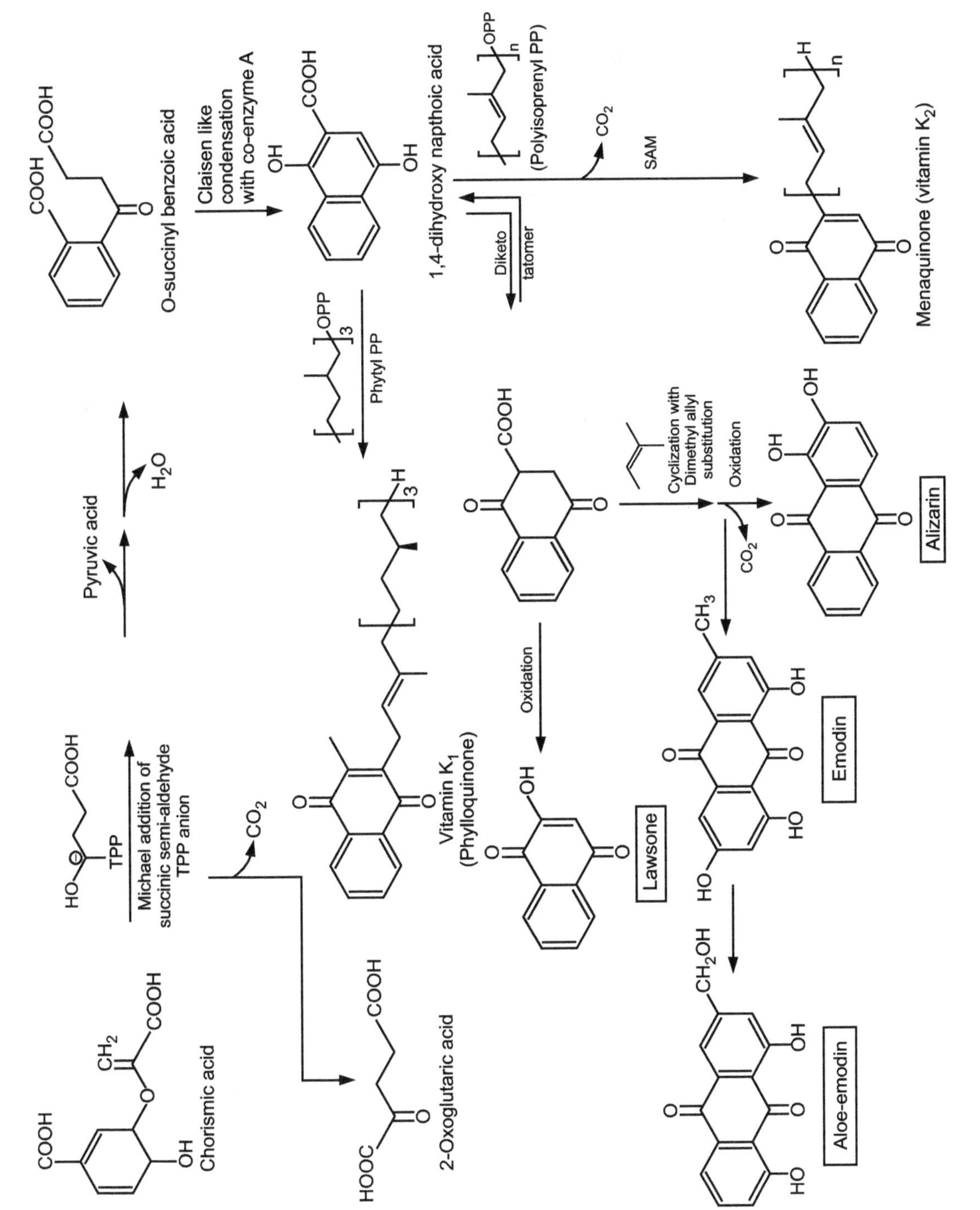

Fig. 5.11

acetate as well as shikimate pathway. Alizarin, (1, 2-dihydroxyanthraquinone) is a very important red colour dye present in *Rubia tinctorium*, *R. cordifolia*, family : Rubiaceae. Lawsone (2-hydroxy-1,4-naphthoquinone), is a very anciently known red-orange dye present in the leaves of the *Lawsonia inermis*, family : Lythraceae and *Impatiens balsamica*, family : Balsaminaceae.

The proper length of terpenoid fragment (n=1...13) and nature of the starting compound obtained from shikimic acid pathway determines the different derivatives. (Chorismic acid derived 1, 4-dihydroxynapthoic acid gives menaquinones, phylloquinones; coumaric acid derived 4-hydroxybenzoic acid gives ubiquinones, while 4-hydroxy-phenylpyruvic acid derived homogentisic acid gives plastoquinones and tocopherol.) Tautomer of 1, 4-dihydroxynapthoic acid gives rise to napthaquinone derivatives through oxidative sequence. (Fig. 5.11) Dimethyl allyl cyclization with napthaquinones gives anthraquinons. Phylloquinones (vit. K) involve phytyl subtituents which is actually the reduced form of GGPP.

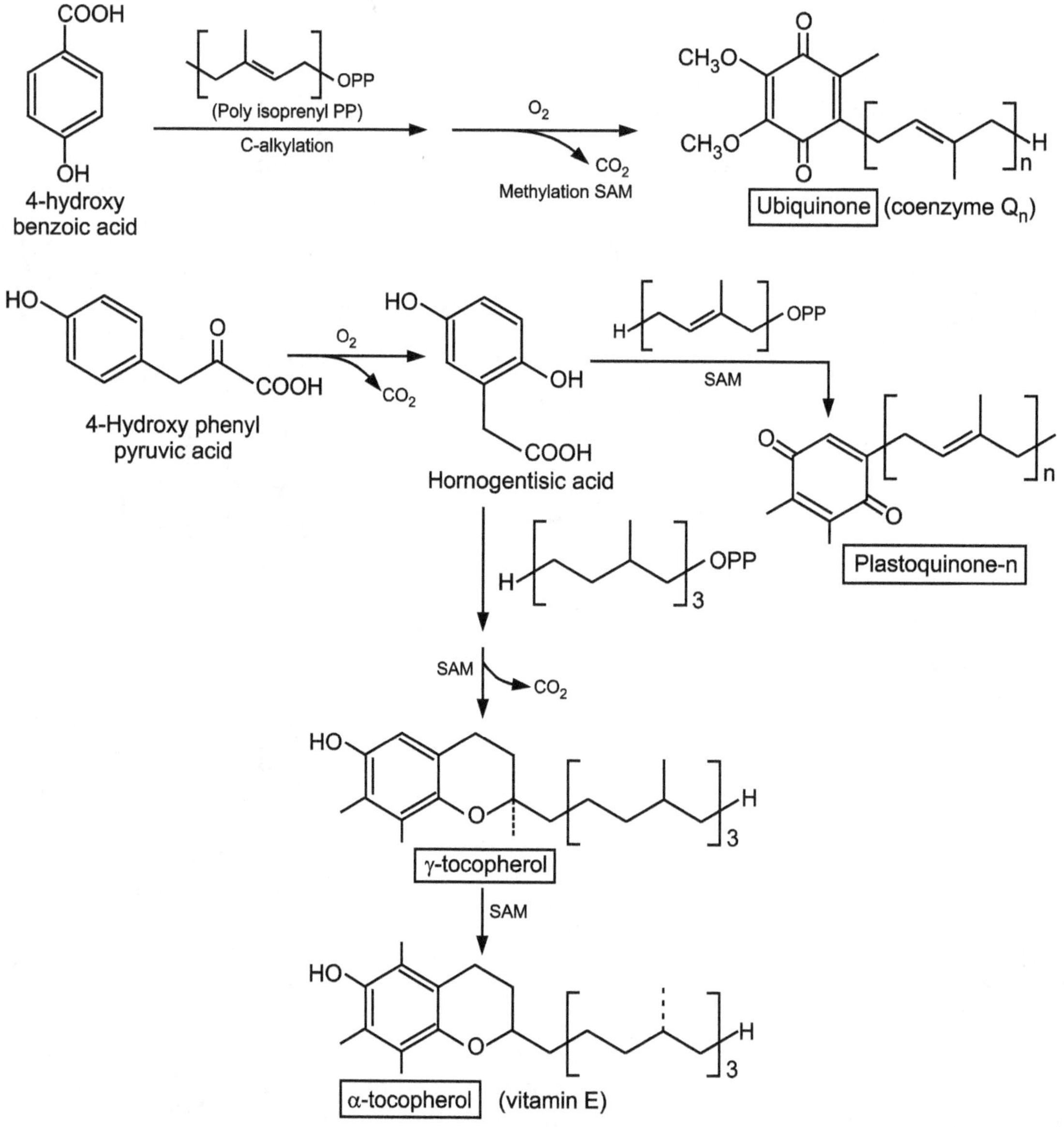

Fig. 5.12

CHAPTER

ISOPRENOID PATHWAY / ACETATE MEVALONATE PATHWAY

- Introduction: Isoprenoid Pathway, D-L-deoxyxylulose-3-phosphate Pathway
- Classification of Terpenoids
- Monoterpenoide Biosynthesis: Pinene, Limonene, Phellandrene, Linalool, Fenchone, Camphor, Cineol, Thujone, Geraniol, Carvone, Menthol
- Monoterpenoid irridoide Biosynthesis: Loganin, Secologanin, Valtrate, Gentiopicroside
- Sesquiterpenoide Biosynthesis: Gossypol, Artemisinin, Humulene, Cadinene
- Diterpenoide Biosynthesis: Forskolin, Ginkgolide, Abietic acid, Steviol, Taxol
- Triterpenoide Biosynthesis: α-Amyrin, β- Amyrin, Lupeol, Euphol, Cucurbitacin-E
- Modified Triterpenoid Biosynthesis:
- Steroids and Steroidal Saponin Biosynthesis: Diosgenin, Hecogenin, Tigogenin, Sarsapogenin, Ginsenoside,
- Cardioactive sterol Biosynthesis: Digitoxigenin, Digoxigenin, Gitoxigenin, Scillaren A, Hellebrigenin
- Phytosterol Biosynthesis: Stigmasterol, Sitosterol, Ergosterol, Fucosterol
- Pentacyclic triterpenoid Biosynthesis: Quillaic acid, Glycyrrhezetic acid, Limonoids, Quassinoids, Azadirachtin.
- Tertaterpenoide Biosynthesis: Lycopene, α-Carotene, β-Carotene, Capsanthin, Lutein, Vitamin A

6.1 INTRODUCTION

Isoprenoid pathway is also known as *terpenoid pathway* or *acetate mevalonate pathway*. This pathway contributes about one third of all known secondary metabolites. Acetate mevalonate pathway leads to the important class of secondary metabolites i.e. terpenoids. The isoprene unit from this pathway is contributed to the biosynthesis of many other metabolites such as anthraquinones, napthaquinones, furanocoumarins and terpenoid, indole alkaloids.

Acetate mevalonate pathway begins with a molecule of acetyl CoA which is produced from pyruvic acid, the end product of glycolysis. Firstly, two molecules of acetyl CoA forms acetoacetyl CoA through Claisen condensation. The third molecule of acetyl CoA forms important intermediate β-hydroxy β-methylglutaryl-CoA (HMG-CoA) by aldol addition. Further, a two step reduction gives rise to mevalonic acid, the main precursor for biosynthesis of terpenoids. Mevalonic acid on ATP mediated phosphorylation results in mevalonic acid diphosphate which on decarboxylation provides first isoprene unit, Isopentenyl pyrophosphate (IPP). Mevalonate kinase and mevalonate-5-phosphate kinase form mevalonate diphosphate which is decarboxylated via ATP to form IPP. IPP by an isomerase enzyme gives a second isoprene unit dimethyl allyl pyrophosphate

6.2 Isoprenoid Pathway / Acetate Mevalonate Pathway

(DMAPP). The allylic phosphate group of DMAPP is an excellent leaving group which yields a carbonium ion, a reactive alkylating agent easily reacts with IPP.

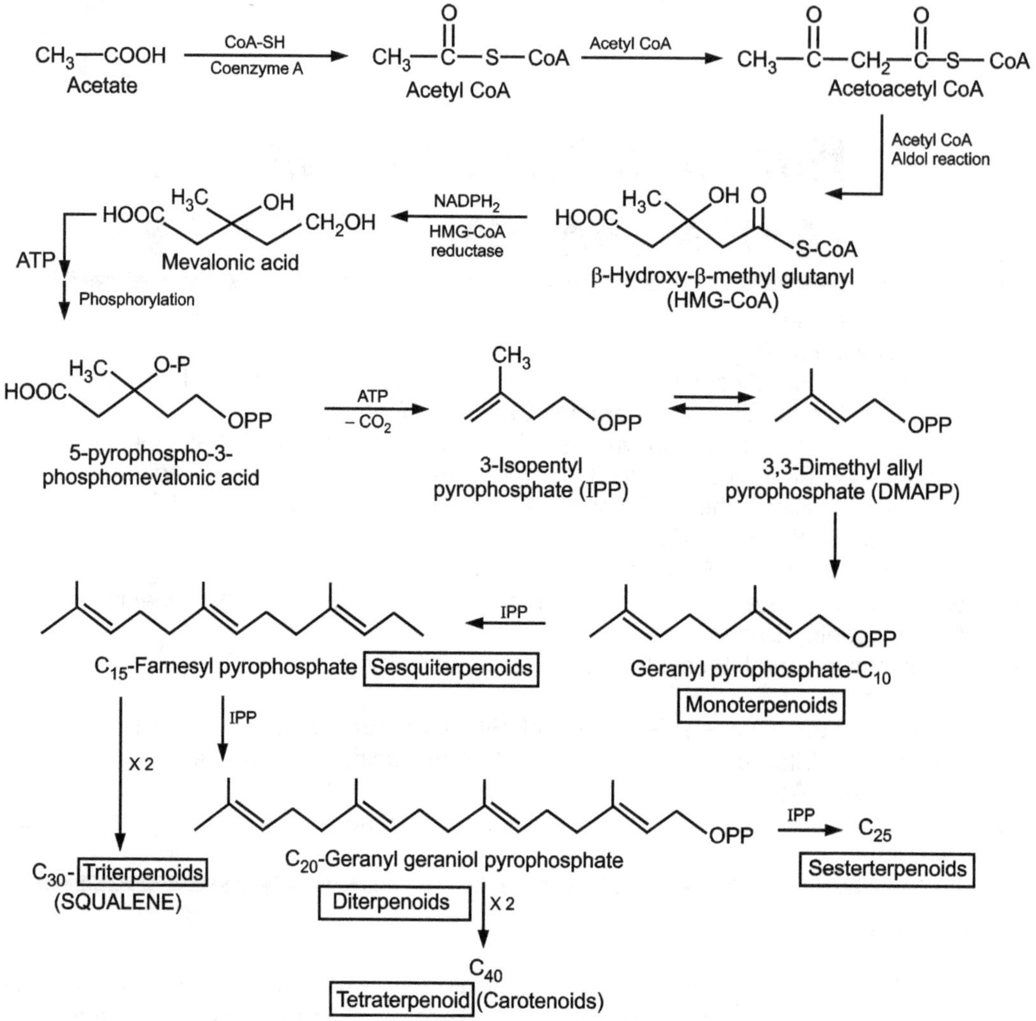

Fig. 6.1 : Acetate Mevalonate Pathway

Enzyme prenyltransferase (prenyl = isoprene) yields C_{10}, C_{15}, C_{20} units. C_{10}, C_{20} and C_{40} compounds are synthesized in plastids via D-L-deoxyxylulose-3-phosphate pathway and C_{15}, C_{30} compounds are formed in cytosol via mevalonate pathway.

Electrophilic addition of IPP with DMAPP via enzyme prenyl transferase yields the C_{10} unit, geranyl diphosphate (GPP) precursor for synthesis of monoterpenes. Combination of another IPP unit again via with GPP gives rise to the farnesyl diphosphate (FPP) C_{15} unit, precursor for sesquiterpene synthesis. Further addition of another molecule of IP forms the C_{20} unit, geranylgeranyl diphosphate (GGPP) to produce range of diterpenes. Similarly, further addition of IPP units yield rare terpenoids i.e. geranyl farnysyl/pyrophosphal (GFPP), C_{25} unit called as *sesterterpenes*. Tail to tail addition of two FPP units yields C_{30} unit, triterpene. Similarly, two units of GGPP form C_{40} unit, tetraterpenes.

Recent studies have uncovered the existence of an alternative, non-mevalonate pathway for the formation of isopentenyl pyrophosphate and dimethylallyl pyrophosphate, the two building blocks of terpene biosynthesis. A hypothetical mechanism was suggested with a head-to-head condensation of glyceraldehyde 3-phosphate and activated acetaldehyde derived from pyruvate, resulting in the formation of 1-deoxy- -xylulose 5-phosphate as the first precursor of the novel pathway which on specific enzyme reaction gives 2-C-methylerythritol-4-phosphate to 4-(cytidine-5'-diphospho)-2-C-methylerythritol and finally 2-C-methyl-D-erythritol-2, 4-cyclodiphosphate. The lateral product gives IPP and DMAPP by unknown mechanism.

6.2 CLASSIFICATION

In chapter 1, we have already discussed the classification of terpenoids. Here we will focus on the classification of volatile oils. Volatile oils are generally classified on the basis of functional groups present viz. hydrocarbon, alcohol, phenol, ketone, aldehyde, ether etc.

Acyclic Hydrocarbon Volatile Oils : These are the simplest hydrocarbons found in nature. Beta myrcene found in oil of Bay (*Myrcia acris*, Myricaceae), Oil of turpentine (*Pinus longifolia*, Pinaceae) is used as an intermediate in the synthesis of perfumes. Similarly, trans- beta- ocimine (*Ocimum basilium*, Labiatae) is also one of the common examples from acyclic monoterpenes used in perfume manufacturing.

The Monocyclic Hydrocarbon Volatile Oils : Terpene, phellandrene, limonine and sylvestrene are the main examples of monocyclic hydrocarbon monotepenoides. Limonene is used as a perfume in cosmetics, flavouring agent, in resin manufacturing, wetting and dispersing agent.

Bicyclic Hydrocarbon Volatile Oils : These are divided into five main categories viz. thujane (sabinine isolated form *Juniperus Sabina*, Cupressaceae.), pinane (alpha and beta pinene from turpentine oil), carane (3-carene which is part of turpentine form *Pinus longifolia*, Pinaceae), camphane (camphene commonly found in various plants such as *Anethum graveolens, Foeniculum vulgare, piper nigrum, Myristica fragans* etc.) and fenchane (d- fenchone from *Foeniculum vulgare* and *Lavondula stochas*).

Alcohol Volatile Oils : Acyclic alcohol volatile oils have the broken six membered ring at some point. Geraniol, nerol, linalool are the typical examples of this class.

Aldehyde Volatile Oils : Most of the acyclic aldehyde volatile oils are of less significance as compared to citral (isolated from *Cymbopogon flexuosus*, Graminae which is usually used as a precursor in the synthesis of vitamin A) and citronallal (isolated *Cymbopogon nardus*, Graminae used as an insect repellant and artificaial flavour). Safranal (*Crocus sativus*, Iridaceae) and phellandral (*Eucalyptus globules*, Myrtaceae) are example from monocyclic aldehyde volatile oils. Anisaldehyde, banzaldehyde, Cinnamaldehyde, cumminaldehyde and salicylalaldehyde are the most common aromatic aldehydes found in different essential oils. Vanillin, the extensively useful flavouring agent in food products, confectioneries and beverages, is the chief example of this class.

Ketone Volatile Oil : Menthone (*Mentha piperita*, Labiateae), carvacol and carvone (*Mentha spicata*, Lamiacea) are the typical examples of monocyclic ketone volatile oils. Camphor and d-fenchone are bicyclic ketone volatile oils.

Phenol Volatile Oil : Carvacrol obtained from *Origanum vulgare*, Labiatae is used as a disinfectant and as an anthelmintic.

Phenolic Ether Volatile Oil : Anethole, the chief constituent of *Foeniculum vulgare*, belongs to this class. Safrol, cineole myristicin and ascaridole are the other very important volatile oil constituents. Cineole from various species of eucalyptus which is also a part of many essential oils of other species is used as an antiseptic, local anti-inflammatory, expectorant and a flavouring agent. Ascaridole is the chief constituent of *Chenopodium ambrosioides*, family : Chenopodiaceae is used to evacuate hook worms and round worms.

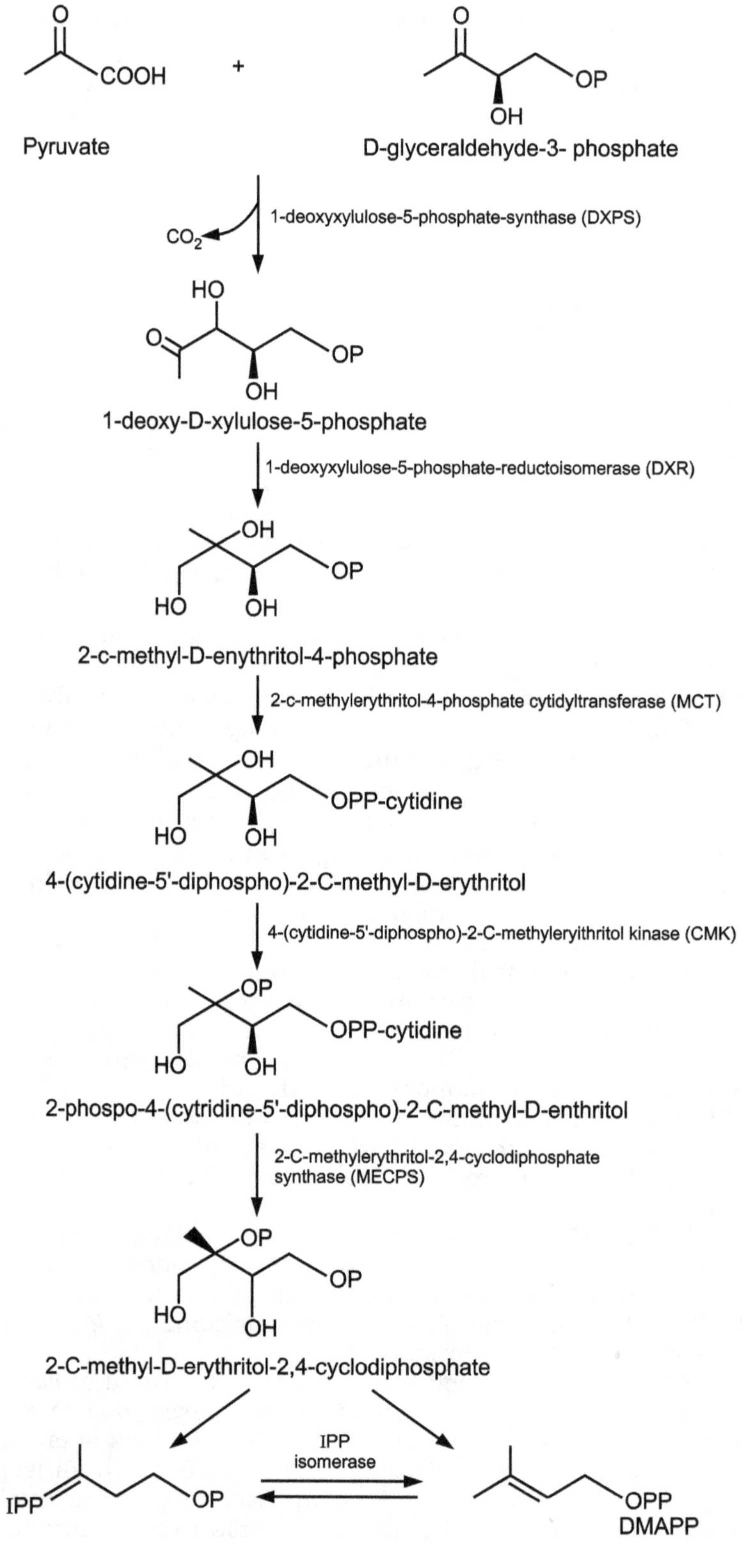

6.4 Isoprenoid Pathway / Acetate Mevalonate Pathway

Fig. 6.2 : DXP Pathway

6.3 MONOTERPENOIDS

Monoterpenoids are derived from geranyl pyrophosphate and are composed of two isoprene units. Monoterpenoids are found in plants, animals, as well as in insects. They are mostly present in higher plants and their parts such as seed (nutmeg), bark (cinnamon), fruits (*umbelliferae*), leaves, roots and flowers.

Prominent families containing monoterpenoids are *Umbelliferae, Lauraceae, Labiateae, Myrtaceae, Burseraceae* and *Pinaceae*. Most commonly occurring terpenoids are limonene, cineole and pinene. Many of these compounds have been found to be carminative, antiseptic, anthelmintic, stimulant, sex attractant, and antimicrobial due to which plants shows defensive properties.

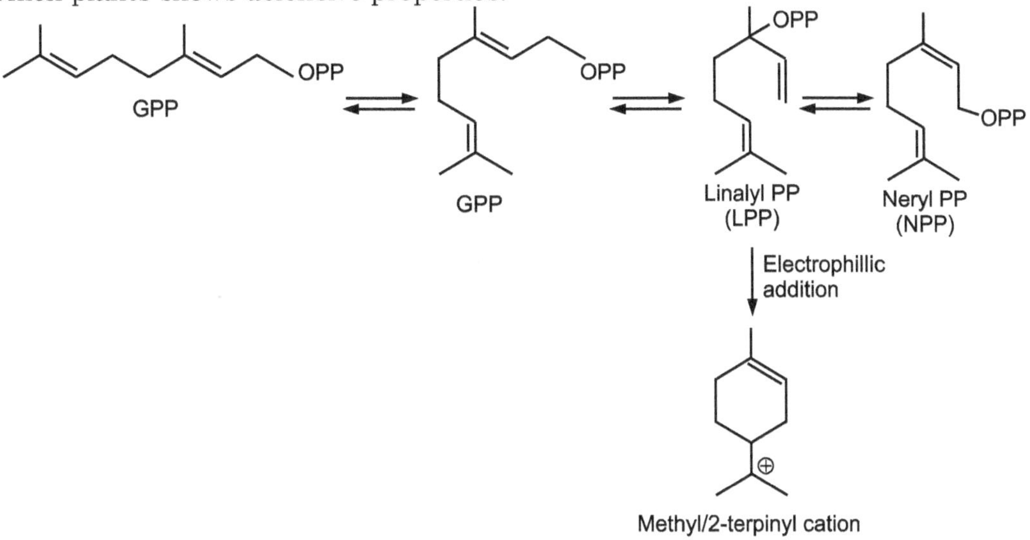

Fig. 6.3

Geranyl diphosphate (GPP) generated carbocations (Fig. 6.3) lead to acyclic linalyl PP (LPP), neryl PP (NPP) and the monocyclic menthane skeleton. This basic skeleton leads to the formation of a range of monoterpenes through reactions such as hydration, dehydrogenation, cyclization and Wagner-Meerwein rearrangement.

Linalyl pyrophosphate is the more favourable direct intermediate for the monoterpenoid biosynthesis than neryl and geranyl pyrophosphates (Fig. 6.9 and Fig. 6.10). The direct cyclization of linalyl pyrophosphate may take place in the biosynthesis of the cyclic monoterpenoids in the higher plants.

Folding of cation : The cationic side-chain of monocyclic menthane ring to the double bond and cyclization generates various bicyclic skeletons as shown in Fig. 6.4. The three isomers of menthane viz. para, ortho and meta yield respective monoterpenes.

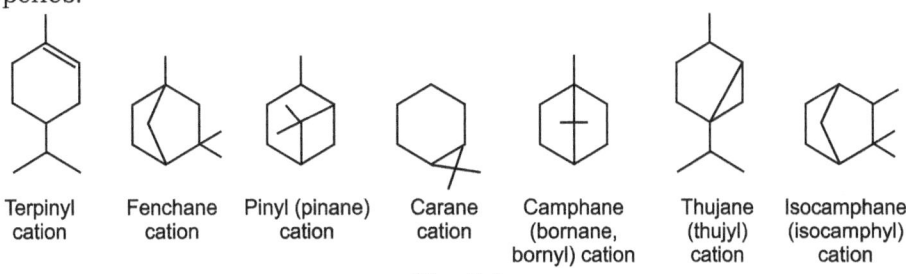

Fig. 6.4

6.6 Isoprenoid Pathway / Acetate Mevalonate Pathway

Biosynthesis of various monoterpenoids especially depends on Wagner Meerwein rearrangement involving migration of carbons or hydrogen. Generally 1, 2 alkyl or hydride shifts are involved in the formation of various bicyclic skeletons which either on hydroxylation, oxidation or dehydrogenation gives a number of bicyclic monoterpenoids (Fig. 6.5, Fig. 6.6, Fig. 6.7 and Fig. 6.8).

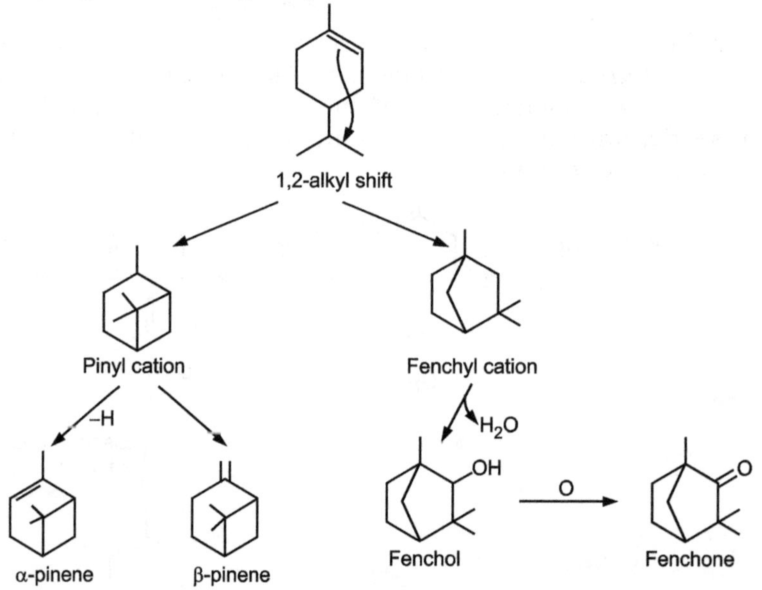

Fig. 6.5

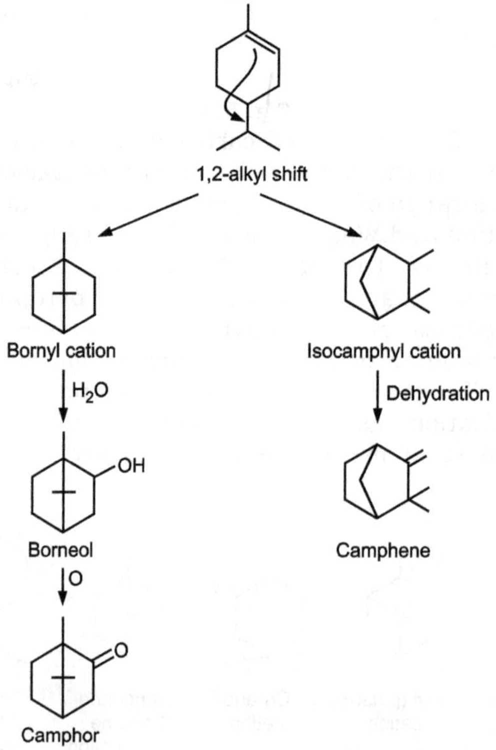

Fig. 6.6

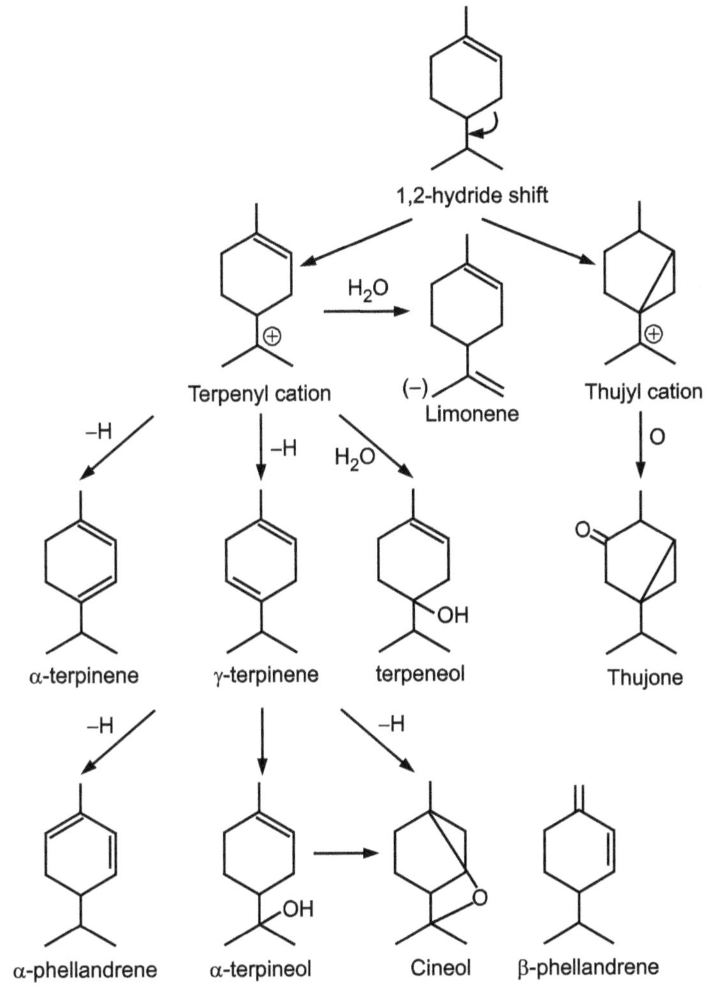

6.7 Isoprenoid Pathway / Acetate Mevalonate Pathway

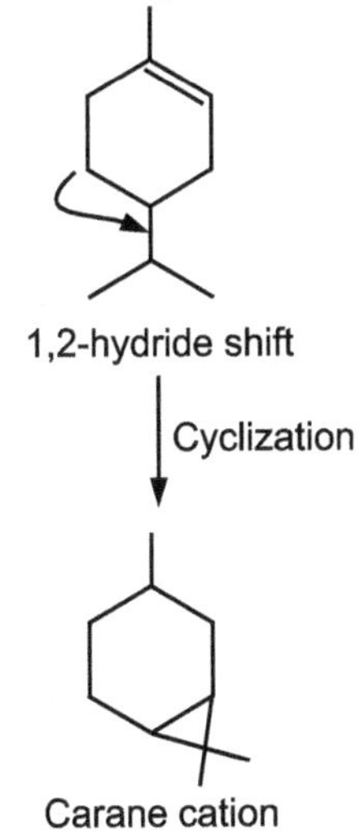

Fig. 6.7

Fig. 6.8

Sometimes a mixture of stereoisomers is also found for a single constituent when the single compound plays the role of a precursor for various terpenoids. E.g. limonene is the precursor for carvone, piperitone and menthol (Fig. 6.11).

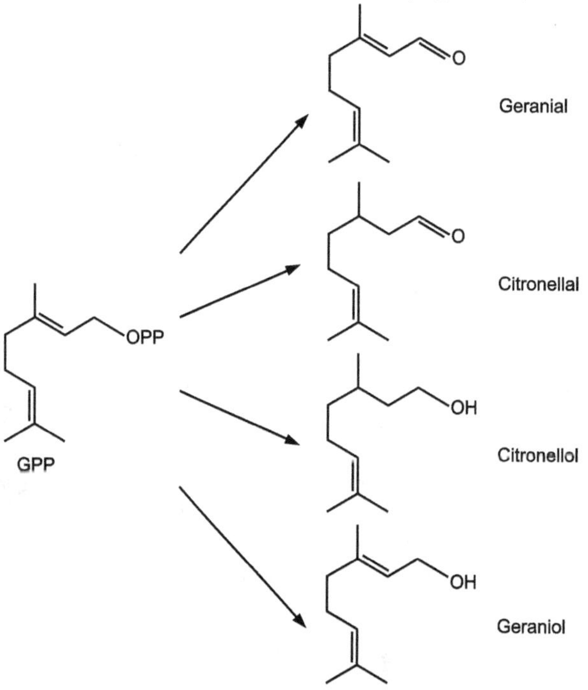

Fig. 6.9

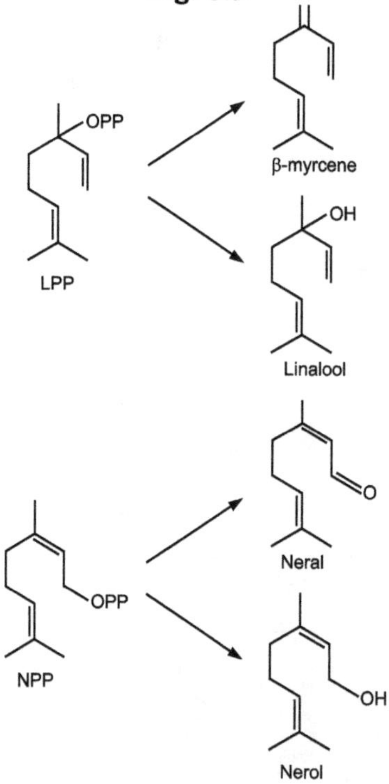

Fig. 6.10

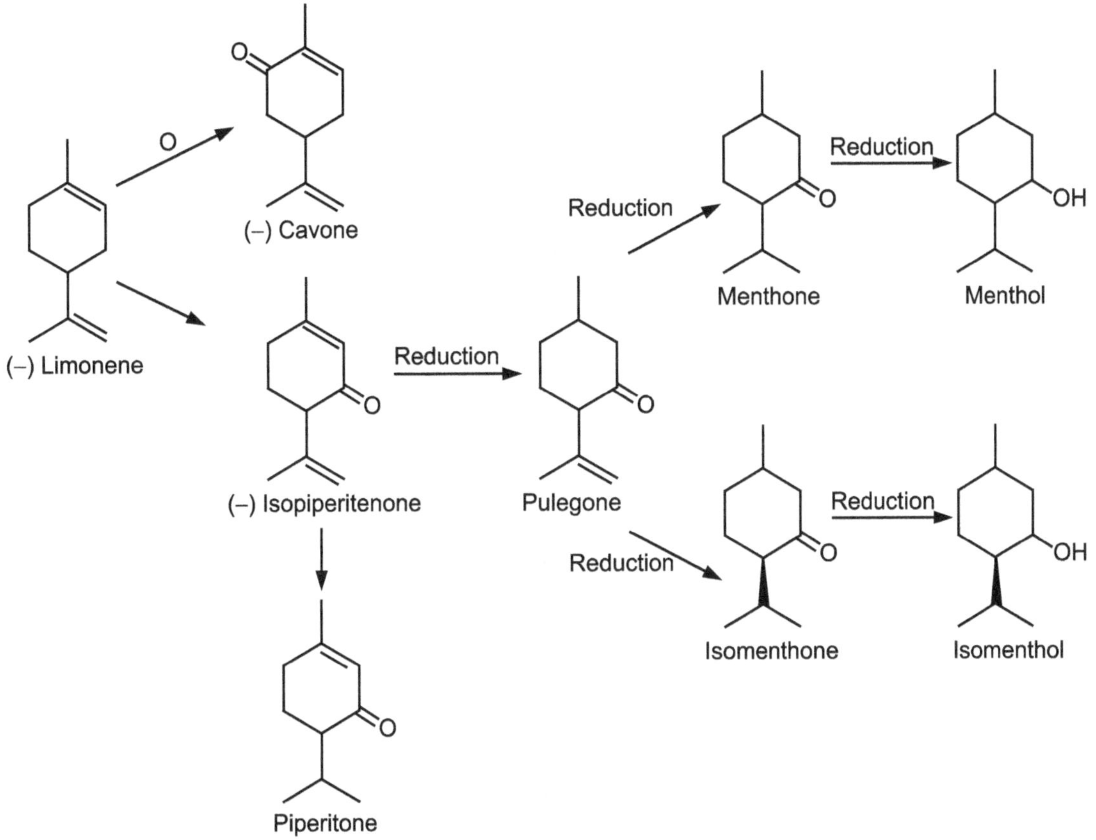

Fig. 6.11

6.3.1 Heterocylic Monoterpenoids-Irridoids (C_{10})

Irridoids have been found as natural components in countless families of plants and are found to have antimicrobial, choleretic, antitumor, antimicrobial and hepatoprotective properties. Gentiopicroside (*Gentiana lutea*, Gentianaceae) and valtate (*Valeriana officinalis*, Valerianceae) are typical examples of irridoides. Iridane, irridoid, secoiridoid, and nepet`alactone are examples of heterocyclic monoterpenoids. Irridoids constitute the larger family of cyclopentanoid monoterpene derivatives and can be subdivided into four groups : irridoid glycosides, simple irridoids or non-glycosidic irridoids, secoiridoids and bisiridoids.

Irridoids usually consist of a cyclopentane ring fused to a six-membered oxygen heterocycle. Nepetalactone is a bicyclic terpenoid, i.e. it is a ten-carbon compound derived from isoprene with two fused rings, a cyclopentane and a lactone. Oxidative cleavage of a bond in the cyclopentane ring by redox enzyme gives rise to seco-irridoids and its derivatives by secondary modifications such as oxidation, epoxidation, hydroxylation and esterification. Epoxyiridoids (e.g. Valtrate from valeriana officinalis) are typically related to loganins.

Irridoids are structurally characterized by the presence of a partially hydrogenated cis fused cyclopentane pyran system which arises from the intramolecular acetalization of a 1, 5-cyclopentanedialdehyde moiety and is usually stabilized by acetalization or esterification. Cyclization of irridoid skeleton occurs via attack of hydride on the dialdehyde to form hemiacetals of irodotrial which on oxidation, glycosylation

6.10 Isoprenoid Pathway / Acetate Mevalonate Pathway

esterification and hydroxylation produces loganin (Fig. 6.12) the main precursor for the synthesis of irridoids and terpenoid indole alkaloids. Loganin on ring cleavage via cytochrome P_{450} dependent monoxygenase forms secologanin to produce a range of secoiridoids e.g. Gentiopicroside (Fig. 6.12).

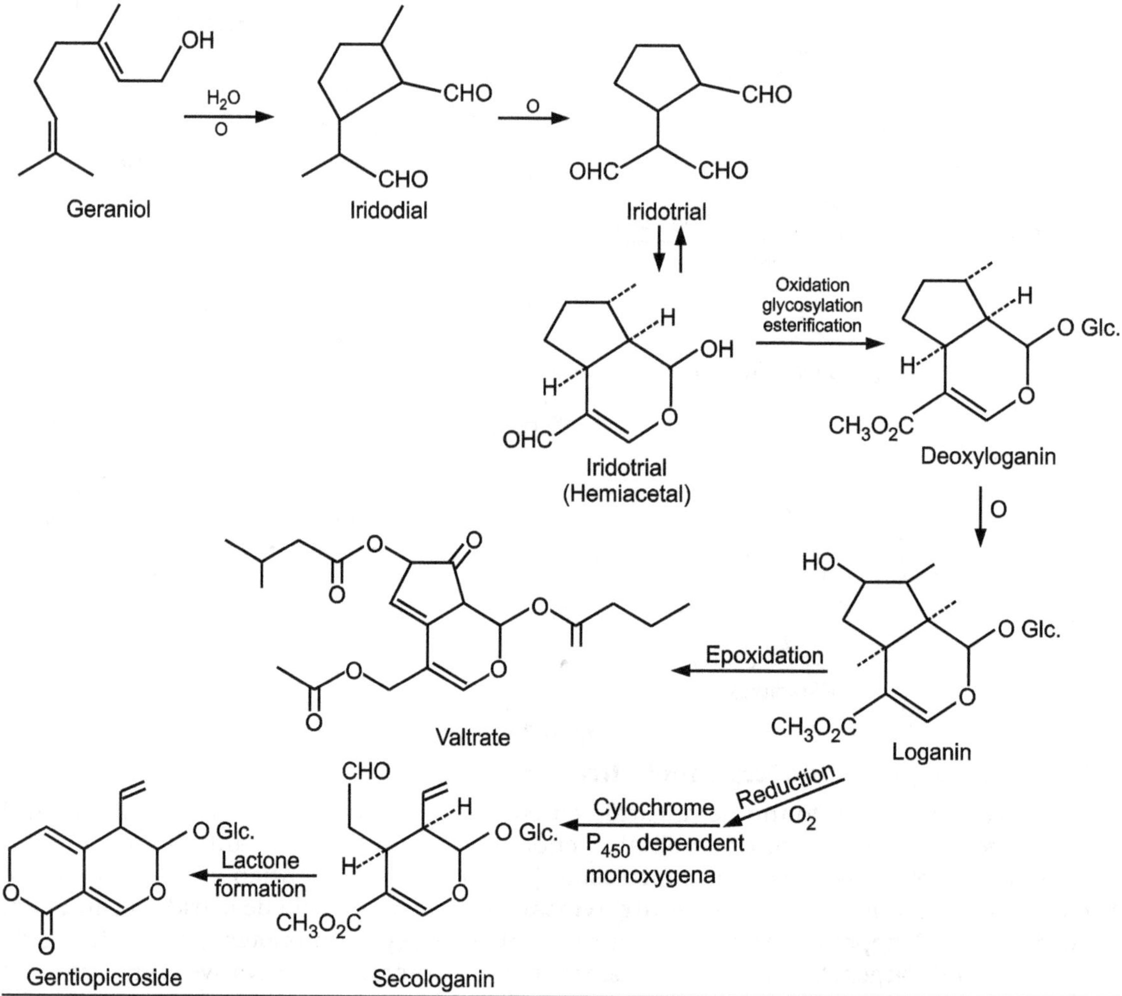

Fig. 6.12

6.4 SESQUITERPENOIDS

Sesquiterpenes are less volatile principles than monoterpenoids. These are among the most widely occurring and the best understood products from the point of view of biological origin, biochemistry and chemistry. These metabolites display a broad range of physiological properties including antibiotic, antitumor, antiviral, cytotoxic, immunosuppressive, phytotoxic, antifungal, insect antifeedant and hormonal activities. Numerous sesquiterpenes hydrocarbons, alcohols and derived metabolites are found in plants. Essential oils are also highly valued for their desirable odour characteristics.

Artemisinin form *Artemisia annuna*, family : Asteraceae is a popular antimalarial agent and santonin from *Artemisia cina, A. maritime*, Family : Compositae is used as an anthelmintic agent. Davanone, the most costly constituent of perfumes, obtained from

Plant Biosynthesis 6.11 Isoprenoid Pathway / Acetate Mevalonate Pathway

Artemisia pallens, Family : Compositae. α and β santalol, obtained from sandal wood oil (*Santalum album*, santalaceae) is used in cosmetics, in the symptomatic treatment of dysurea and micturation. Eugenol and caryophyllene obtained from *Eugenia caryophyllus*, Myrtaceae are traditionally used as dental analgesic.

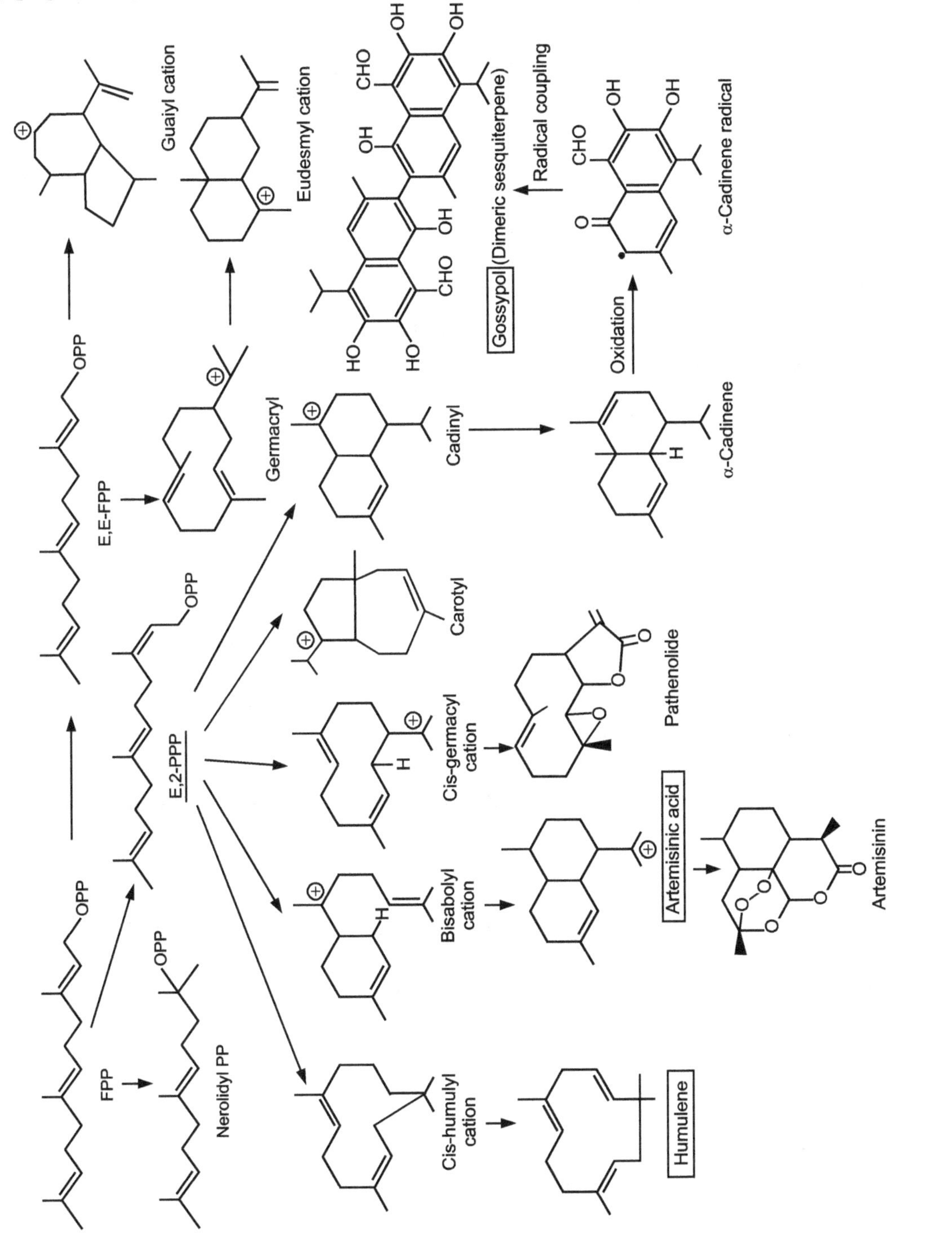

Fig. 6.13

Sesquiterpenes are derived from a single acyclic precursor farnesyl diphosphate (FPP) and can be cyclized to produce about 300 known skeletal structures. Sesquiterpenoid biosynthesis begins with the loss of pyrophosphate from FPP under the action of sesquiterpene synthesis enzymes, generating an allylic cation that is highly susceptible to intramolecular attacks. Cyclization of the farnesyl cation may take place onto either of the remaining double bonds with the result of ring systems larger than six carbons i.e. 10 (germacryl and cis germacryl), or 11 (hymulyl and cis-humulyl cations) membered rings may be formed (Fig. 6.13).

Sesquiterpenoids are synthesized from farnesyl diphosphate (FPP) again via carbocation mechanism. As the FPP molecule has more number of double bonds, this allows a number of possible foldings at appropriate bonds to give a variety of linear and cyclic sesquiterpenes that may be mono, bi or tri cyclic structures. Most of the structures are due to 1, 3 shift of hydride and Wagner Meerwein rearrangements.

Fig. 6.13 explains all possible carbo-cation formations with related examples.

6.5 DITERPENOIDS

Diterpenoids are C_{20} carbon compounds, derived from four isoprene units, i.e. geranyl-geranyl pyrophosphate. They are non-volatile in nature. They are present in plants, animals, and marine organisms. The plant families rich in diterpenoids are Pinaceae, Leguminosae, Burseraceae, Labiateae and the like. They are also found in marine animals such as soft corals, sea fans.

Taxol, a potent anticancer agent, obtained from the stem bark of *Taxus breviofolia*, Taxaceae and forskolin, a potent vasodilator, obtained from roots of *Coleus forskohlii*, Labiateae are typical examples from the class of diterpenoides. Stevioside obtained from *Stevia rebaudiana*, Family : Asteraceae is a very famous natural sweetener.

Diterpenes are also produced from GGPP mediated carbocation mechanism through cyclization and Wagner-Meerwein rearrangements. (Fig. 6.14).

Loss of diphosphate group and attack of water leads to a heterocyclic ring of forskolin, further, via a sequence of oxidation and esterification gives the final product of forskolin.

Taxol, an anticancer agent is produced via an important skeleton, taxadiene. The side chains of taxol are obtained from shikimate pathway via phenylalanine. Protonation of GGPP can initiate a concerted cyclization sequence, terminated by loss of a proton from a methyl, yielding copalyl PP or its enantiomer labdadienyl PP.

Copalyl PP on Wagner-Meerwein rearrangements removal of diphosphate group yields ent-kaurene to ent-kaureonic acid which is the actual precursor of steviol glycosides. kj

The enatiomer of labdadienyl PP generates abietenyl cation to give abietic acid through a series of oxidation.

Ginkgolides are (*Ginkgo biloba*, Ginkgoaceae) potent antagonists of platelet activating factor, also produced from copalyl PP through a series of Wagner-Meerwein and lastly lactone formation. Sesterpenes, e.g. ophiobolene are obtained from the plant pathogen *(Helminthosporium maydis)*.

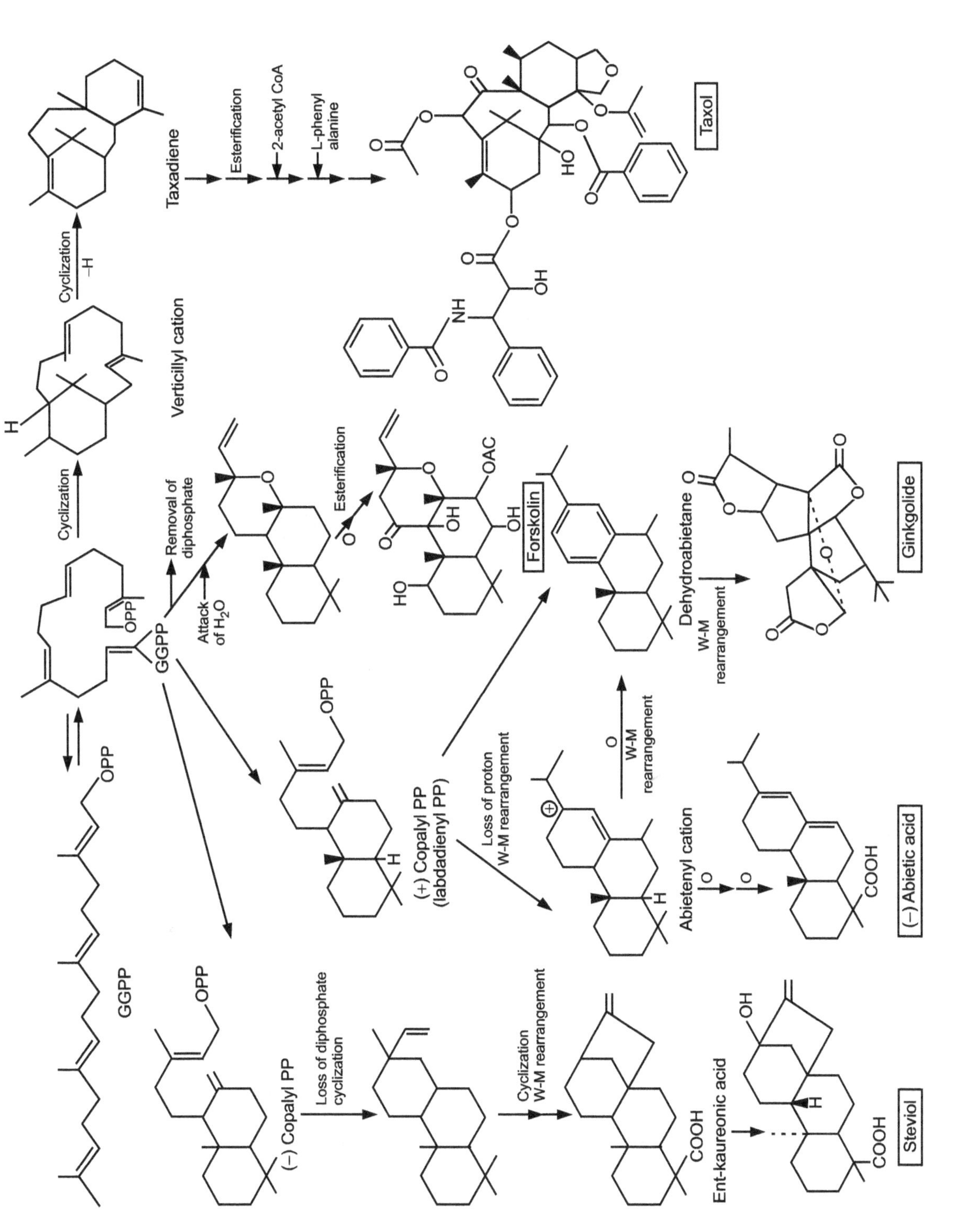

Plant Biosynthesis 6.13 Isoprenoid Pathway / Acetate Mevalonate Pathway

Fig. 6.14

6.6 TRITERPENOIDS

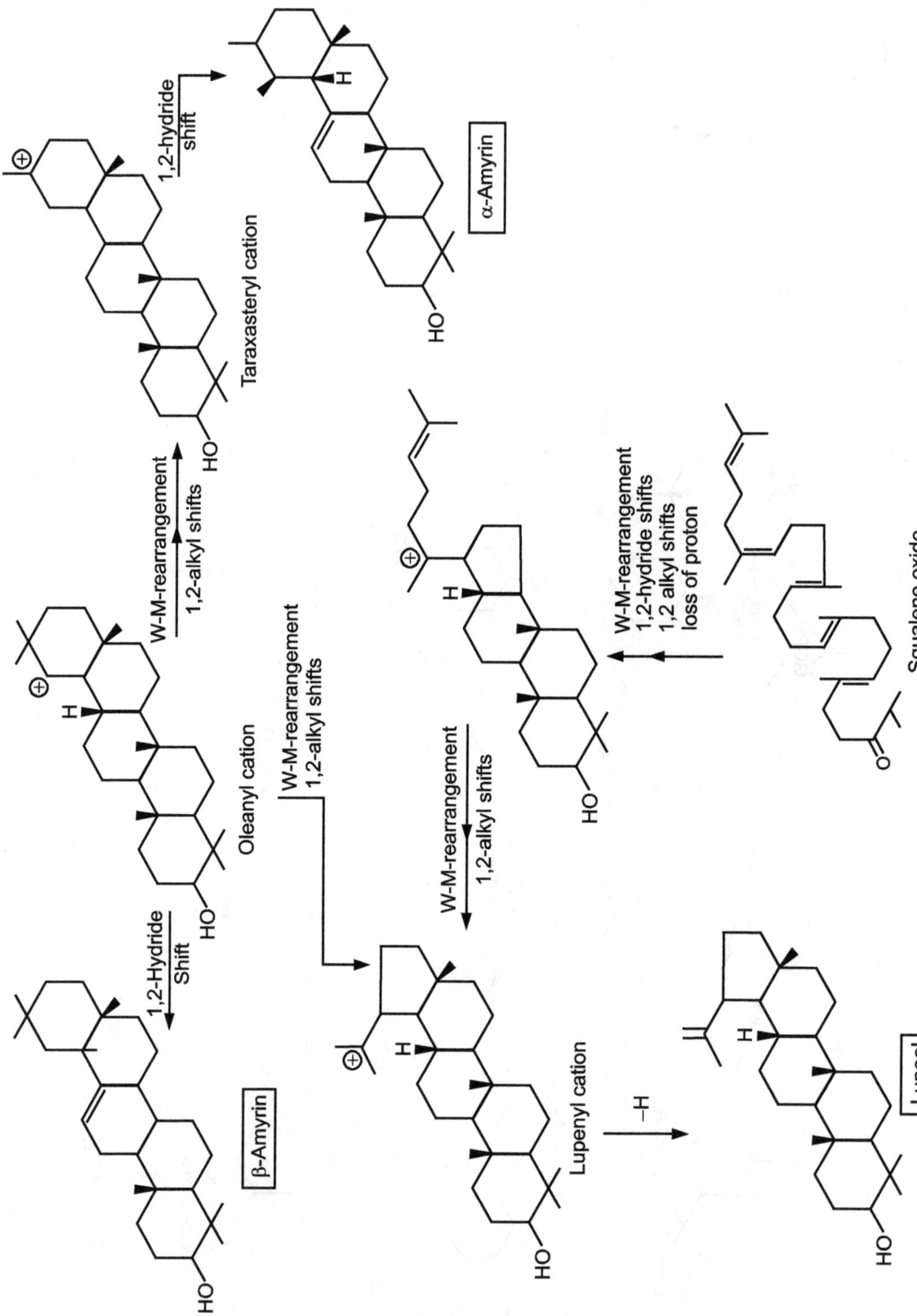

Fig. 6.15   Continued

Continued

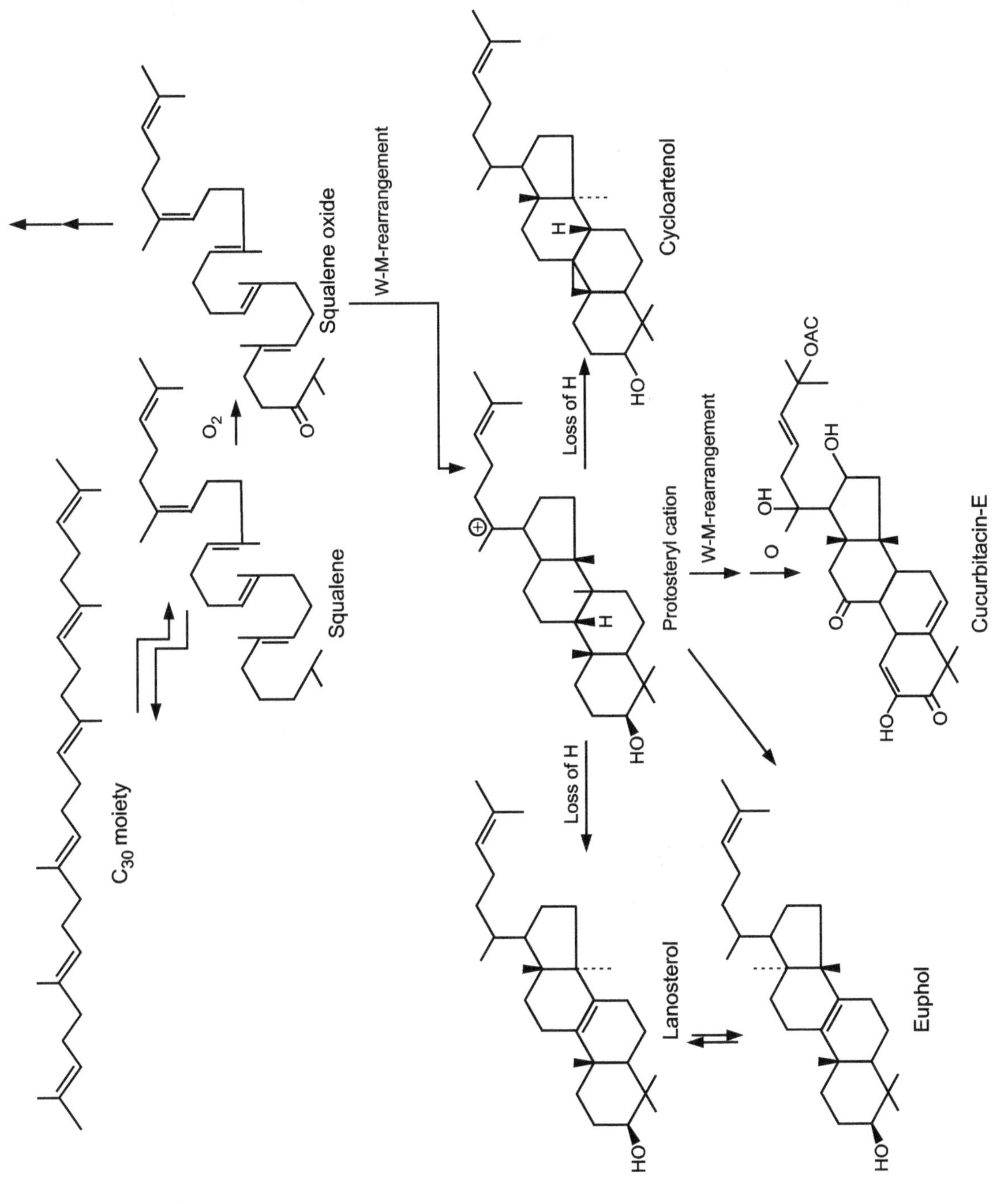

Fig. 6.15

Triterpenoids are C_{30} carbon compounds prepared from a six isoprene unit having molecular formula $C_{30}H_{48}$. They can be tetracyclic triterpenoids (steroids) or pentacyclic triterpenoids. Triterpenes are distributed in plant families like Cucurbitaceae, Apocynaceae and Leguminosae. They are also found in marine sources like squalene from shark.

Two molecules of fanesyl PP on tail to tail condensation via squalene synthase yields triterpene skeleton squalene. Squalene is the main precursor for the biosynthesis of a variety of terpenoid and steroid derivatives.

Hopanoids a part of composition of bacterial membrane are pentacyclic triterpenoids based on the hopane skeleton (with a five-membered ring E). They are widely distributed in prokaryotes.

Squalene on cyclization forms cycloartenol in plants and lanosterol in animals and fungi through Wagner-Meerwein migrations of methyl and hydrides. The protonation of epoxide group allows ring opening to form carbocation where electrophilic addition to double bond forms six membered rings. This process continues until protostenyl cation containing 4-6 membered fused ring is formed (Fig. 6.15).

Variation in position of double bond gives cucurbitacin E from protosteryl cation. Euphol stereoisomer of lanosterol is the most simple squalene derivative.

Dammarenyl cation is one more modification of squalene oxide. Cyclization of double bond gives pentacyclic ring to form lupenyl cation on reduction / loss of proton give lupeol.

The ring expansion of lupenyl cation forms a six membered ring to give oleanyl cation and taraxasteryl cation which on loss of proton yields beta amyrin and alpha amyrin respectively.

6.7 MODIFIED TRITERPENOIDS

Modified triterpenoids includes steroids e.g. cardioactive sterols, steroidal saponins, phytosterols and bile acids.

Steroids :

Steroids are modified triterpenes which are derived from squalene by cyclization, unsaturation and substitution. Steroids are present naturally as a steroidal saponins, cardioactive steroids, steroidal alkaloids, phytosterol or in the form of other steroids (e.g. withanolides, cucurbitacins). The larger amount of steroids, including sterols, is present in plants and animals but only small amounts in bacteria, while hopanoids are very abundant in prokaryotes where they replace cholesterol.

The nucleus of all steroids is the tetracyclic C_{17} hydrocarbon 1, 2-cyclopentano-perhydrophenanthrene (gonane or sterane) moiety substituted by methyl groups at C_{10} and C_{13}, as well as an alkyl side-chain at C_{17}.

Steroids consist of four fused rings (A, B, C and D). The spiroketal function at C_{22} of steroidal saponins is obtained via oxygenation and hydroxylation. All natural steroids have trans B/C ring fusion. CD ring fusion (cholestane type backbone) is also trans except in the case of cardioactive sterols.

Chemically, these hydrocarbons are cyclopentanoperhydrophenanthrenes, they contain a five member cyclopentane (D) ring plus rings of phenanthrene. A perhydrophenanthrene (Rings A, B and C) is the completely saturated derivative of phenanthrene. The polycyclic hydrocarbon known as cholestane will be used to illustrate the numbering system for steroids.

The term cholestane refers to steroids with 27 carbons that include a side-chain of eight carbons at position 17. The basic steroid structure becomes a plane with two surfaces; upper the plane of the molecule, denoted by solid line; below the plane, are designed by dotted lines. The 5 α notation is used to denote the configuration of the hydrogen atom at C_5, which is opposite from the C_9 angular methyl group, making the A/B ring junction trans.

The C_{19} angular methyl group is assigned the β side of the molecule. Similarly, the configuration for the 8 β and 9 α hydrogen and 14 α hydrogen and C_{18} angular methyl group, denotes transfusion for rings B/C and C/D. The C_{18} and C_{19} angular methyl group always have β axial orientation. 5 α cholestane is said to have a trans-trans-trans backbone, all the fused rings have trans-stereochemistry i.e. the A/B fused ring, the B/C fused ring and C/D fused ring are all trans.

6.7.1 Steroidal Saponins

The biosynthesis of steroids involves the acyclic form of squalene on oxidation and cyclization leading to cycloartenol in plants and lanosterol in animals and fungi. The conversion of cycloartenol to cholesterol involves cyclopropane ring opening via enzyme and trans elimination. However, when lanosterol produces cholesterol, it loses three methyl groups at C_4 and C_{14} via cytochrome P_{450} mono-oxygenase.

Sequential oxidation of 4-methyl group to carboxyl, oxidation of 3-OH to keto group and reduction followed by decarboxylation loses C_4 methyl groups. Firstly, the C_{14} methyl group is lost as formic acid. This conversion produces a variety of steroidal saponins e.g. diosgenin (*Dioscorea deltoida*, Dioscoreacea), yamogenin, hecogenin, tigogenin, netigogenin, sarsapogenin (*Smilax febrifuga*, Liliaceae) and smilagenin (*Agave species*, Agavaceae) (Fig. 6.16).

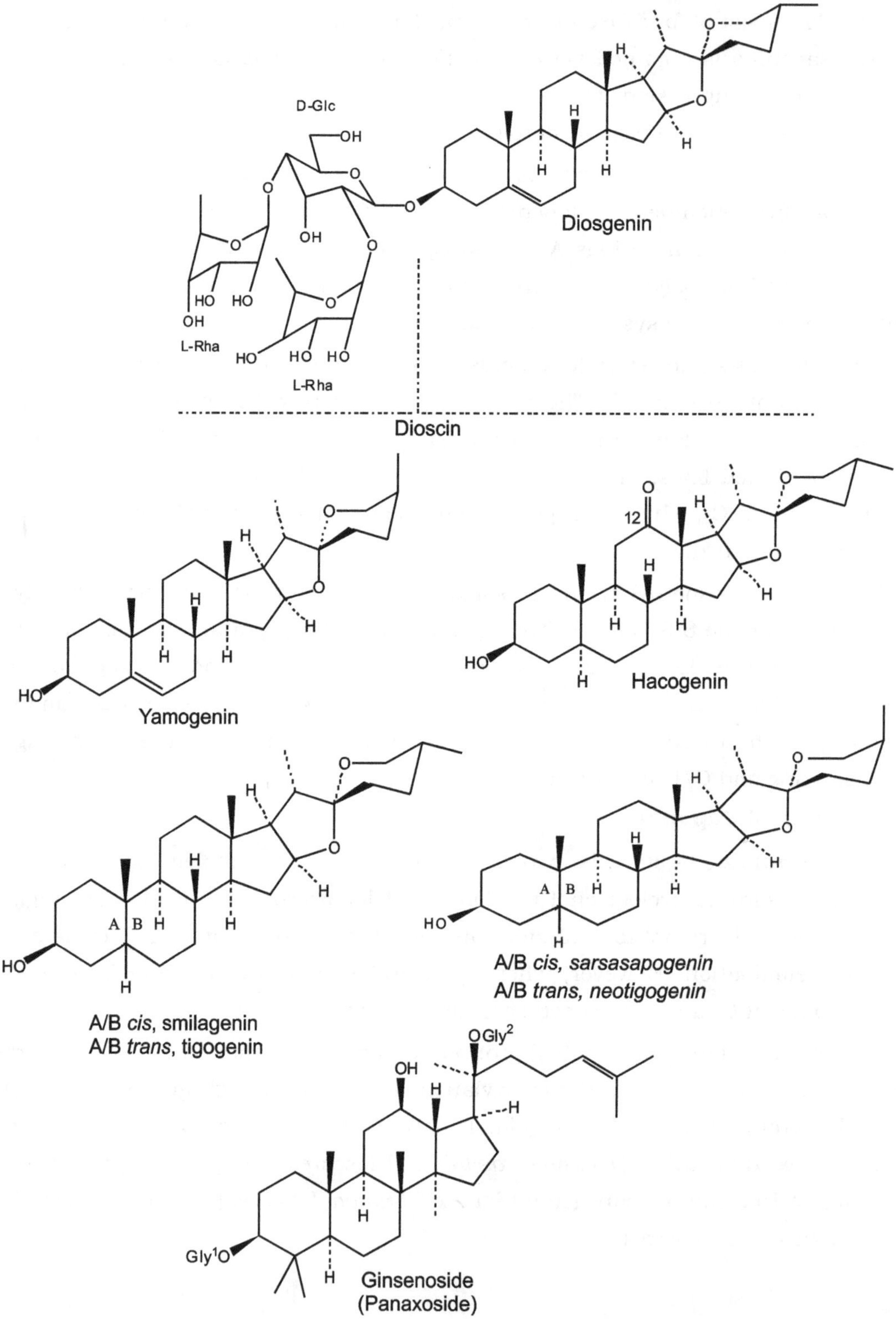

6.18 Isoprenoid Pathway / Acetate Mevalonate Pathway

Diosgenin

Dioscin

Yamogenin

Hacogenin

A/B *cis*, smilagenin
A/B *trans*, tigogenin

A/B *cis*, sarsasapogenin
A/B *trans*, neotigogenin

Ginsenoside
(Panaxoside)

Fig. 6.16

6.7.2 Cardioactive Glycosides

Cardiac glycosides are drugs used in the treatment of congestive heart failure and cardiac arrhythmia, found as secondary metabolites in several plants, but also in some animals. Here the aglycone part is a steroidal nucleus. Chemically the aglycone part of cardiac glycosides is a steroidal moiety. They are either C_{23} or C_{24} steroids because of either five membered or six membered lactone rings respectively. Those with five membered lactone rings are called as cardenolides, e.g. digitoxin, digoxin, gitoxin present in Digitalis (*Digitalis purpurea, D. lanata*, Scrophulariaceae), k-stropanthine present in stropanthus (*Stropanthus kombe, Stropanthus gratus*, Apocynaceae), thevetine in Thevetia (*Thevetia nerifolia*, apocynaceae), while those with six membered lactone ring are termed as bufadienolides, e.g. hellebrigenin from black hellebore (*Helleborus niger*, ranunculaceae) and scillaren A from Squill (*Urginea indica*, liliaceae).

Heart diseases can be primarily grouped into three major disorders : cardiac failure, ischemia and cardiac arrhythmia. Cardiac failure can be described as the inability of the heart to pump blood effectively due to weak muscles contraction. Thus, cardiac failures primarily arise from the reduced contractility of heart muscles, especially the ventricles. Reduced contraction of heart leads to reduced heart output but new blood keeps coming in, resulting in increase in heart blood volume. The heart feels congested. Hence, the term congestive heart failure.

Congested heart leads to lowered blood pressure and poor renal blood flow which results in the development of edema in the lower extremities and the lung (pulmonary edema) as well as renal failure.

Cardiac glycosides inhibit the membrane bound Na^+-K^+-ATPase pump responsible for Na^+-K^+ exchange. Inhibition causes increase in intracellular calcium levels. Elevated intracellular calcium concentration triggers a series of intracellular biochemical events that ultimately result in an increase in the force of the myocardial contraction or a positive inotropic effect.

Hydroxylation of cholesterol at C_{22} and C_{20} and then cleavage of C_{20}/C_{22} bond gives pregnenolone. Oxidation of pregnenolone to 3-keto group and its tautomerisaton gives progesterone. Further two step reduction produces 3-β-hydroxy-5-β-pregnan-20-one. 14-β and 21-β–hydroxylation yields one trihydroxy moiety 3-β, 14-β, 21-trihydroxy-5-β-pregnan-20 one. Malonyl CoA addition to this trihydroxy moiety produces digitoxigenin (cardenolide). Addition of oxaloacetyl CoA produces bufadienolide skeleton via lactone formation. 12-β and 16-β hydroxylation of digitoxigenin yields trihydroxy moiety-digoxigenin and gitoxigenin (Fig. 6.17).

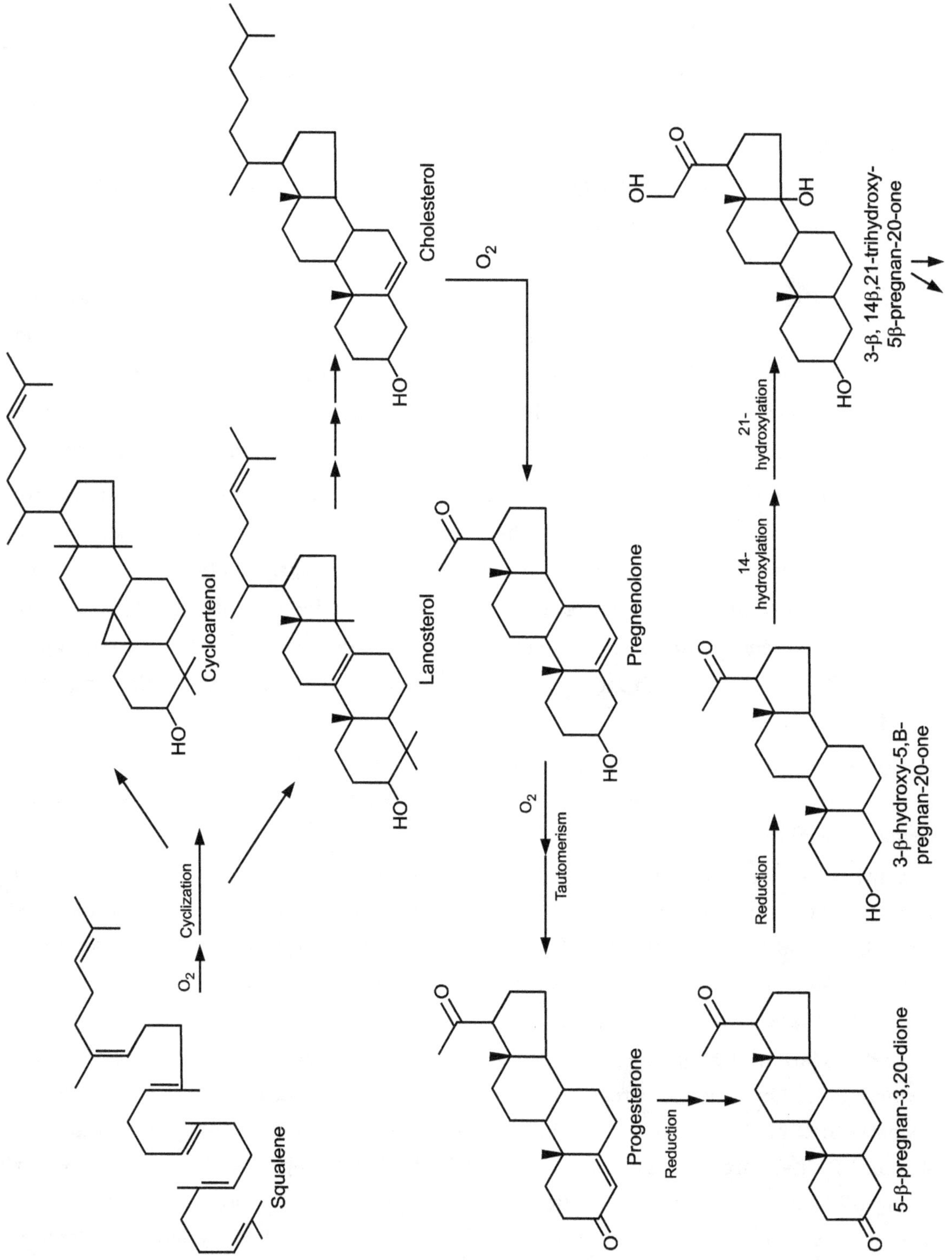

Plant Biosynthesis   6.20 Isoprenoid Pathway / Acetate Mevalonate Pathway

Fig. 6.17   **Continued**

6.21 Isoprenoid Pathway / Acetate Mevalonate Pathway

Continued

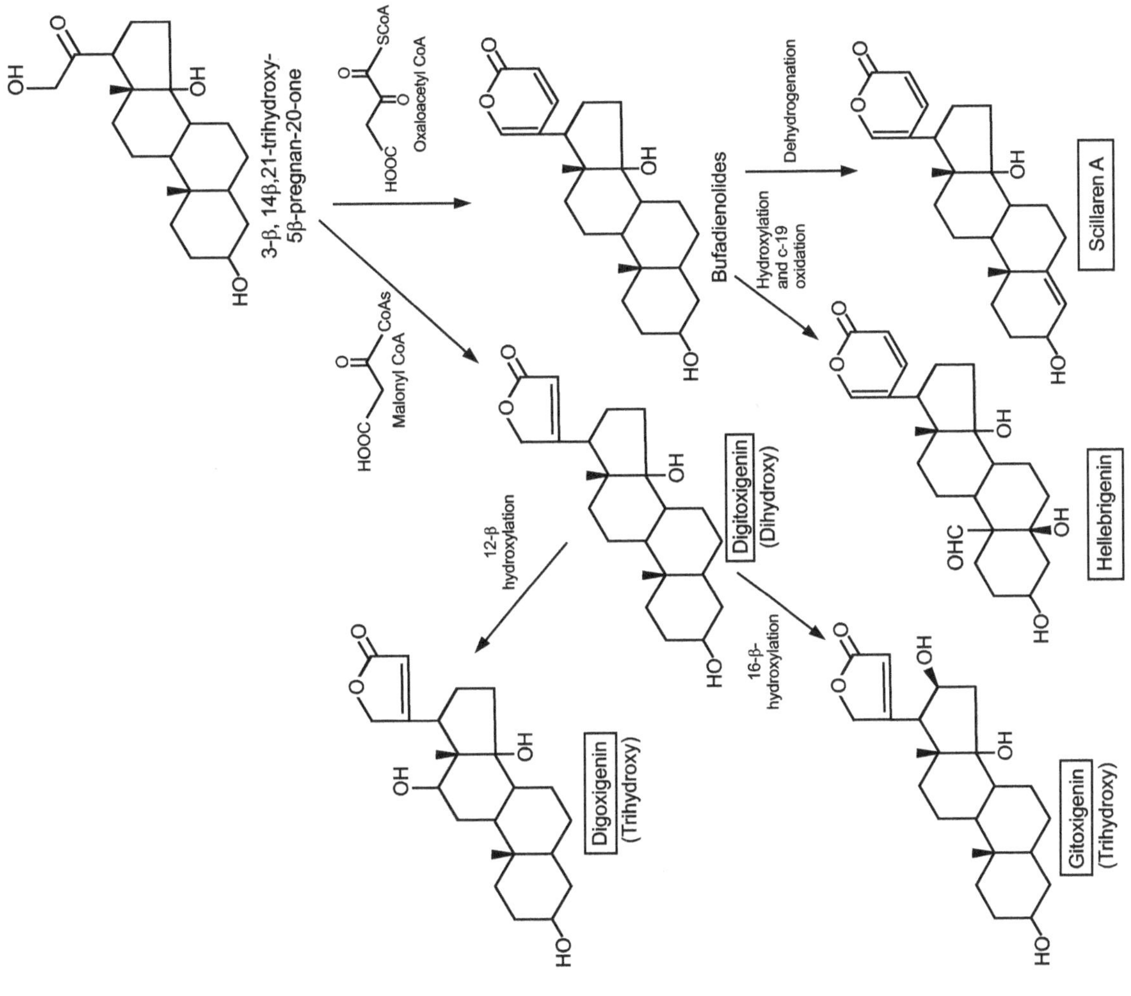

Fig. 6.17

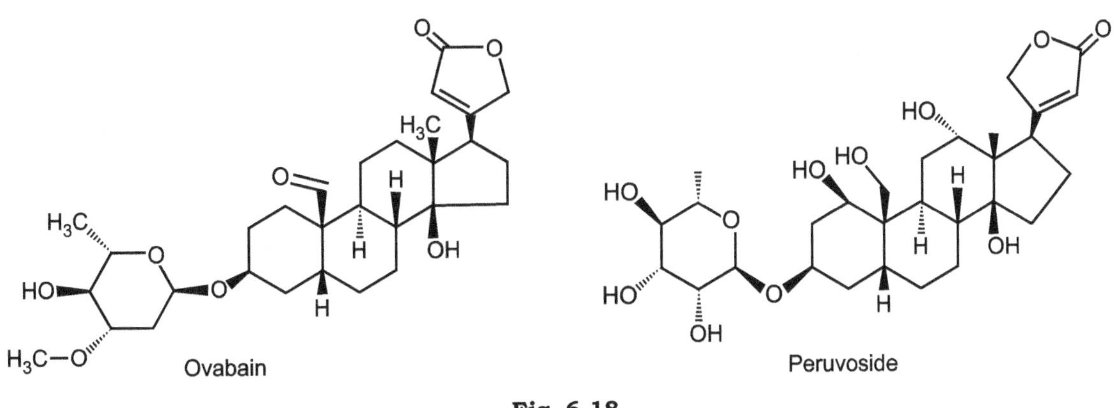

Fig. 6.18

6.7.3 Phytosterols

Phytosterols are SAM mediated 24-methyl and 24-ethyl substituted derivatives of cholesterol. C_{24} alkylation, C_4 and C_{14} demethylation, dehydrogenation followed by reduction along with side-chain modification produces stigmasterol, sitosterol in plants and ergosterol, fecosterol in fungi (Fig. 6.18).

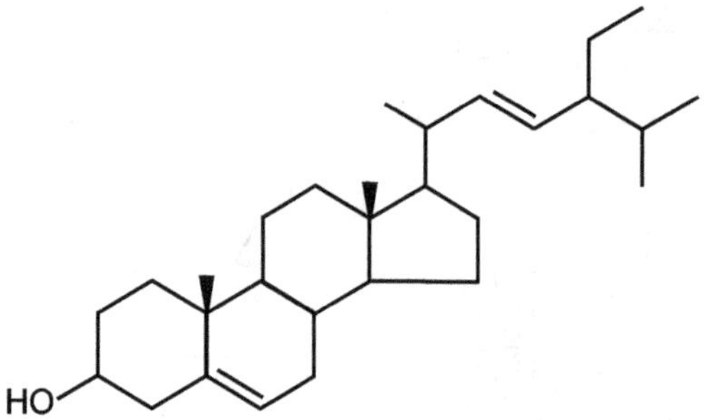

Stigmasterol

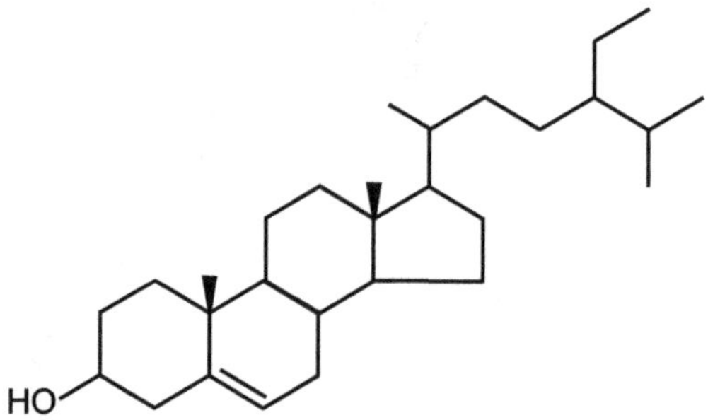

Sitosterol

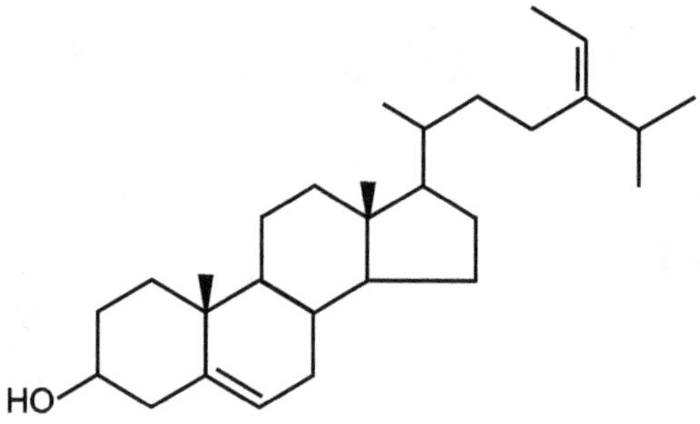

Fucosterol

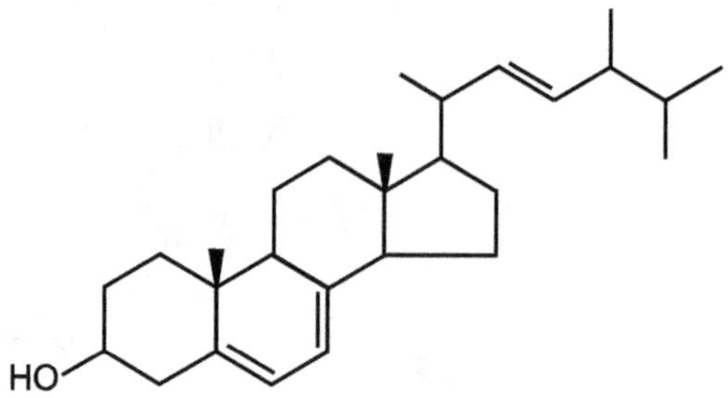

Ergosterol

Fig. 6.19

Cholesterol, phytosterol and many other steroids are major precursors for the synthesis of steroids hormones i.e. adrenocortical hormones or corticosteroids. Synthetic glucocorticoids are used in the treatment of arthritis or inflammation, dermatitis, allergic reactions, asthma, hepatitis, blood electrolyte levels, and behaviour and inflammatory bowel disease. The corticosteroids are produced from cholesterol via pregnenolone and progesterone which further produce corticosterone, and hydrocortisone (cortisol) (Figure 6.20 and 6.21) through a series of hydroxylation steps catalysed by cofactors.

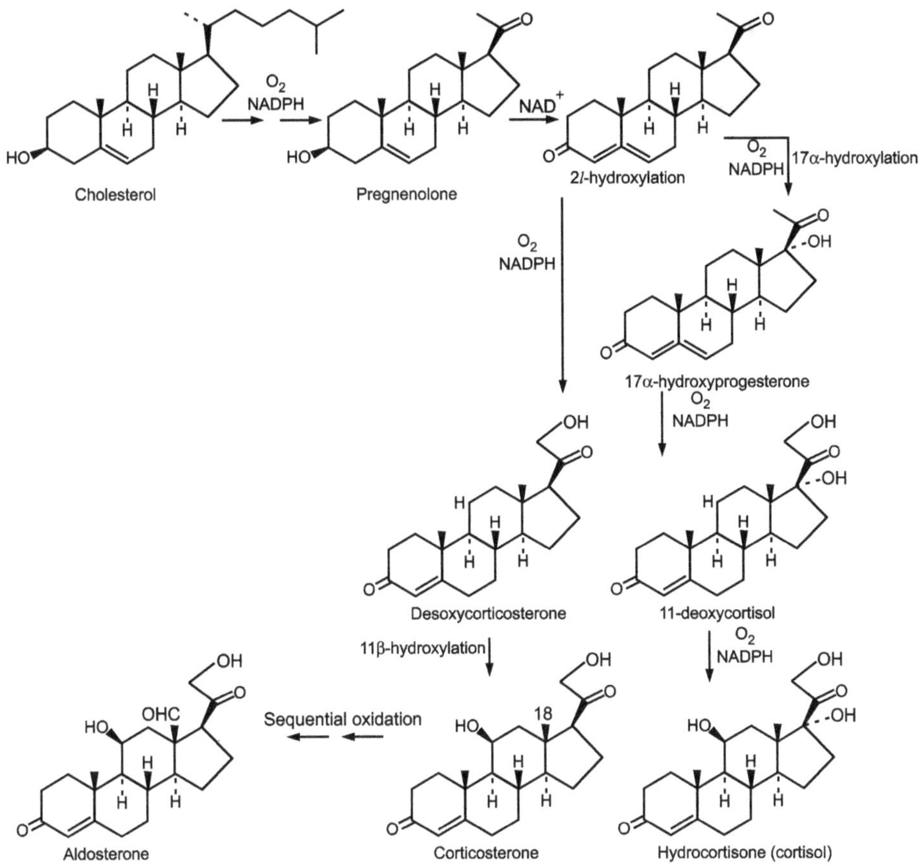

6.23 Isoprenoid Pathway / Acetate Mevalonate Pathway

Fig. 6.20

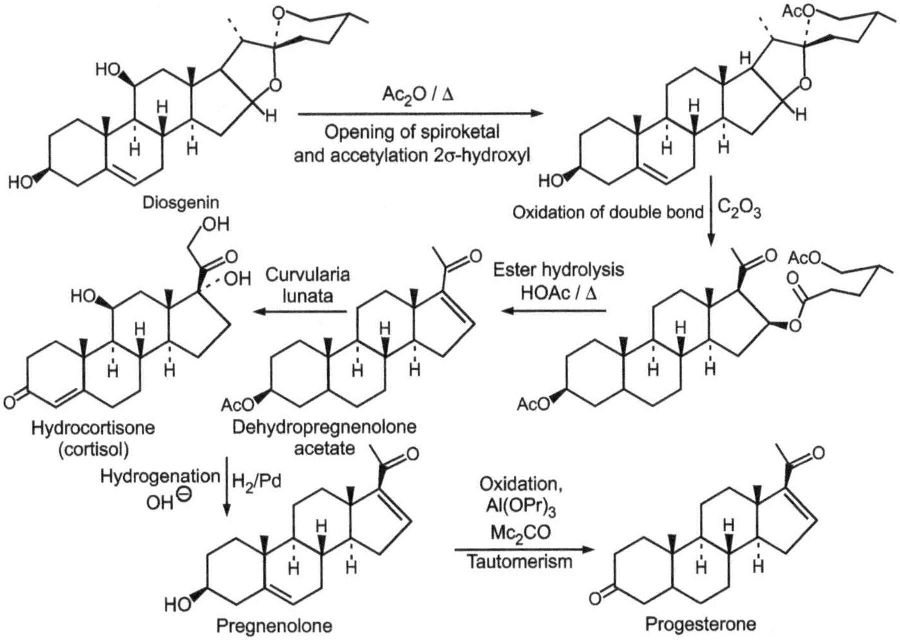

Fig. 6.21

6.7.4 Pentacyclic Triterpenoids

Pentacyclic triterpenoids have a number of pharmacological properties such as anti-tumor, anti-AIDS, anti-bacterial and anti-inflammatory activities. Lupeol, alpha-amyrin and β-amyrin are the important triterpenoid skeletons. Mostly β-amyrin is the part of triterpenoid saponins.

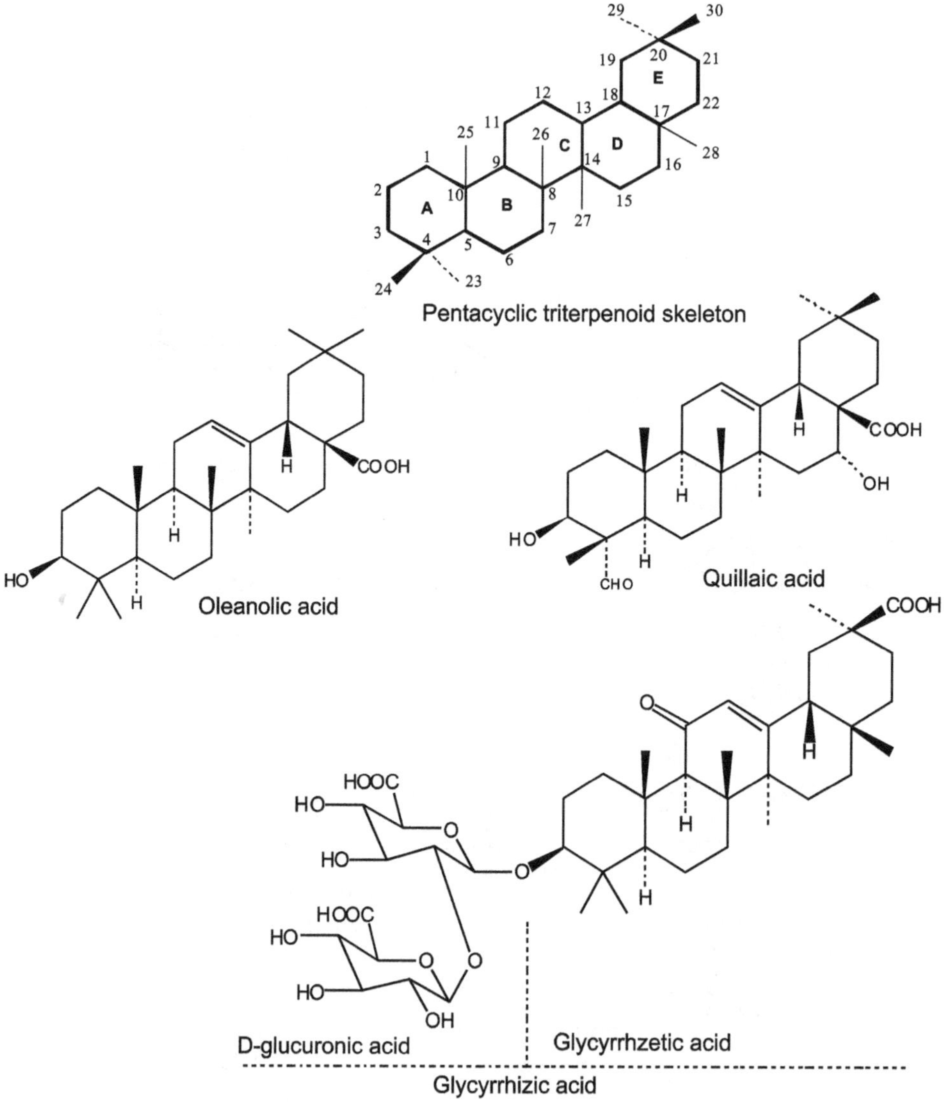

Fig. 6.22

Series of oxidation and glycosylation of methyl groups at position C_3, C_4, C_{11}, C_{16}, C_{17} or C_{20} gives rise to a variety of triterpenoid saponins like quillaic acid (*Quillaja saponaria*, Rosaceae) oleonolic acid (*Olea europaea*) and glycyrrhizin (*Glycyrrhiza glabra*, Leguminoseae) (Fig. 6.19). Glycyrrhizin is 50 times as sweet as sucrose. Glycyrrhizin on hydrolysis gives aglycone glycyrrhetinic acid which possesses monocorticoidal activity hence is useful in the treatment of arthritis and inflammation. Oleanolic acid possesses antitumour, hepatoprotective, antiviral properties and has been recently found to exhibit strong anti-HIV activity.

6.25 Isoprenoid Pathway / Acetate Mevalonate Pathway

Limonoids and quassinoids are structurally modified triterpenoids obtained from loss of several carbon atoms. Loss of 4 carbons from the terminal side chain yields limonoids and loss of 10 carbons yields quassinoids (Fig. 6.20). Azadirachtin, belonging to the class of limonoides, obtained from *Azadirachta indica*, Meliaceae is used as a spermicidal and insect repellant agent.

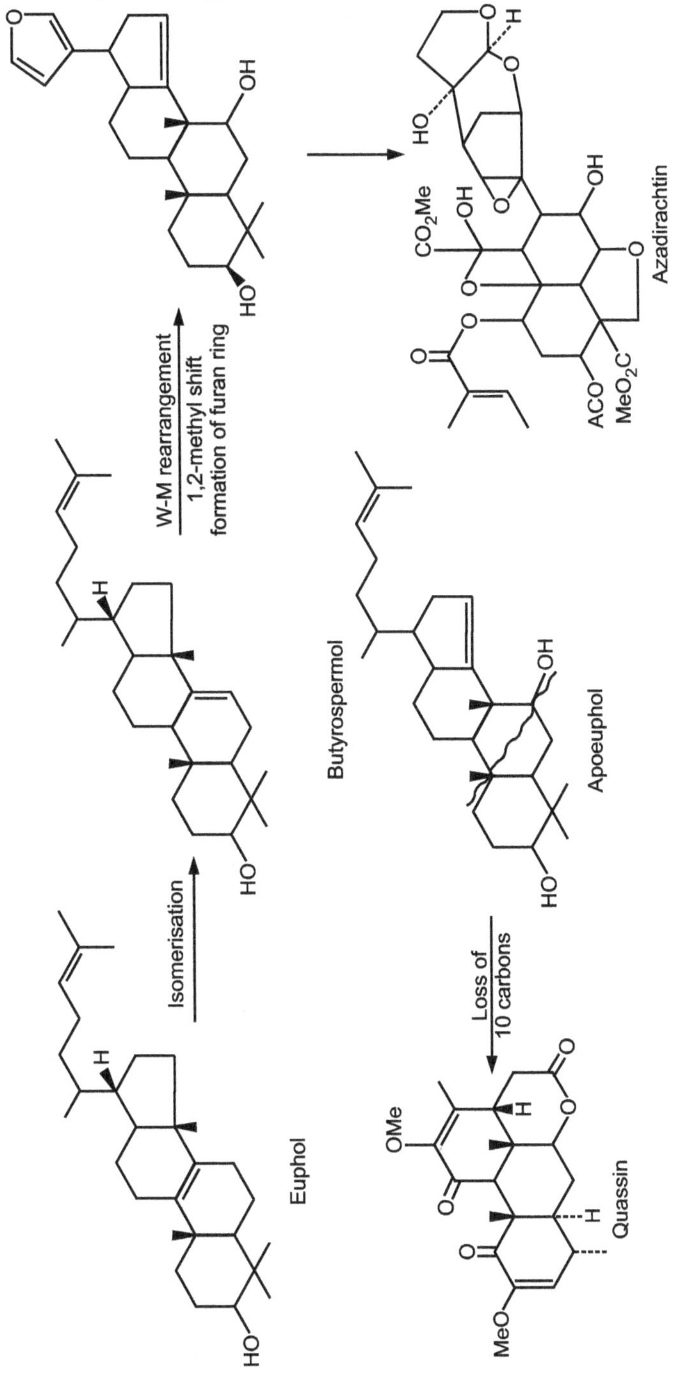

Fig. 6.23

6.8 TETRATERPENOIDS

They are C_{40} compounds of terpenoids group. They contain a long sequence of conjugated double bonds. Carotenoids are a prominent group of natural colouring matter exhibiting purple, red, yellow, orange colour to flowers, roots or fruits of plants in the form of photosynthetic accessory pigment. Carotenoids are a very popular source of vitamins and antioxidants. Due to their antioxidant, free radical scavenging property these are the part of a number of marketed nutraceuticals, herbal supplements and functional foods which are used to prevent ageing, cancer, diabetes and many age related diseases, e.g. – β-carotene (from *Daucus carota*, Apiaceae), Crocetin (from saffron, *Crocus sativus*, Iridaceae), bixin (from Annato, *Bixa orellana*, Bixaceae).

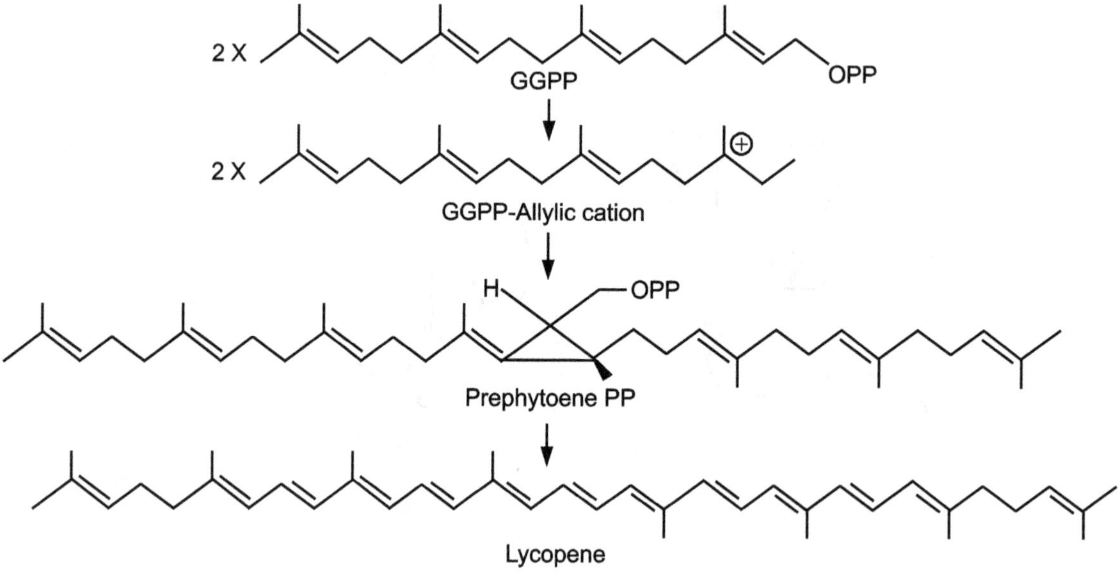

Fig. 6.24

Tetraterpenes which are called carotenoids are obtained by tail to tail condensation of 2 moles of geranylgeranyl diphosphate (GGPP) mediated by the enzyme phytoene synthase which creates first phytoene (Fig. 6.21).

The allylic cation of GGPP loses the proton to generate a double bond at the centre. The sequence of desaturation reactions via enzymes phytoene desaturase gives conjugated skeleton of lycopene. The end of the cyclic form of allylic cation gives three types of ring systems, β, ε and γ (Fig. 6.22). These ring systems are on the basis of 'which proton is lost'. Vitamin A is actually the metabolite of carotenoids as shown in Fig. 6.23 which occurs in mammals after consumption of carotenoids in diet.

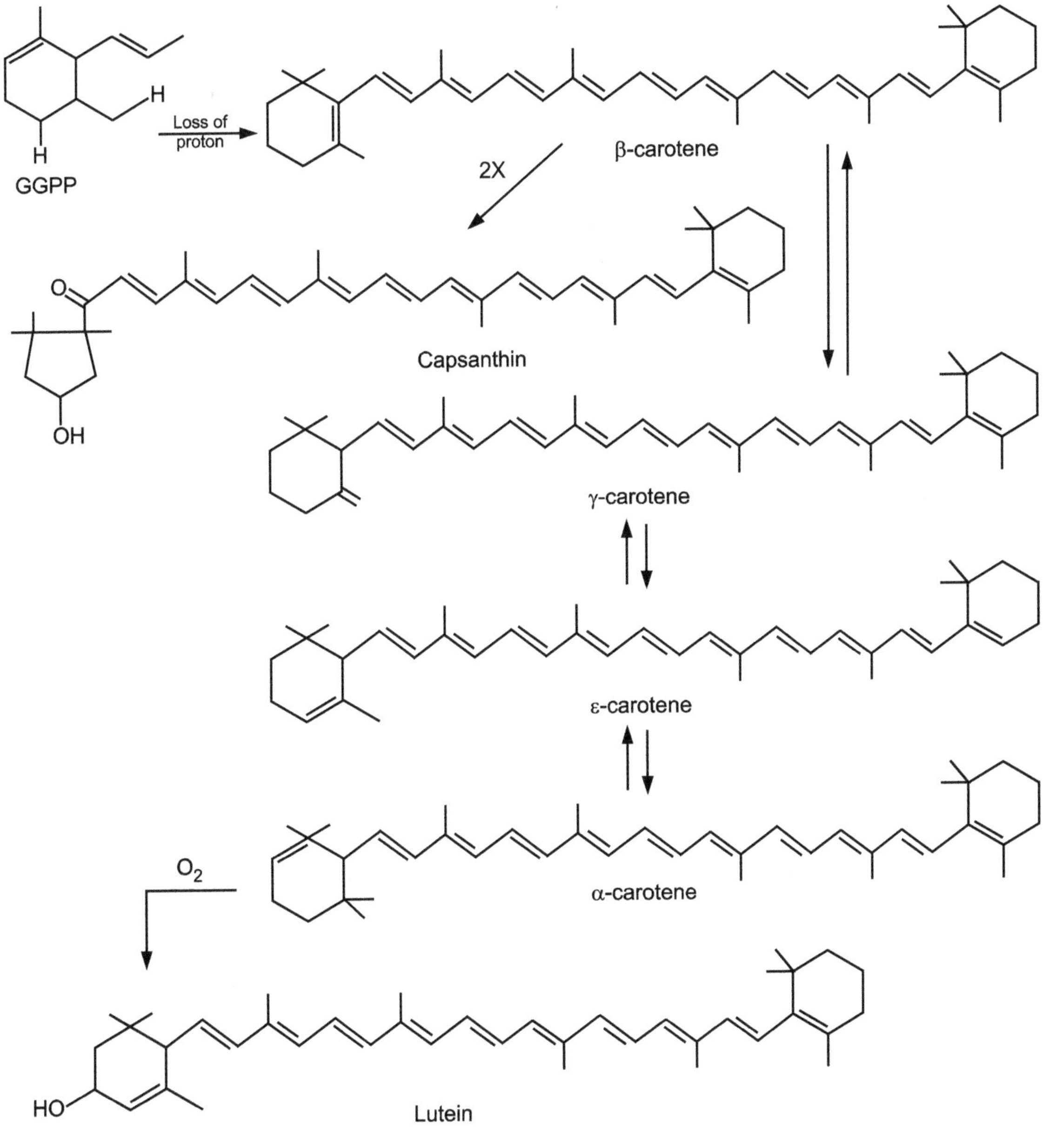

Plant Biosynthesis
6.27 Isoprenoid Pathway / Acetate Mevalonate Pathway

Fig. 6.25

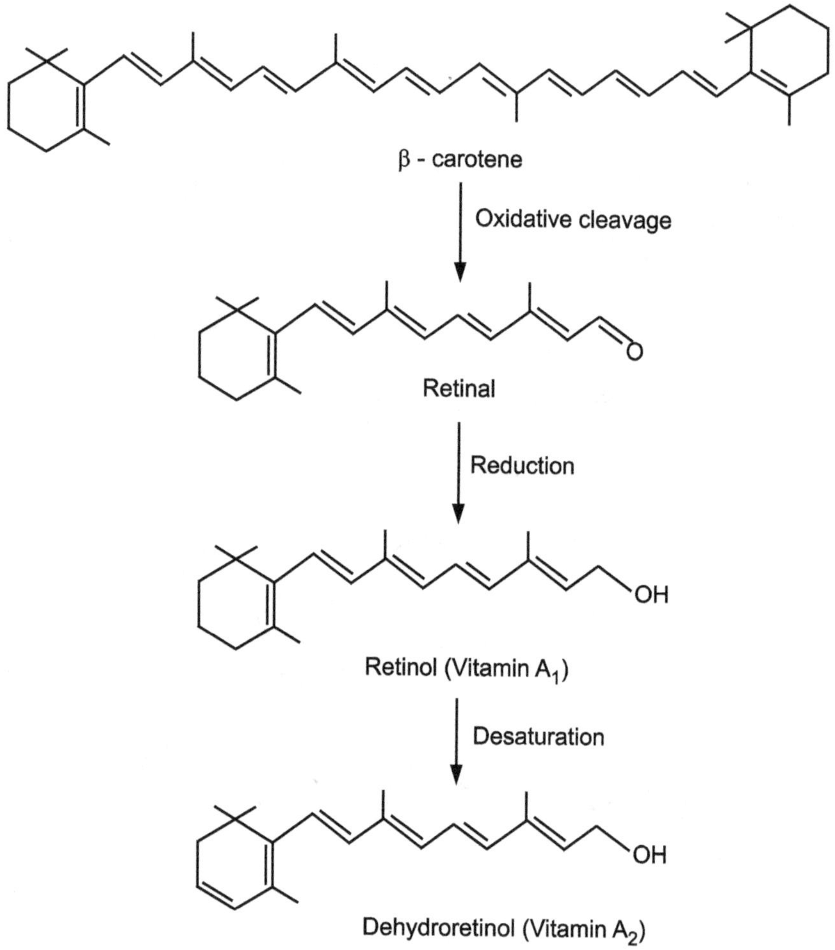

6.28 Isoprenoid Pathway / Acetate Mevalonate Pathway

β - carotene

↓ Oxidative cleavage

Retinal

↓ Reduction

Retinol (Vitamin A_1)

↓ Desaturation

Dehydroretinol (Vitamin A_2)

Fig. 6.26

In higher plants, carotenoid isomerase then acts to catalyze cis-trans-isomerisation of the lycopene to produce trans-lycopene. Once trans-lycopene has been produced, two possible outcomes can occur :

1. If two cyclic β rings are added (b,b branch) then β-carotene, zeaxanthin, neoxanthin, violaxanthin and antheraxanthin are created.
2. If a β and an ε ring (b, e branch) are added to the cyclic end then α-carotene is created.

Table 6.1 : Monoterpenoid and Sesquiterpenoid Containing Plants

Plant	Biological Source	Constituents	Uses
Ajwain	Dried ripe fruits of *trychyspermum ammi*, Umbelliferae	Thymol, cymene, terpinene, pinene	Flavouring agent, antiseptic, antispasmodic, carminative

Plant	Biological Source	Constituents	Uses
Anise	Ripe fruits of *Pimpinella anisum*, Umbelliferae	Anethol, chavicol, anisaldehyde	Stimulant, carminative, flavouring agent
Camphor	*Cinnamomum camphora*, Lauraceae	Camhor, cineole	Ingredient of soaps
Caraway	Fruits of *Carum carvi*, Umbelliferae	(+) Carvone, limonene	Flavouring agent, carminative
Cardamom	Ripe fruits of *Elettaria cardamomum*, Zingiberaceae	Cineole, linalool, alpha terpinyl acetate	Flavouring agent, carminative
Cassia	Bark of *Cassia cinnamomum*, Lauraceae	Cinnamaldehyde	Flavouring agent, carminative
Chamomile	Dried flowers of *Chamaemelum nobile*, Compositae	Angelic acid, tiglic acid, isovaleric acid	Flavouring agent
Chenopodium	Fresh flowering plant of *Chenopodium ambrosiodes*, Chenopodiaceae	Ascaridol, cymene, myrcene	Anthelmintic
Cinnamon	Bark of *Cassia cinnamomum*, Lauraceae	Cinnamaldehyde, eugenol	Flavouring agent, carminative
Citronella	Leaves of *Cymbopogon nardus*, Gramineae	Citronellal, citronellol, geraniol	Insect repellant
Clove	Dried flowering buds of *Eugenia caryophyllus*, Myrtaceae	Sesquiterpenoid: Eugenol, beta caryophyllene	Dental nalgesic, antiseptic,
Coriander	Fruits of *Coriandrum sativum*, Umbelliferae	Linalool, alpha pinene, terpinene	Flavouring agent, carminative
Davana	Flowering herb of *Artemisia pallens*, Compositae	Sesquiterpenoids: davanone, cineole, borneol, eugenol, linalool	Flavouring agent, perfume
Dill	Fruits of *Anethum graveolens*, Umbelliferae	Carvone	Flavouring agent, carminative
Eucalyptus	Leaves of *Eucalyptus globulus*, Myrtaceae	Cineole, citronellal	Perfume
Fennel	Fruits of *Foeniculum vulgare*, Umbelliferae	Anethole, fenchone	Flavouring agent, carminative

Geranium	Fresh leaves of *Pelargonium graveolens*, Geraniaceae	Geraniol, citronellol, geranyl acetate	Flavouring agent
Ginger	Dried rhizomes of *Zingiber officinale*, Zingiberaceae	Zingiberine, phellandrene, bisabolene	Flavouring
Gualtheria	Leaves of *Gualtheria procumbens*, Ericacae	Methyl salicylate	Antirheumatic, antiseptic
Lavender	Fresh flowering tops of *Lavandula angustifoila*, Labiateae	Linalool, linalyl acetate	Perfume
Lemon	Peels of fruit *Citrus limonis*, Rutaceae	Limonene, citral, alpha pinene, terpinene	Flavouring agent, carminative, perfume
Lemongrass	Leaves of *Cymbopogon flexuolus*, Gramineae	Citral	Flavouring agent, perfume
Mentha	Leaves of *Mentha piperita*, Labiateae	Menthol, menthone	Flavouring agent,
Musk	Secretion from Perputial follicles of *Moschus moschiferus*	Muskone	Perfume
Nutmeg	Seeds of *Myristica fragrans*, Myristicacea	Myristicin, α and β pinene, sabinene	Stimulant carminative
Orange	Peels of fruit *Citrus aurantium*, Rutaceae	Limonene, myrcene	Flavouring agent
Palmrosa	Leaves of *Cymbopogon martini*, Gramineae	Linalool, geraniol	Flavouring agent, antirheumatic
Rose	Fresh flowers of *Rosa damascena*, Rosaceae	Citronellol, geraniol	Perfume
Sandal wood	Heartwood of *Santalum album*, Sanatalaceae	Sesquiterpenoid: α and β santalol	Perfume, cosmetic, cooling agent
Spearmint	Leaves of *Mentha spicata*, Labiateae	(-) Carvone, (-) limonene	Flavouring agent, carminative
Tea tree	Fresh leaves of *Melaleuca alternifolia*, Myrtaceae	Terpeniol, cineole, terpinene	Antiseptic, perfume
Tulsi	Fresh leave of *Ocimum sanctum*, Labatae	Eugenol, carvacrol, methyleugenol	antibacterial, insecticidal, stimualnt,
Turpentine	Oleoresin of *Pinus roxburghii*, Pinaceae	Alpha and beta pinene, limonene	Counter irritant, rubefacient
Valerian	Rhizomes and stolons of *Veleriana walichii*, Valerianaceae	Camphene, borneol acetate, Sesquiterpenoid: valeopotriates	Antispasmodic, antidepressant

Table 6.2 : Mevalonate Pathway derived Phytoconstituents

Plant	Biological Source	Constituents	Uses
Cardio active Sterol			
Digitalis (fox glove leaves)	Dried leaves of *Digitalis purpurea, Digitalis lanata,* Scrophulariaceae.	Cardenolides, purpurea glycosides A,B.,glucogitaloxin,odoroside H, gitaloxin, verodoxin, glucoverodoxin, digitoxin, gitoxin, gitaloxin,2 saponin-digitonin,gitonin.	Treatment of congestive heart failure.
Thevetia (lucky-nut tree)	Dried seeds of *Thevetia nerifolia,* Apocynaceae	Theventin A, cereberoside (thevetin B), cerberin, nerifolin, peruvoside, theveneriin, peruvosidic acid.	Abortifacient, purgative, treatment of mild cardiac insufficiency and weak heart.
Indian squill (jangli pyas)	Dried bulbs of *Urginea indica,* Liliaceae	Scillaren A, B., mucilage, calcium oxalate, glucoscillaren A.	Cardiotonic, stimulant, expectorant, diuretic, emetic, cathartic, anti-cancer.
European squill	Dried sliced bulbs of *Urginea maritima,* Liliaceae	Bufadienolide type cardiac glycosides, Scillaren A. B., mucilage, calcium oxalate, glucoscillaren A, proscillaridin A, xanthoscillide, flavonoids, sinistrin.	Cumulative, expectorant.
Strophanthus	Dried ripe seeds of *Strophanthus kombe,* Apocynaceae	K-strophanthin, k-strophanthoside (strophoside), K-strophanthoside β cymarin, cymaril, mucilage, resin, trigonelline, choline, fixed oil.	Cardio tonic.
Ouabain	Dried seeds of *Strophanthus gratus,* Apocynaceae	Ouabain	Cardio tonic
Oleander	Dried leaves of *Nerium oleander,* Apocynaceae	Oleandrin	In cardiac insufficiency
Black hellebore	Dried rhizome and root of *Helleborus niger,* Ranunculaceae	Hellebrin	Cardiac stimulant.
Red squill	Dried scaly bulbs of *Urginea maritime,* Liliaceae	scilliroside	Rat poison
Saponins			
Dioscorea (yam)	Tubourous roots of *Dioscorea deltoida,* Dioscoreaceae	Starch, diosgenin, smilagenin, epismilagenin, β-isomer yammogenin.	Precursor for synthesis of several corticosteroids, sex-hormones, and oral contraceptives. Used in treatment of rheumatic arthritis.

Safed musali	Peeled tuberous roots of *Chlorophytum borovillianum*, Liliaceae	Carbohydrates, proteins, saponin, sapogenin (hicogenin), elements like zinc, copper, phosphorus fibre.	Tonic, aphrodisiac.
Liquorice (glycyrrhiza)	Dried roots and stolon of *Glycyrrhiza glabra*, Leguminosae	Glycyrrhizin, glycyrrhizinic acid, flavonoids (liquiritin, isoliquiritin), 2-methylisoflavones, coumarin, carbenoxolone.	Expectorant, demulcent, cough mixtures, flavouring agent, anti-ulcer, anti-spasmodic, treatment of rheumatoid arthritis, inflammation, Addison's disease.
Shatavari (shatmuli)	Dried roots and leaves *Asparagus racemosus*, Liliaceae	Shatavarin I-IV, quercetin, rutin, hyperoside, diosgenin, quercetin.	Galactogogue, tonic, diuretic, antioxytocic, and treatment of rheumatism and nervine disorders, in ayurveda in threatened abortion and safe delivery is justified by uterine blocking activity.
Brahmi (jalbrahmi)	Leaves and stems *Bacopa moniera*, Scrophulariaceae	Brahmine, herpestine, saponin (bacosides A,B), betulic acid, asiatic acid, brahmic acid, stigmasterol, monnierins A, B.	Nervine tonic, treatment of asthma, epilepsy, insanity. Diuretic, anti-cancer, treatment of dementia.
Ginseng (panax)	Dried roots of *Panax ginseng*, Araliaceae	Ginsenosides, panaxosides (oleanolic acid, panaxadiol, panaxatriol), chikusetsusaponin,	Immunomodulator, stimulant, sedative, aphrodisiac, adrenal and thyroid dysfunction, demulcent.
Karela (momordica)	Dried fruits of *Momordica charantia*, Cucurbitaceae	Charantin, momordicin, carbohydrates, mineral matter, ascorbic acid.	Stomachic, carminative, tonic, cooling, treatment of rheumatism, treatment of diabetes mellitus.
Senega (rattlesnake root)	Dried roots of *Polygala senega*, Polygalaceae	Senegin, polygalic acid, senegenic acid, senegenin, presenegenin (senegin II), sterol, polygalitol, starch.	Stimulant, expectorant, treatment of chronic bronchitis.
Quillaia (soap bark)	Dried inner bark of *Quillaia saponaria*, Rosaceae	Quillaic acid, quillaia-sapotoxin, sucrose, tannin.	Emulsifying agent, expectorant, detergent, preparation of shampoo.
Gokhru (puncture vine)	Dried fruits of *Tribulus terrestris*, Zygophyllaceae	Alkaloids, harmine, Harman, saponins, sapogenins like diosgenin, gitogenin, chlorogenin and ruscogenin, flavonoids, kaemferol, tribuloside.	Diuretic, tonic, treatment of calculous affections and painful micturition, aphrodisiac, ayurvedic preparation (dashmoolarishta, chyavanprash).

✱✱✱

CHAPTER 7
ALKALOID BIOSYNTHESIS

- Introduction: Alkaloid Classification, Biosynthetic Origin of Alkaloids
- Tropane Alkaloids : Hygrine, Hyoscyamine, Hyoscine
- Quinoline Alkaloids: Quinine, Quinidine, Cinchonine, Cinchonidine, Cinchonamine
- Isoquinoline/Opium Alkaloids: Thebaine, Morphine, Codeine, Papaverine, Berberine
- Amine Alkaloids: Ephedrine, Pseudoephedrine
- Purine Alkaloids : Caffeine, Theophylline, Theobromine
- Indole Alkaloids: Lysergic acid, Ergotamine, Ajmalicine, Yohimbine, Catharanthine, Vincristine, Vinblastine, Strychnine, Brucine
- Imidazole Alkaloids: Pilocarpine, Pilosine

7.1 INTRODUCTION

Alkaloids are defined as "physiologically active basic compounds of plant origin, in which at least one nitrogen atom forms part of a cyclic system".

Alkaloids are widely distributed in higher plants particularly in the dicotyledonous families such as Apocynaceae, Rubiaceae, Rutaceae, Ranunculaceae, Papaverace, Solonaceae, Papilionaceae. Labiatae (Lamiaceae) and Rosaceae do not contain alkaloids, less frequently found in monocotyledons plants viz. Amaryllidaceae, Liliaceae.

All alkaloids are biosynthesized from amino acid precursors. Usually the amino acid precursors incorporate the nitrogen atom and the basic moiety but sometimes the residues from acetate, shikimate or mevalonate pathway are also found to be involved in the formation of alkaloid structure. Hence, the alkaloids with different taxonomic distribution and physiological activities can be classified on the basis of amino acid precursors from which they are bio-synthesized.

However, a few of the alkaloids are not derived from the amino acids viz. purine, terpenoid and steroid alkaloids. On this basis, the alkaloids are grouped in three classes as true, proto and pseudo alkaloids.

The true alkaloids are toxic in nature and contain heterocyclic N which is derived from amino acids, and always basic in nature. E.g. morphine, emetine, hyoscyamine.

Proto alkaloids also called as amino alkaloids or simple amines in which N is not in a heterocyclic ring, but derived from amino acids and basic in nature, sometimes are considered as biological amines viz. mescaline, colchicines, ephedrine.

Pseudo alkaloids are also called as alkaloids but are not derived from amino acids and give the standard qualitative tests for alkaloids. These include terpenoid alkaloids, steroidal alkaloids and purines viz. Caffeine, conessine.

Alkaloids are also classified as heterocyclic and non-heterocyclic alkaloids. The common heterocyclic alkaloids, basic structure and their examples are given in Table 7.1 and 7.2.

7.2 TROPANE ALKALOIDS

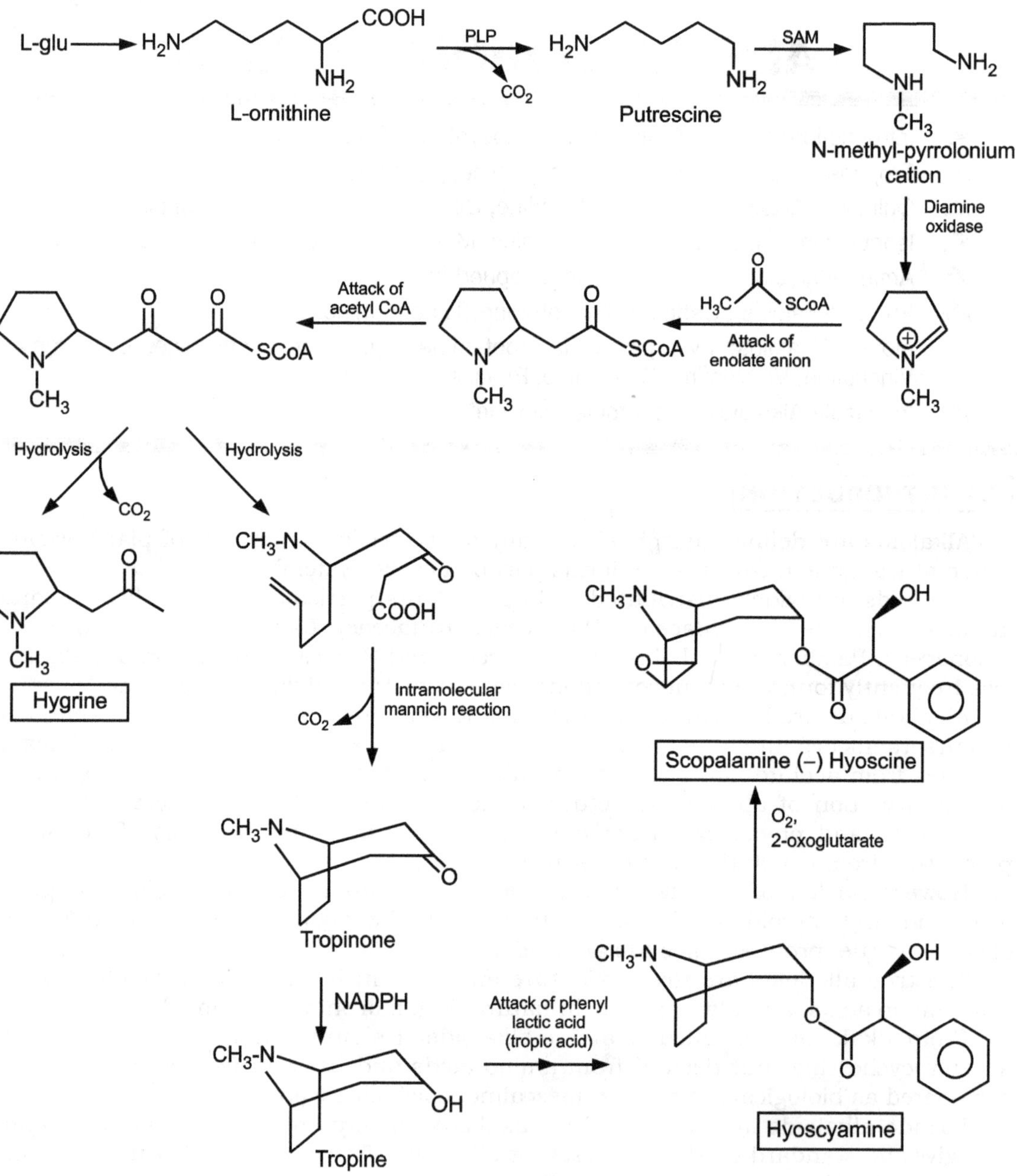

Fig. 7.1

Tropane alkaloids viz. (−) hyoscine and its racemic form (±) hyoscine (atroscin), (−) hyoscyamine and its racemic form (±) hyoscyamine (atropine) are derived from ornithine which is part of urea cycle in animals and in plants it is mainly derived from L-glutamate. L-ornithine forms putrescine via PLP- decarboxylation which further on N- methylation and action of diamine oxidase to cause deamination gives N-methyl-pyrrolinium cation (Fig. 7.1). This cation acts as a main precursor for the synthesis of various tropane alkaloids. The addition of two acetyl Co-A moieties forms the side chain containing intermediate. This intermediate on hydrolysis and immediate decarboxylation gives hygrine. But on the other side after the hydrolysis the intermediate undergoes Intramolecular Mannich like reaction and then on decarboxylation gives tropinone. The reduction of tropinone yields tropine. This tropine reacts with tropic acid obtained from phenylalanine to give (-) hyoscyamine. Hydroxylation and oxidation forms epoxide ring of n (-) hyoscine.

7.3 QUINOLINE ALKALOIDS

Quinoline alkaloids are derived from amino acid L-tryptophan. Benzylpyrrole ring of tryptophan moiety cleaves and a further rearrangement reaction forms the quinoline nucleus. The non-tryptamine derived portion is obtained from monoterpene glycoside, secolganine. The condensation of secologanin and tryptamine through Mannich reaction gives strictosidine (Fig. 7.2). The ring opening and conversion of strictosidine to its aldehyde form on hydrolysis and decarboxylation produces another intermediate, coryntheal. The cleavage of C-N bond of the side chain and formation of the C-N bondagain to aldehyde portion gives cinchonamine. When there is cleavage of indole C-N bond and hydrolysis it produces ketone moiety cinchonione. The reduction of cinchonione on one side forms cinchonidine and quinine. The epimerisation and then reduction on another side forms cinchonine and quinidine.

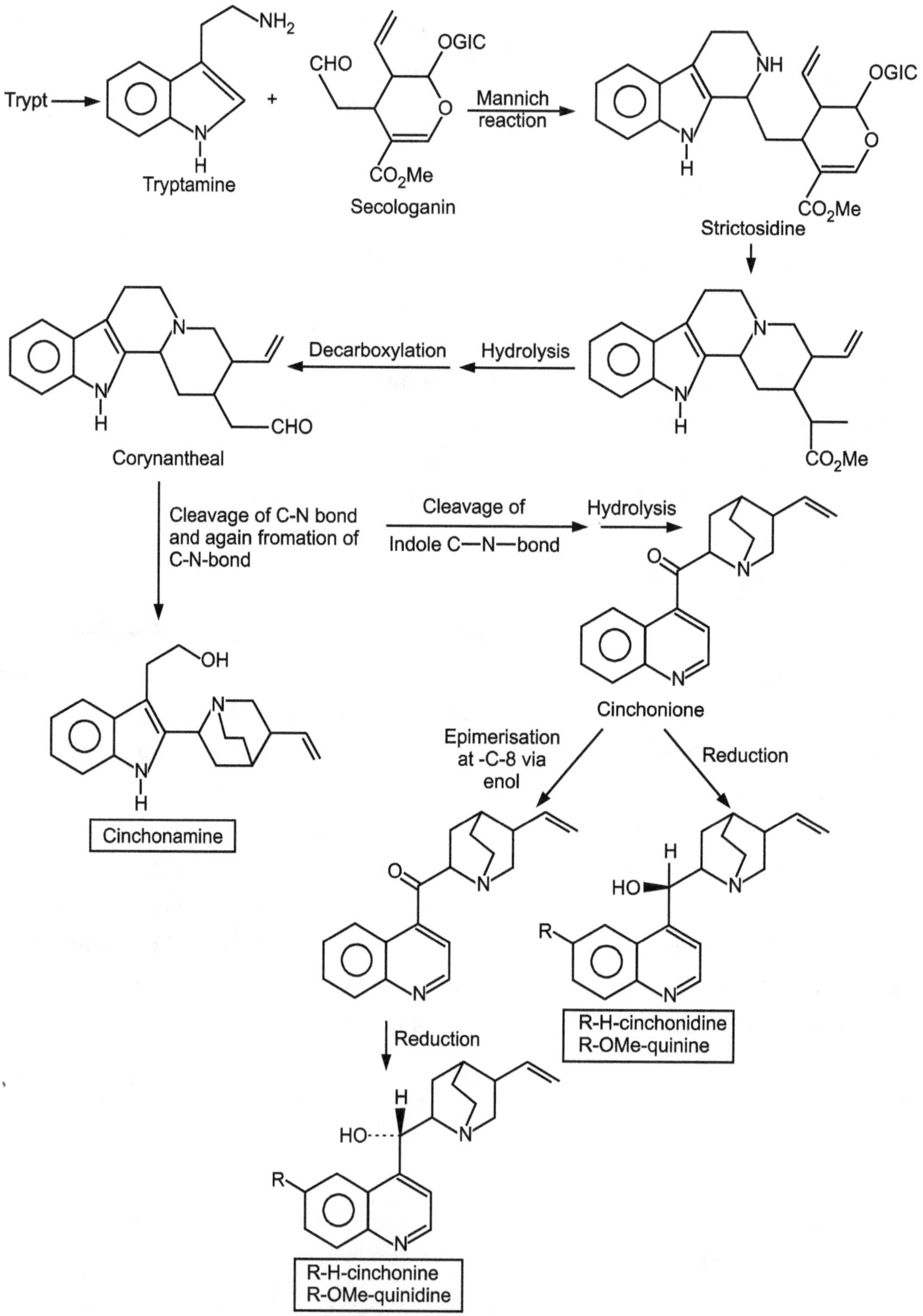

Fig. 7.2

7.4 ISOQUINOLINE / OPIUM ALKALOIDS

7.4.1 Opium Alkaloids

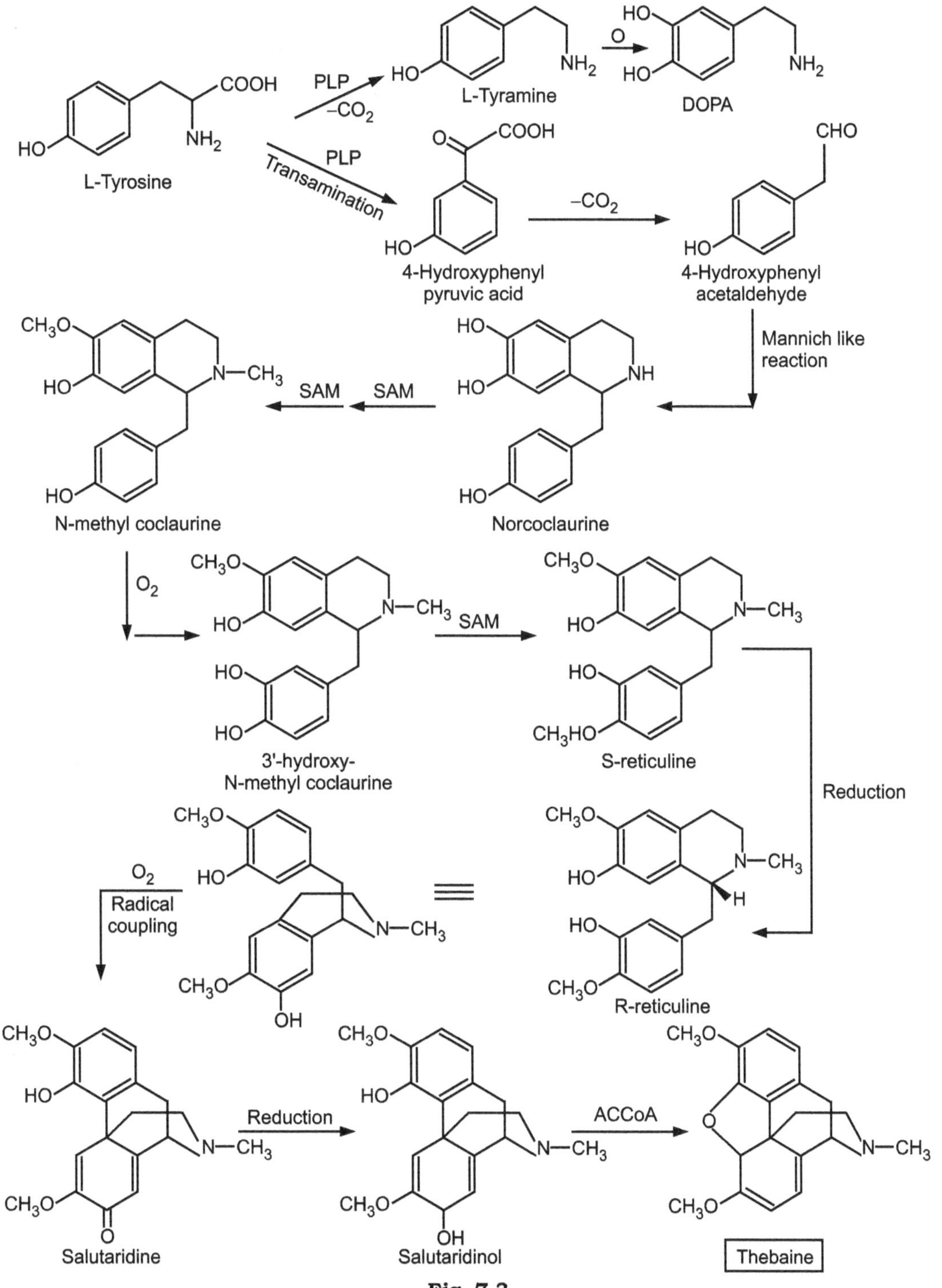

Fig. 7.3

Opium alkaloids, the benzyltetrahydroisoquinoline alkaloids viz. morphine, codiene, thebaine are derived from two molecules of L-tyrosine through phenolic oxidative coupling. One L-tyrosine on PLP decarboxylation forms L-tyramine and another molecule on PLP transamination forms 4-hydroxyphenylpyruvic acid. Tyramine on hydroxylation yields DOPA which incorporates the phenylethylamine portion of benzyltetrahydroisoquinoline ring. The phenylpyruvic acid moiety on decarboxylation gives aldehyde moiety which reacts with DOPA through Mannich like reaction and forms norcoclaurine (Fig. 7.3).

The methylation of norcoclaurine forms N-methyl coclaurine which on hydroxylation and again methylation forms an important intermediate S-reticuline. The isomer of S-reticuine i.e. R-reticuline is incorporated to form salutaridine and its reduced form salutaridol via oxidative coupling. The nucleophilic attack of acetyl CoA forms ether linkage of thebaine. The products of demethylation and sterospecific reduction of thebaine are morphine and codeine (Fig. 7.4).

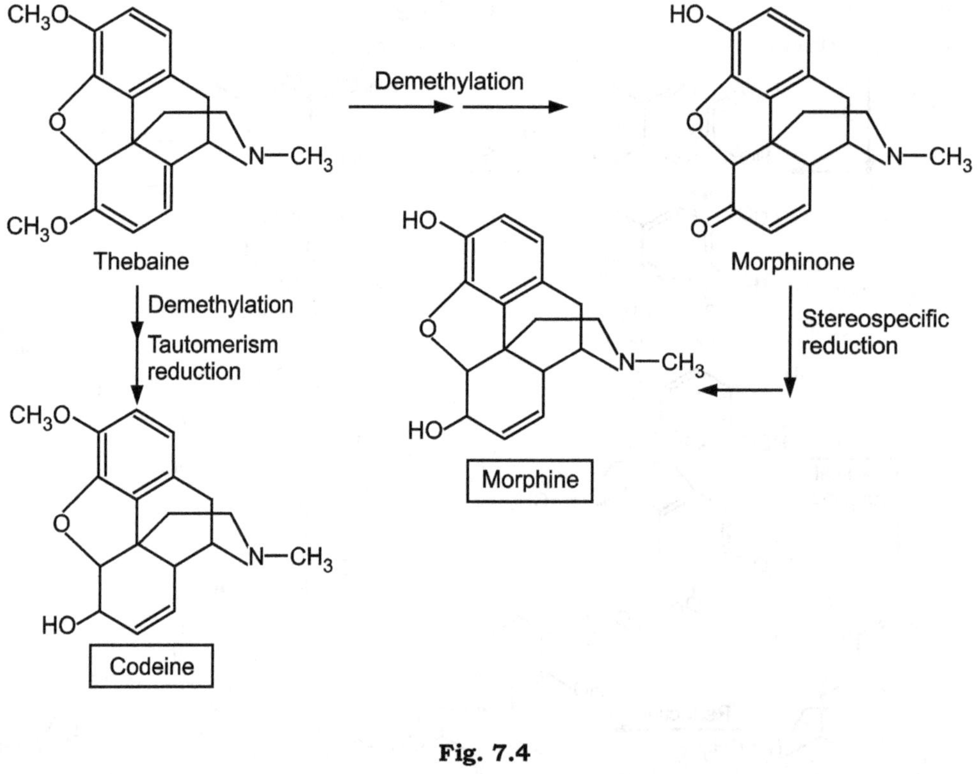

Fig. 7.4

The SAM mediated methylation and further oxidation of norcoclaurine produces s-coclaurine and then N-nor-reticuline respectively. The successive o-methylation and oxidation yields papaverine (Fig. 7.5).

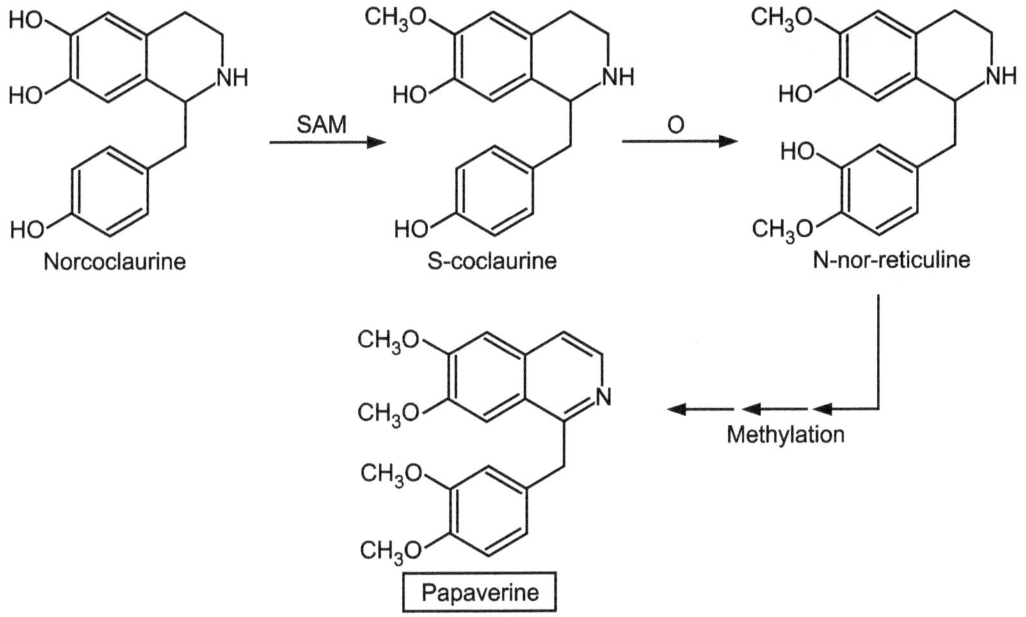

Fig. 7.5

7.4.2 Berberine Alkaloids

Berberine, benzyltetrahydroisoquinoline alkaloid biosynthesis starts with S-reticuline which undergoes oxidation and Mannich like reaction via berberine bridge enzyme to give s-scoulerine. Methylation and oxidative cyclization produces berberine with methylenedioxy group (Fig. 7.6).

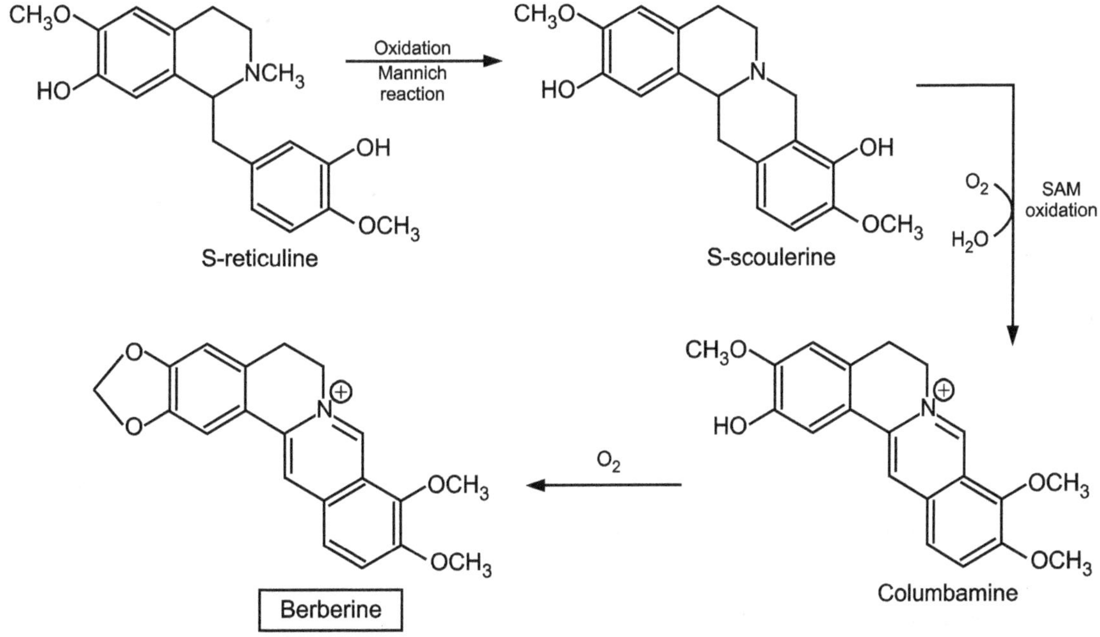

Fig. 7.6

7.5 AMINE ALKALOIDS

7.5.1 Ephedra Akaloids

L-Phenylalanine is the precursor for the synthesis of ephedra alkaloids which is metabolized through cinnamic acid. The nucleophilic attack of pyruvic acid and transamination reaction produces the important intermediate cathinone which on reduction and methylation forms ephedrine and pseudoephedrine (Fig. 7.7).

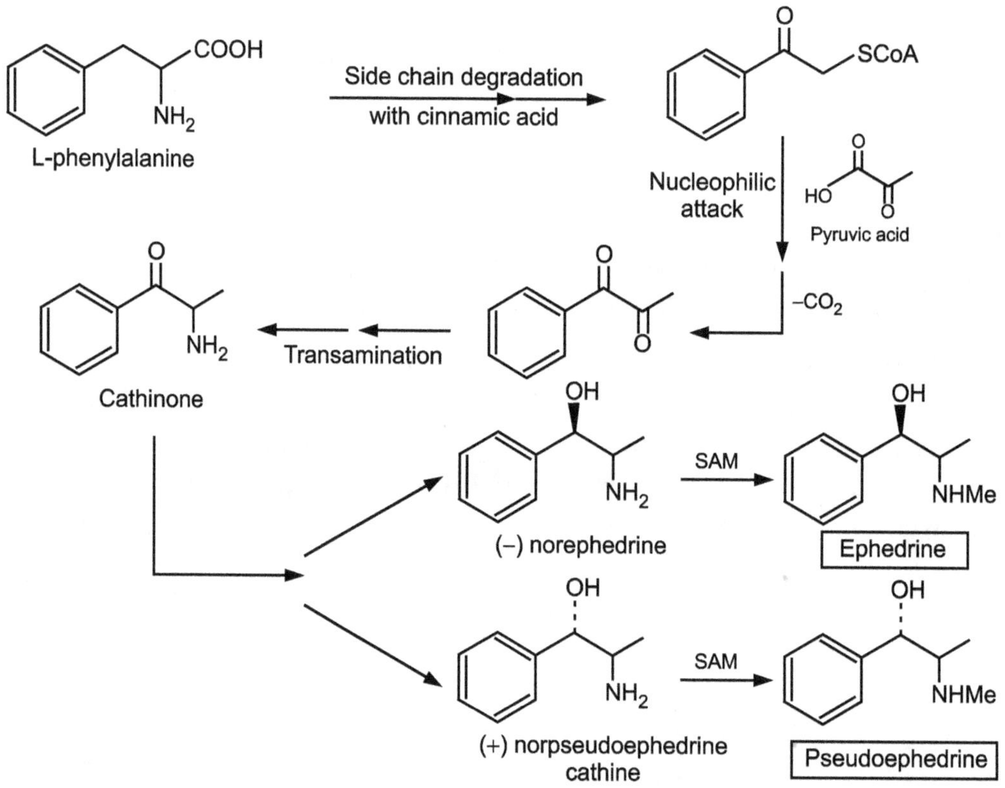

Fig. 7.7

7.6 PURINE ALKALOIDS

Purine rings are formed by the residues of various amino acids like glycine, glutamine, aspartate and folic acid.

Oxidation of inosine monophosphate (IMP) forms xanthosine monophosphate (XMP) which on methylation and hydrolysis yields 7-methyl xanthine. The sequence of methylation produces caffeine and theobromine. Methylation of xanthine, the product of hydrolysis of XMP, gives rise to theophylline (Fig. 7.8).

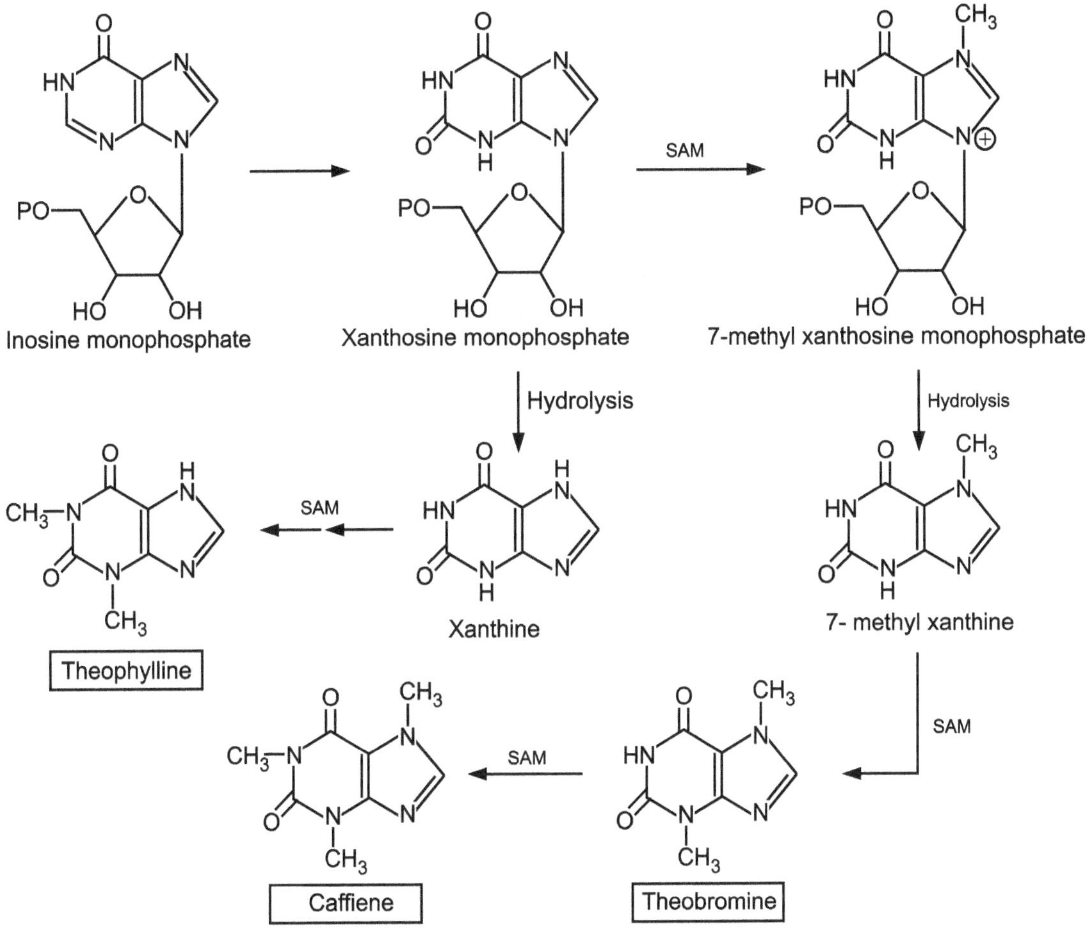

Fig. 7.8

7.7 INDOLE ALKALOIDS

7.7.1 Ergot Alkaloids

The condensation of L-trptophan and isoprene unit gives rise to various ergot alkaloids viz. ergotamine, ergometrine, ergocrystine and the like. Lysergic acid is an important intermediate of ergot alkaloids. Alkylation of tryptophan and isoprene produces dimethylallyl-L-tryptophan which on methylation, epoxidation and decaroxylation yields chanoclavine I (Fig. 7.9). The cyclization of chanoclavine produces argoclavine which on oxidation forms paspalic acid, isomer of lysergic acid. This lysergic acid gives a peptide moiety containing the most complex ergot alkaloid, ergotamine, through the addition of residues of amino acid L-alanine, L-phenylalanine and L-proline. Ergocristine is the isomer of ergotamine. Lysergic acid substituted with 2-aminopropanol is ergotametrine also called as ergonovine.

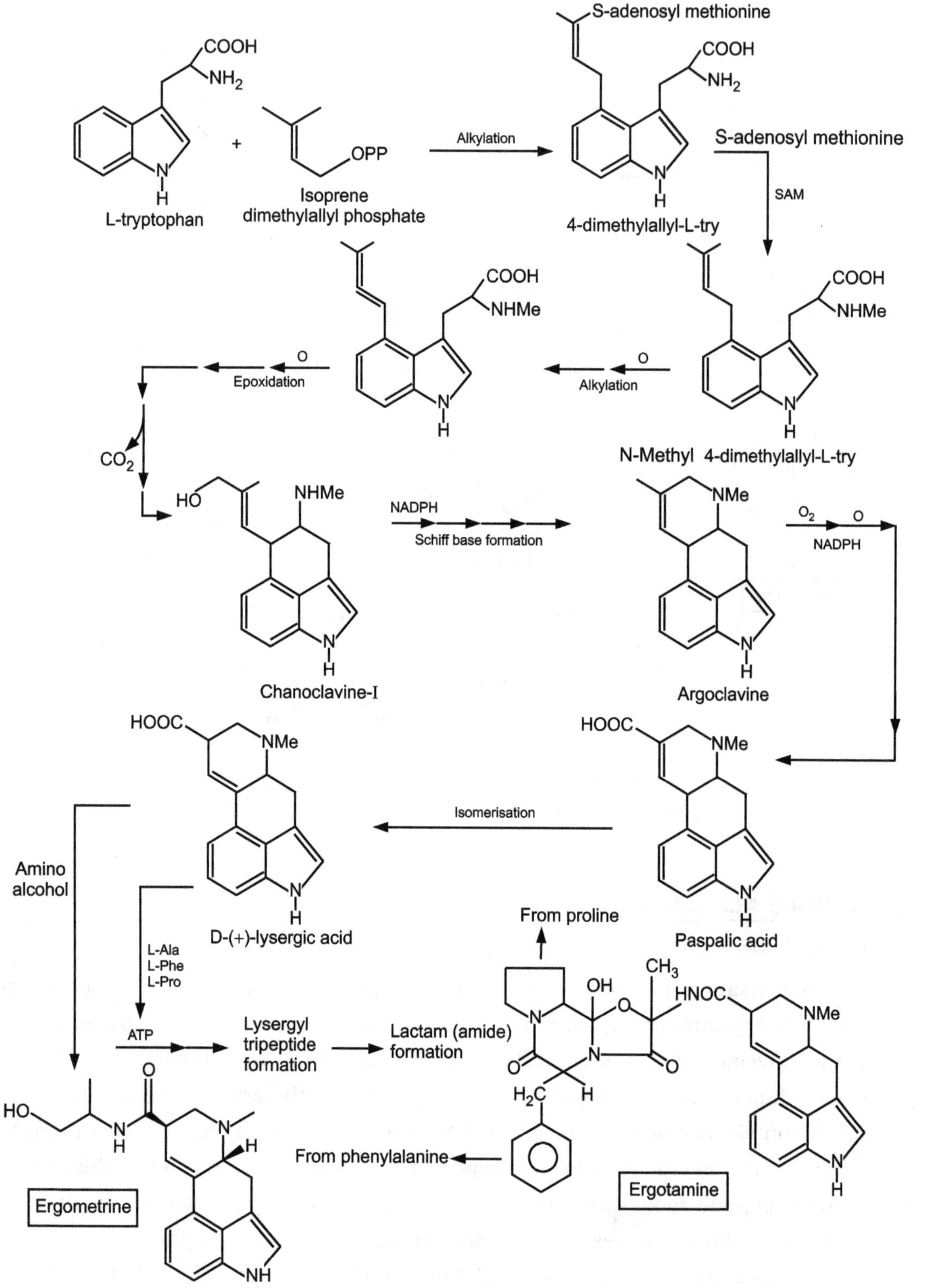
S-adenosyl methionine
COOH
NH2
L-tryptophan
+
OPP
Isoprene
dimethylallyl phosphate
Alkylation
4-dimethylallyl-L-try
S-adenosyl methionine
SAM
NHMe
Epoxidation
Alkylation
N-Methyl 4-dimethylallyl-L-try
CO2
NADPH
Schiff base formation
O2
NADPH
Chanoclavine-I
Argoclavine
HOOC
NMe
Isomerisation
D-(+)-lysergic acid
Paspalic acid
Amino
alcohol
L-Ala
L-Phe
L-Pro
ATP
Lysergyl
tripeptide
formation
Lactam (amide)
formation
From proline
CH3
OH
HNOC
From phenylalanine
Ergometrine
Ergotamine

Fig. 7.9

7.7.2 Vinca Alkaloids

Hydrolysis and Schiff base reaction of strictosidine (see Fig. 7.2) produces dehydrogeissoschizine in keto and enol form. Enol form of dehydrogeissoschizine on reduction generates ajmalicine via canthenamine while the reduction of keto form generates yohimbine (Fig. 7.10).

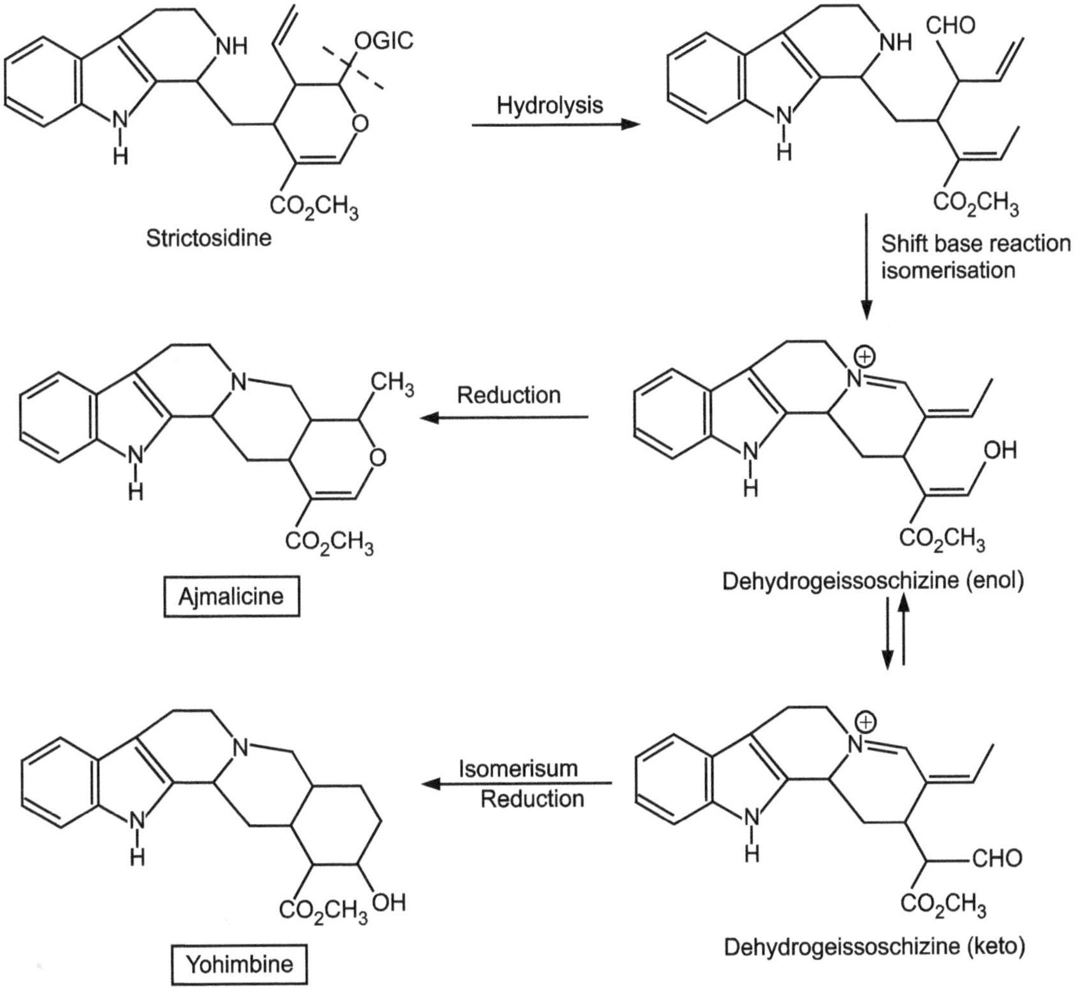

Fig. 7.10

The biosynthesis of vinca alkaloids viz. vinblastine, vincristine, vindoline and Nux-vomica alkaloids involves rearrangement of enol form of dehydrogeissoschizine to form preakummicine which on breakage of C-beta carbon yields vindoline followed by stemmadenine. The ring opening of catharanthine, the product of rearrangement and Diels –Alder reaction of stemmadenine, via peroxidase generates the intermediate which is attacked by vindoline to produce vinblastine through NADH mediated 1, 4-addition and hydroxylation (Fig. 7.11).

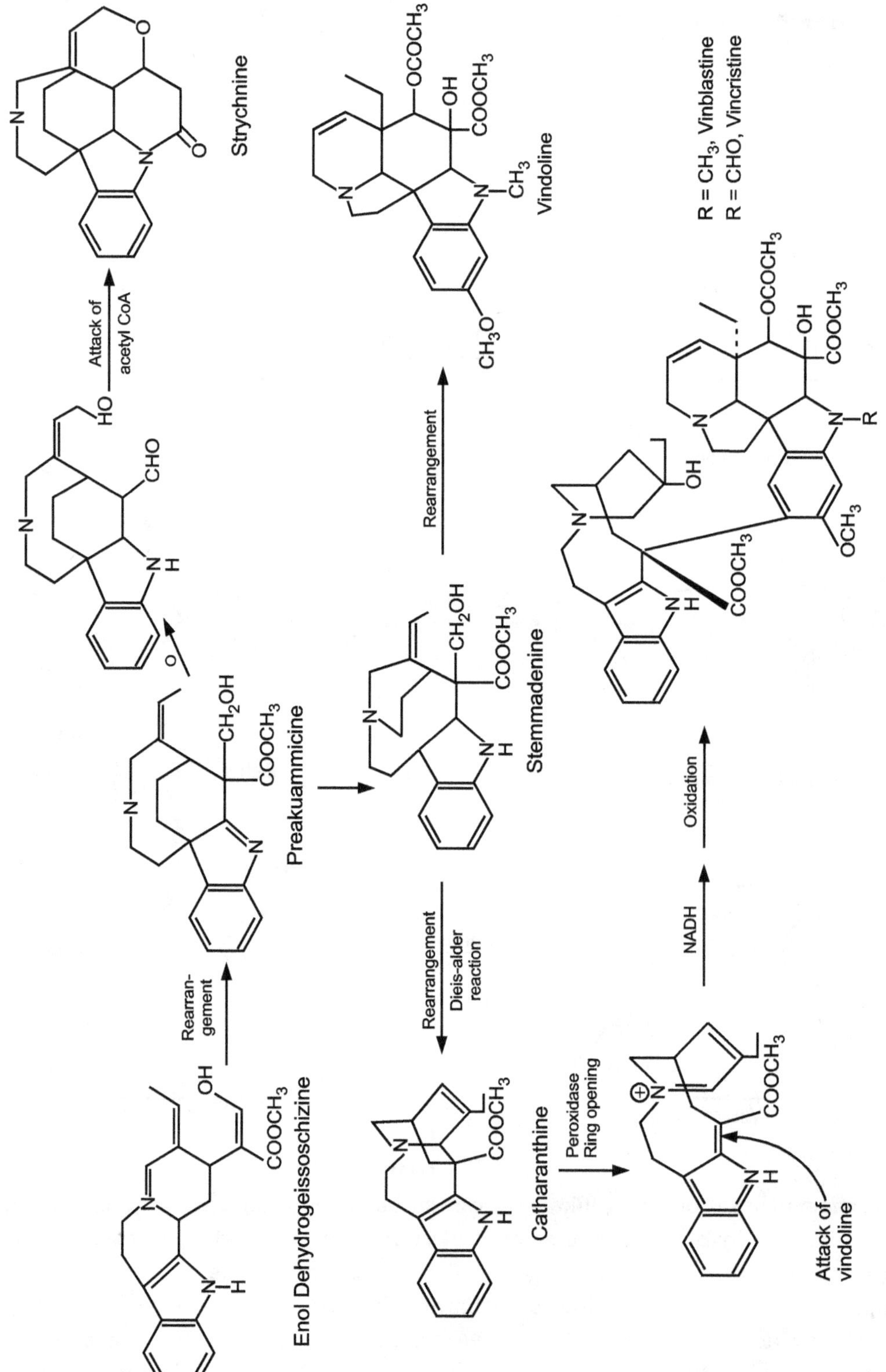
Enol Dehydrogeissoschizine
Rearran-
gement
Preakuammicine
Attack of
acetyl CoA
Strychnine
Rearrangement
Dieis-alder
reaction
Stemmadenine
Rearrangement
Vindoline
Catharanthine
Peroxidase
Ring opening
Attack of
vindoline
NADH
Oxidation
R = CH3, Vinblastine
R = CHO, Vincristine

Fig. 7.11

7.7.3 Nux-vomica Alkaloids

The hydrolysis and decarboxylation of preakummicine leads to the loss of one carbon to form an aldehyde intermediate. The aldol reaction of acetyl CoA with this intermediate forms strychnine. Brucine is the dimethoxy analogue of strychnine (Fig. 7.11). Strychnine and brucine obtained from *strychnos nux-vomica* (loganiaceae) are used as a CNS-stimulant and appetizer.

7.7.4 Ruwolfia Alkaloids

Rauwolfia serpentina contains a number of bioactive chemicals, including yohimbine, reserpine, ajmaline, deserpidine, rescinnamine, serpentinine useful in hypertension and anxiety. Reserpine, deserpidine (Figure 7.12), both having additional methoxyl substituent on the indole system at position 11 and opposite stereochemistry at position 3 to yohimbine and strictosidine, are trimethoxybenzoyl esters of yohimbine-like alkaloids, whilst rescinnamine is a trimethoxycinnamoyl ester.

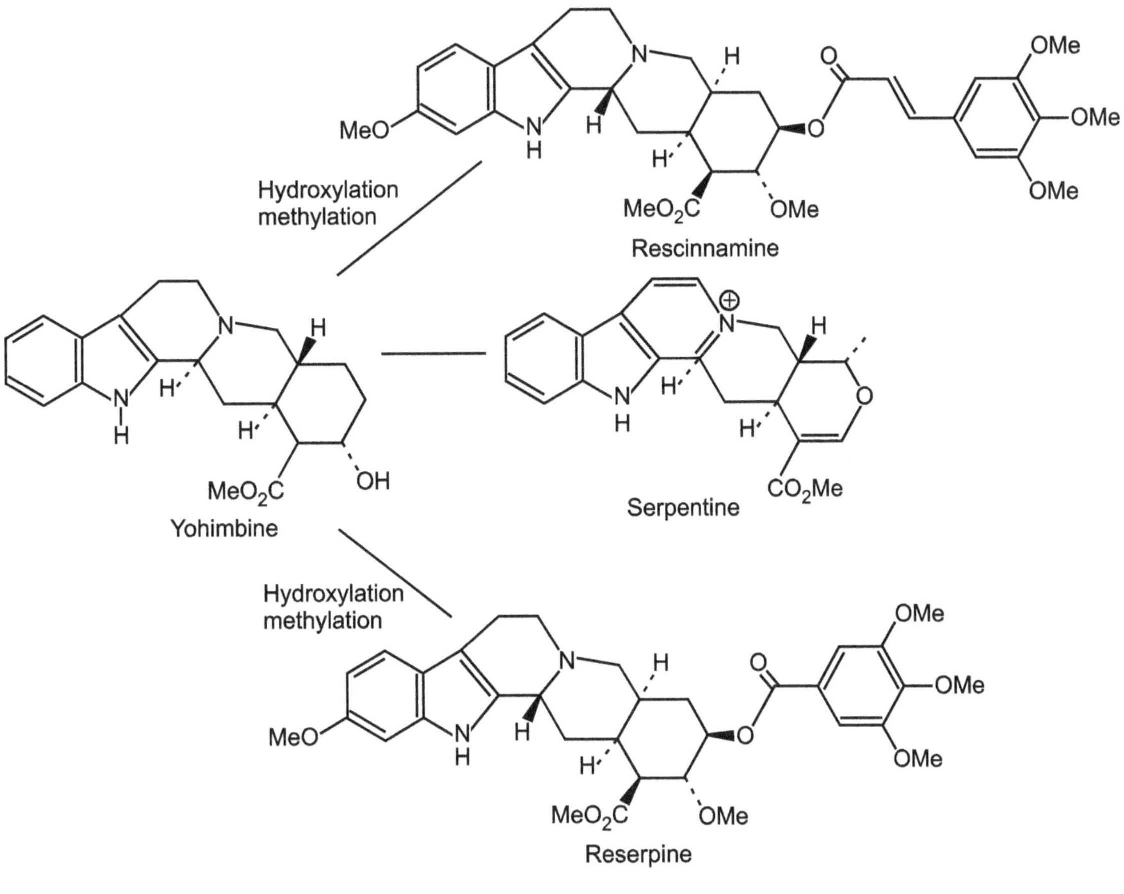

Fig. 7.12

7.8 IMIDAZOLE ALKALOIDS

Imidazoles are a small group of very few alkaloids reported from families such as Rutaceae, Euphorbiaceae and Fabaceae, of which pilocarpine obtained from Pilocarpus spp is the only pharmaceutically important alkaloid useful for the treatment of glaucoma. As per research the amino acid L-histidine might be a precursor of imidazole alkaloids found in Pilocarpus jaborandi leaves which is elaborated in fig 7.13, but experimental proofs of such a biosynthetic origin is lacking.

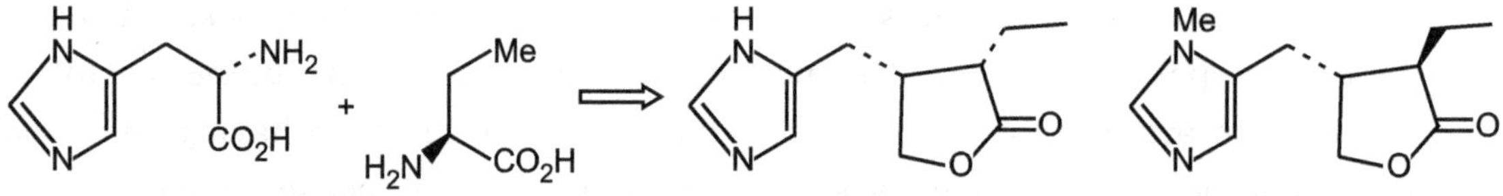

L-His L-Thr Pilocarpine Isopilocarpine

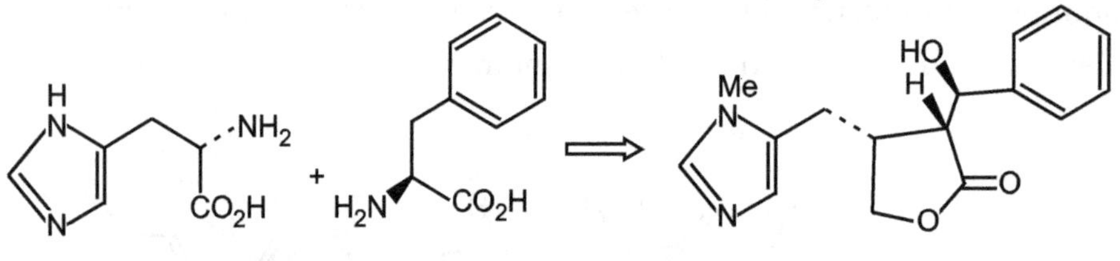

L-His L-Phe Pilosine

Fig. 7.13

Table 7.1 : Different Chemical Classes of Alkaloids

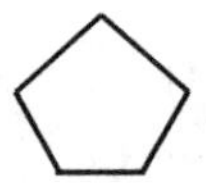 Pyrrolidine	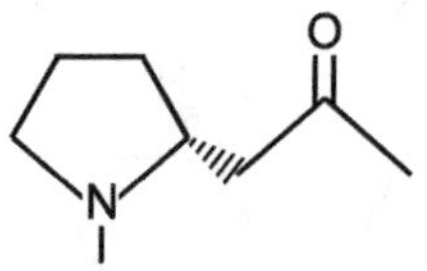 Hygrine, *Erythroxylon coca,* Erythroxylaceae
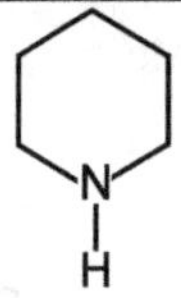 Piperdine	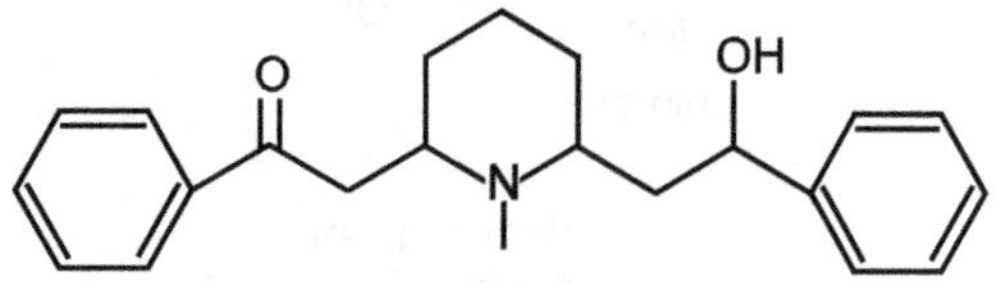 Lobeline, *Lobelia inflara,* Lobeliaceae
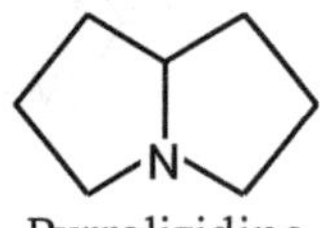 Pyrrolizidine	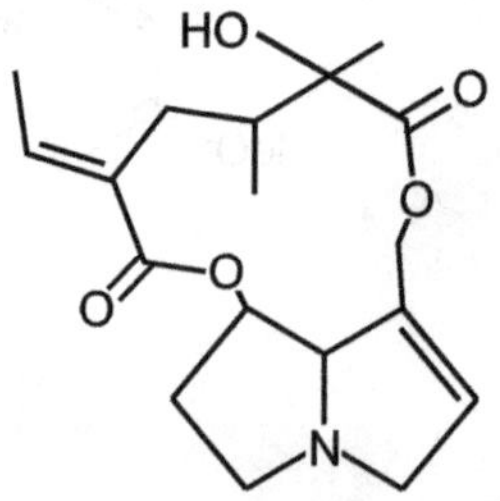 Senecionine, *Senecio brasiliensis,* Asteraceae

Tropane	Atropine, *Atropa belladonna*, Solanaceae
Quinoline	Quinine, *Cinchona officinalis*, Rubiaceae
Isoquinoline	Morphine, *Papaverum somniferum*, Papaveracea
Aporphine	Boldine, *Peumus boldus*, Monimiaceae
Indole (Benzpyrrole)	Ergometrine, *Clavicepus purpurea*, Clavicepataceae

Imidazole	Pilocarpine, *Pilocarpus jaborandi*, Rutaceae
Purine	Caffeine, *Thea sinensis*, Theaceae
Steroid	Solasodine, *Solanum nigrum*, *S. tuberosum*
Diterpene	Aconitine *Aconitum napellus*, Ranunculaceae

Table 7.2 : Examples and Biosynthetic Origin of Different Classes of Alkaloids

Sr. No.	Type	Examples	Biosynthetic Origin
1	Tropane alkaloids	Hygrine (sedative), methylecogine and cocaine (CNS stimulant, *Erythroxylum coca*, erythroxylaceae), hyoscine, hyoscyamine and atropine (anticholinergic,	Ornithine

		Datura metel, *Datura stramonium*, *Atropa belladonna*, solanaceae)	
2	Pyrrolizidine	Senecionine (oxytocic, controls heamorrhage, *Senecio Aegyptius*, Asteraceae) lycospamimne (*Symphytum officinalis*, Boraginaceae), Indicine-N-oxide (*Heliotropium indicum*, Boraginaceae)	
3	Piperidine	Pelletriene (*Punica granatum*, Punicacae), anaferine (*Withania somnifera*, solanaceae), lobeline (Respiratory stimulant, *Lobelia inflata*, Campanulaceae), sedamine (*Sedum acre*, Crassulaceae), piperine (*Piper nigrum*, piperaceae)	Lysine
4	Quinolizidine	Lupinine (*Lupinis luteus*, Fabaceae) sparteine (*Cytisus scoparius*, Fabacaeae), cytisine (*Cytisus laburnum*, Fabaceae)	
5	Indolizidine	Swainsonine (*Swainsona canescens*, Fabaceae), castanospermine (*Castanospermum australe*, Fabaceae)	
6	Pyridine	Nicotine and anabasine (Insectiside, *Nicotiana tabacum*, Solanaceae), ricinine (*Ricinus communis*, Euphorbiaceae), arecoline (*Areca catechu*, Arecaceae)	Niconitic acid
7	Tetrahydro-isoquinoline	Hordenine (Cardiotonic, *Hordeum vulgare*, Graminae), mescaline, anhalamine and anhalonine, (hallucinogenic : *Lopophora williamsii*, Cactaceae), lophocerine : *Lophophora schotti*, Cactaceae), papaverine and narceine (Narcotic analgesic, *Papaverum somniferum*, Papavaraceae), tubocuranine (arrow poison, *Chondrodendron tomentosum*, Menispermaceae)	Tyrosine
8	Benzyltetrahydro-isoquinoline	Morphine (analgesic), codiene (analgesic) and thebaine (Morphine antagonist), (*Papaverum somniferum*, Papavaraceae), salturadine, stephanine (*Stephania bancroftii*, Menispermaceae) aristolochic acid (*Aristolochia serpentina*, aristolochiaceae) berberine (antinflammatory, *berberis aristata*, Berberidaceae), hydrastine (*Hydrastis canadensis*, Ranunculacese)	
9	Phenthyl isoquinoline	Autumnaline, colchicine, demecolcine, and deacetylcholchicine (antigout, *Colchicum autumnale*, Liliaceae)	
10	Terpenoid tetrahydro-isoquinoline	Emetine, cephaline (antiamoebic, *Cephalis ipecacuhana*, Rubiaceae)	

11	Indole alkaloids		
	Simple indole	Psilocine (Halucinogenetic, *Psilocybe mexicana*, Strophariaceae)	Tryptophan
	Beta carboline Indole	Harmine, harman (Narcotic hallucinogenic, *Peganum harmala*, Rutaceae)	
	Terpenoid indole	Coryanthe type : Ajmalicine (Antiarythmic, *Catharanthus roseus*, Apocynaceae), yohimbine, reserpine and deserpidine (Antihypertensive, *Rauwolfia serpentina*, Apocynaceae) Akuammicine, strychnine, brucine (anticancer, *Strychnos nux-vomica*, Loagniaceae),	
		Aspidosparma type : tabersonine (*Tabernaemontana corymbosa*, Apocynaceae), vindoline and vincamine (*Catharanthus roseus*, Apocynaceae)	
		Iboga type : ibogaine (pcychoactive, *Taberanthe iboga*, Apocynaceae), catharanthine (antihypertensive, *Catharanthus roseus*, Apocynaceae)	
12	Pyrroloindole	Physostigmine (cholinergic, *Physostigma venenosum*, Fabaceae) Ergometrine (oxytocic) and ergotamine (migrane treatment), (*Claviceps purpurea*, Clavicipataceae)	
13	Quinoline alkaloids	Quinine, quinidine, chinchonine, chinchonidine (Antimalarial, *Chinchona succirubra*, Rubiaceae) camptothecin (Potent anticancer, *Camptotheca acuminata*, Nyssaceae),	
14	Quinazoline	Vasicine (peganine) (brochodialator, *Adhatoda vasica*, Acanthaceae)	Anthranilic acid
15	Acridine	Dictamnine (*Dicatamus albus*, Rutaceae), skimmianine (*Skimmia japonica*, Rutaceae)	
16	Imidazole	Pilocarpine and pilosine (Mitotic, *Pilocarpus jaborandi*, Rutaceae)	Histidine
17	Amine	Connine (Anticonvulsant, *Conium maculatum*, Apiaceae), pinidine (Pinus species)	Acetate
		Ephedrine and pseudoephedrine, (CNS stimulant, brocnchodialtor, *Ephedra geriardiana*, Ephedraceae) capsaicine (counter irritant, *Capsicum annum*, Solanaceae)	Phenylalanine
18	Terpenoid	Actinidine (*Actinidia polygama*, Actinidiaceae), gentianine (Apetizer, *Gentiana lutea*, Gentianaceae) aconitine (*Aconitum napellus*,Ranunculaceae)	Monoterpenes
19	Steroid	Solasodine (*Solanum nigrum, S. tuberosum*, Solanaceae), tomatidine (*Lycopersicon esculente*, Solanaceae), conessine (*Holarrhena antidysentrica*, Apocyanceae)	Steroids
20	Purine	Caffiene (*Coffea arabica, C. liberica*, Rubiaceae) theobromine and theophylline (*Thea sinesis*, Theaceae, *Theobroma cacao*, Sterculiaceae)	Purine

ABBREVIATIONS

SAM	:	S-Adenosyl Methionine
PLP	:	Pyridoxal 5'-Phosphate
O	:	Hydroxylation
O_2	:	Oxidation
WM	:	Wagner-Meerwein rearrangement
PP	:	Pyrophosphate
CoA	:	Coenzyme A
IPP	:	Isopentyl Pyrophosphate
DMAPP	:	Dimethyl Allyl Pyrophosphate
FPP	:	Farnesyl Pyrophosphate
GPP	:	Geranyl Pyrophosphate
GFPP	:	Geranyl Farnesyl Pyrophosphate
HMG-GoA	:	β-Hydroxyl-β-Methyl Glutaryl CoA
PEP	:	Phosphoenol Pyruvate
ACP	:	Acyl Carrier Protein
PKS	:	Polyketids
MUFA	:	Monounsaturated Fatty Acids
PUFA	:	Polyunsaturated Fatty Acids
FAD	:	Flavin Adenine Dinucleotide
FMN	:	Flavin Mononucleotide
ATP	:	Adenosine-5'-triphosphate
DHA	:	Docosahexanoic Acid

***

FURTHER READINGS

1. Abe I and Prestwich GD (1999) Squalene epoxidase and oxidosqualene:lanosterol cyclase–key enzymes in cholesterol biosynthesis. Comprehensive Natural Products Chemistry, Vol 2. Elsevier, Amsterdam, pp 267–298.
2. Abe I, Rohmer M and Prestwich GD (1993) Enzymatic cyclization of squalene and oxidosqualene to sterols and triterpenes. Chem Rev 93, 2189–2206.
3. Abe I, Tomesch JC, Wattanasin S and Prestwich GD (1994) Inhibitors of squalene biosynthesis and metabolism. Nat Prod Rep 11, 279–302.
4. Alberts, Bruce (2002). Molecular biology of the cell. New York: Garland Science.
5. A. M. Bezborodov (1978) Discussion On secondary metabolites: Their functions and biogenesis Folia Microbiologica 23: 6, 509-510.
6. Ashutosh Kar (2003), Pharmacognosy & Pharmacobiotechnology, New Age International, Delhi.
7. Atta-ur-Rahman and Choudhary MI (1990) Purine alkaloids. The Alkaloids, Chemistry and Pharmacology (ed Brossi A) Vol 38. Academic, San Diego, pp 225–323.
8. Bentley KW (2000) β-Phenylethylamines and the isoquinoline alkaloids. Nat Prod Rep 17, 247–268. Earlier reviews: 1999, 16, 367–388; 1998, 15, 341–362.
9. Berg, J. Tymoczko, J. and Stryer, L., (2002) Biochemistry. W. H. Freeman and Company.
10. Bochar DA, Friesen JA, Stauffacher CV and Rodwell VW (1999) Biosynthesis of mevalonic acid from acetyl-CoA. Comprehensive Natural Products Chemistry, Vol 2. Elsevier, Amsterdam, pp 15–44.
11. Bosch J, Bonjoch J and Amat M (1996) The Strychnos alkaloids. The Alkaloids, Chemistry and Pharmacology (ed Cordell GA) Vol 48. Academic, San Diego, pp 75–189.
12. Brock, T. D. Madigan, M. T. Martinko, J. and Parker J., (2002) Brock's Biology of Microorganisms. Benjamin Cummings.
13. Brown GD (1998) Biosynthesis of steroids and triterpenoids. Nat Prod Rep 15, 653–696.
14. Brown GD (1998) Biosynthesis of steroids and triterpenoids. Nat Prod Rep 15, 653–696.
15. Cane DE (1999) Sesquiterpene biosynthesis: cyclization mechanisms. Comprehensive Natural Products Chemistry, Vol 2. Elsevier, Amsterdam, pp 155–200.
16. Chappell J (1995) Biochemistry and molecular biology of the isoprenoid biosynthetic pathway in plants. Annu Rev Plant Physiol Plant Mol Biol 46, 521–547.
17. Connolly JD and Hill RA (2000) Triterpenoids. Nat Prod Rep 17, 463–482. Earlier reviews: 1999, 16, 221–240; 1997, 14, 661–679.
18. Cox, M. and Nelson, D. L., Lehninger (2004) Principles of Biochemistry. Palgrave Macmillan.
19. Crombie L and Whiting DA (1998) Biosynthesis in the rotenoid group of natural products: Applications of isotope methodology. Phytochemistry, 49, 1479–1507.
20. Da Silva, J.J.R.F. and Williams, R. J. P., (1991) The Biological Chemistry of the Elements: The Inorganic Chemistry of Life. Clarendon Press.
21. Dewick PM (1999) The biosynthesis of C5–C25 terpenoid compounds. Nat Prod Rep 16, 97–130. Earlier reviews: 1997, 14, 111–141; 1995, 12, 507–534.

22. Eisenreich W, Schwarz M, Cartayrade A, Arigoni D, Zenk MH and Bacher A (1998) The deoxyxylulose phosphate pathway of terpenoid biosynthesis in plants and microorganisms. Chem Biol 5, R221–R233.
23. Evans W.C.Trease & Evans (2002) Pharmacognosy, 12ed Baillaire Tindal London.
24. Finian J. Leeper, John C. Vederas (2000) Biosynthesis Springer, London.
25. Forkmann G and Heller W (1999) Biosynthesis of flavonoids. Comprehensive Natural Products Chemistry, Vol 1. Elsevier, Amsterdam, pp 713–748.
26. Franz G (1989) Polysaccharides in pharmacy: current applications and future concepts. Planta Med 55, 493–497.
27. Fujii T and Ohba M (1998) The ipecac alkaloids and related bases. The Alkaloids, Chemistry and Biology (ed Cordell GA) Vol 51. Academic, San Diego, pp 271–321.
28. Gokhale, S.S., C.K.Kokate and A.P. Purohit, Pharmacognosy. Nirali Prakashan. Pune. 1994
29. Gross GG (1999) Biosynthesis of hydrolyzable tannins. Comprehensive Natural Products Chemistry, Vol 3. Elsevier, Amsterdam, pp 799–826.
30. Hanson JR (2000) Steroids: reactions and partial synthesis. Nat Prod Rep 17, 423–434. Earlier reviews:1999, 16, 607–617; 1998, 15, 261–273.
31. Harwood JL (1996) Recent advances in the biosynthesis of plant fatty acids. Biochim Biophys Acta 1301, 7–56.
32. Herbert RB (2001) The biosynthesis of plant alkaloids and nitrogenous microbial metabolites. Nat Prod Rep 18, 50–65. Earlier reviews: 1999, 16, 199–208; 1997, 14, 359–372.
33. Herrmann KM and Weaver LM (1999) The shikimate pathway. Annu Rev Plant Physiol Plant Mol Biol 50, 473–503.
34. Hutchinson CR (1999) Microbial polyketide synthases: more and more prolific. Proc Natl Acad Sci USA 96, 3336–3338.
35. Ihara M and Fukumoto K (1996) Recent progress in the chemistry of non-monoterpenoid indole alkaloids. Nat Prod Rep 13, 241–261. Earlier review: 1995, 12, 277–301.
36. Jones, Russell Celyn; Buchanan, Bob B.; Gruissem, Wilhelm (2000). Biochemistry & molecular biology of plants. Rockville, Md: American Society of Plant Physiologists. pp. 371-2.
37. Kaliya.A (2009) Text Book Of Industrial Pharmacognosy, CBS Publishers & Distributors, Delhi.
38. Katz L (1997) Manipulation of modular polyketide synthases. Chem Rev 97, 2557–2575.
39. Knaggs AR (2000) The biosynthesis of shikimate metabolites. Nat Prod Rep 17, 269–292. Earlier reviews: 1999, 16, 525–560; Dewick PM (1998) 15, 17–58.
40. Kokate CK (2005), Practical Pharmacognosy, Edn4, Vallabh Prakashan, Delhi, 7-14.
41. Kren V, Harazim P and Malinka Z (1994) Claviceps purpurea (ergot): culture and bioproduction of ergot alkaloids. Biotechnology in Agriculture and Forestry, Vol 58 Medicinal and Aromatic Plants VII (ed Bajaj YPS). Springer, Heidelberg, pp 139–156.
42. Kutchan TM (1995) Alkaloid biosynthesis – the basis for metabolic engineering of medicinal plants. Plant Cell 7, 1059–1070.
43. Kutchan TM (1998) Molecular genetics of plant alkaloid biosynthesis. The Alkaloids, Chemistry and Pharmacology (ed Cordell GA) Vol 50. Academic, SanDiego, pp 257–316.

44. Kutney JP (1990) Biosynthesis and synthesis of indole and bisindole alkaloids in plant cell cultures: a personal overview. Nat Prod Rep 7, 85–103.
45. Lewis NG and Davin LB (1999) Lignans: biosynthesis and function. Comprehensive Natural Products Chemistry, Vol 1. Elsevier, Amsterdam, pp 639–712.
46. Lewis NG and Yamamoto E (1990) Lignin: occurrence, biogenesis and biodegradation. Annu Rev Plant Physiol Plant Mol Biol 41, 455–496.
47. Lichtenhaler HK (1999) The 1-deoxy-D-xylulose-5- phosphate pathway of isoprenoid biosynthesis in plants. Annu Rev Plant Physiol Plant Mol Biol 50, 47–65.
48. Loewus FA (1999) Biosynthesis and metabolism of ascorbic acid in plants and of analogs of ascorbic acid in fungi. Phytochemistry 52, 193–210.
49. MacMillan J and Beale MH (1999) Diterpene biosynthesis. Comprehensive Natural Products Chemistry, Vol 2. Elsevier, Amsterdam, pp 217–243.
50. Mann J (1994) Chemical Aspects of Biosynthesis. Oxford Chemistry Primers, Oxford.
51. Matern U, L"uer P and Kreusch D (1999) Biosynthesis of coumarins. Comprehensive Natural Products Chemistry, Vol 1. Elsevier, Amsterdam, pp 623–637.
52. McGarvey DJ and Croteau R (1995) Terpenoid metabolism. Plant Cell 7, 1015–1026.
53. Mercer EI (1991) Sterol biosynthesis inhibitors: their current status and modes of action. Lipids 26, 584–597.
54. Michael JP (2000) Quinoline, quinazoline and acridone alkaloids. Nat Prod Rep 17, 603–620. Earlier reviews: 1999, 16, 697–709; 1998, 15, 595–606.
55. Misra N, Luthra R, Singh KL and Kumar S (1999) Recent advances in biosynthesis of alkaloids. Comprehensive Natural Products Chemistry, Vol 4. Elsevier, Amsterdam, pp 25–59.
56. Mohammed Ali (2008) Phramcognosy & Phytochemistry, vol. I 7 II, CBS publishers Delhi.
57. Murray RDH (1997) Naturally occurring plant coumarins. Prog Chem Org Nat Prod 72, 1–119.
58. O'Hagan D (2000) Pyrrole, pyrrolidine, pyridine, piperidine and tropane alkaloids. Nat Prod Rep 17, 435–446. Earlier review: 1997, 14, 637–651.
59. O'Hagan D and Robins RJ (1998) Tropic acid ester biosynthesis in Datura stramonium and related species. Chem Soc Rev 27, 207–212.
60. Ohlrogge J and Browse J (1995) Lipid biosynthesis. Plant Cell 7, 957–970.
61. Parks LW and Casey WM (1995) Physiological implications of sterol biosynthesis in yeast. Annu Rev Microbiol 49, 95–116.
62. Paul M Dewick (2002) Medicinal Natural Products-A Biosynthetic Approach Second Edition John Wiley & Sons Ltd, London.
63. Peters-Golden M and Brock TG (2001) Intracellular compartmentalization of leukotriene synthesis: unexpected nuclear secrets. FEBS Lett 487, 323–326.
64. Poralla K (1999) Cycloartenol and other triterpene cyclases. Comprehensive Natural Products Chemistry, Vol 2. Elsevier, Amsterdam, pp 299–319.
65. Price, N. and Stevens, L., (1999) Fundamentals of Enzymology: Cell and Molecular Biology of Catalytic Proteins. Oxford University Press.
66. Nicholls, D. G. and Ferguson, S. J., (2002) Bioenergetics. (Academic Press Inc.
67. Rangari VD (2008), Pharmacognosy& Phytochemistry, Career Publication, Nashik.

68. Rawlings BJ (1998) Biosynthesis of fatty acids and related metabolites. Nat Prod Rep 15, 275–308. Earlier review: (1997), 14, 335–358.
69. Rawlings BJ (1999) Biosynthesis of polyketides (other than actinomycete macrolides). Nat Prod Rep 16, 425–484. Earlier review: (1997) 14, 523–556.
70. Robins DJ (1995) Biosynthesis of pyrrolizidine and quinolizidine alkaloids. The Alkaloids, Chemistry and Pharmacology (ed Cordell GA) Vol 46. Academic, San Diego, pp 1–61.
71. Rohmer M (1998) Isoprenoid biosynthesis via the mevalonate-independent route, a novel target for antibacterial drugs? Prog Drug Res 50, 135–154.
72. Rohmer M (1999) A mevalonate-independent route to isopentenyl diphosphate. Comprehensive Natural Products Chemistry, Vol 2. Elsevier, Amsterdam, pp 45–67
73. Rohmer M (1999) The discovery of the mevalonateindependent pathway for isoprenoid biosynthesis in bacteria, algae and higher plants. Nat Prod Rep 16, 565–574.
74. Sandmann G (1994) Carotenoid biosynthesis in microorganisms and plants. Eur J Biochem 223, 7–24.
75. Smith WL, Garavito RM and DeWitt DL (1996) Prostaglandin endoperoxide H synthases (cyclooxygenases)-1 and -2. J Biol Chem 271, 33 157–33 160.
76. St¨ahelin HF and von Wartburg A (1991) The chemical and biological route from podophyllotoxin glucoside to etoposide. Cancer Res 51, 5–15.
77. St¨ockigt J (1995) Biosynthesis in Rauwolfia serpentina: modern aspects of an old medicinal plant. The Alkaloids, Chemistry and Pharmacology (ed Cordell GA) Vol 47. Academic, San Diego, pp 115–172.
78. St¨ockigt J and Ruppert M (1999) Strictosidine – the biosynthetic key to monoterpenoid indole alkaloids. Comprehensive Natural Products Chemistry, Vol 4. Elsevier, Amsterdam, pp 109–138.
79. Sujata V. Bhat, Bhimsen A. Nagasampagi, Meenakshi Sivakumar (2005) Chemistry of natural products Birkhäuser, Springer, London.
80. Szantay C, Dornyei G and Blasko G (1994) The morphine alkaloids. The Alkaloids, Chemistry and Pharmacology (ed Cordell GA) Vol 45. Academic, San Diego, pp 127–232.
81. Tayler V.E. & Brady R. (1981) Pharmacognosy, Lea & Febiger, London.
82. Torssell KBG (1997) Natural Product Chemistry. A Mechanistic, Biosynthetic and Ecological Approach. Apotekarsocieteten, Stockholm.
83. Ward RS (1999) Lignans, neolignans and related compounds. Nat Prod Rep 16, 75–96. Earlier reviews: 1997, 14, 43–74; 1995, 12, 183–205.
84. Weymouth-Wilson AC (1997) The role of carbohydrates in biologically active natural products. Nat Prod Rep 14, 99–110.
85. Wise ML and Croteau R (1999) Monoterpene biosynthesis. Comprehensive Natural Products Chemistry, Vol 2. Elsevier, Amsterdam, pp 97–153.

www.ingramcontent.com/pod-product-compliance
Lightning Source LLC
Chambersburg PA
CBHW080557090426
42735CB00016B/3268